*Preacher Woman Sings the Blues*

# Preacher Woman Sings the Blues

## THE AUTOBIOGRAPHIES OF NINETEENTH-CENTURY AFRICAN AMERICAN EVANGELISTS

RICHARD J. DOUGLASS-CHIN

*University of Missouri Press*
COLUMBIA AND LONDON

Library of Congress Cataloging-in-Publication Data
Douglass-Chin, Richard J.
Preacher woman sings the blues : the autobiographies of nineteenth-
century African American evangelists / Richard J. Douglass-Chin
p.   cm.
Includes bibliographical references and index.
ISBN 0-8262-1311-1 (alk. paper)
1. Afro-American evangelists—Biography.
2. Afro-American women—Biography.   I. Title.
BV3780.D68   2001
269'.2'092396073—dc21
[B]                              00-066596

⊗™ This paper meets the requirements of the
American National Standard for Permanence of Paper
for Printed Library Materials, Z39.48, 1984.

Jacket Designer: Susan Ferber
Typesetter: BOOKCOMP, Inc.
Printer and binder: Thomson-Shore, Inc.
Typeface: New Baskerville

Excerpt from *Gifts of Power: The Writings of Rebecca Jackson,
Black Visionary, Shaker Eldress,* edited by Jean McMahon Humez,
used by permission of the University of Massachusetts Press.

FOR

*Amy, Annie, and Pouto,*

through whom the telling came down.

# CONTENTS

# ACKNOWLEDGMENTS

I THANK MARY O'CONNOR for her continued support and her instrumental suggestions for improvement of this work, Donald Goellnicht for the encouragement to begin the undertaking and for his astute editorial observations, and Sylvia Bowerbank for her critiques and her expertise, especially on the subjects of religious enthusiasm and the construction of the "natural" in social discourse. Heartfelt acknowledgments go also to Clover Nixon, Antoinette Somo, Sara Davis, and Jane Lago, who always provided me with much-appreciated assistance in meeting the deadlines (often by extending them) and practical requirements necessary for the preparation of this work. I am forever grateful to my partner, Kathy Brown, for still being here and for the valuable leads and innovative perspectives she provided; the animated discussions we so often had became a testing ground for some of my best ideas. Finally, in the spirit of Alice Walker, I thank the grandmothers for coming, especially my own grandmother Amy Hamilton Alleyne from whom I first heard the word *Yoruba* before I had read about it in any book. She heard it from her mother, who heard it from Amy's grandfather Yoto Pouto, who instilled the memory of his African homeland in all his children.

*Preacher Woman Sings the Blues*

# Introduction

I am preoccupied with the spiritual
survival, the survival *whole* of my people.

Alice Walker, *In Search of Our Mothers' Gardens*

IN 1787, in the *American Museum or Repository of Ancient and Modern
Fugitive Pieces Prose and Poetical,* the petition of one "Belinda," an
"African slave," to the legislature of Massachusetts appeared. The petition, written in the third person, presumably by an amanuensis for the
illiterate Belinda, has been cited by Frances Smith Foster and Joanne
Braxton as the earliest known precursor of black female autobiography in America.[1] In her petition, Belinda relies upon the power of
the West African Orisa—great spiritual forces embodying important
aspects of nature—to aid her in claiming financial compensation from
her master for her aged self and her indigent daughter; she refers to
the Christian God and his worshippers only in a cynical and deroga-
tory fashion, using the very discourse of Christianity to condemn the
hypocrisy of its adherents. But until very recently, serious analyses
of African American women's autobiography have not begun with
Belinda's petition; instead, they have started with the book-length spiritual narrative of Jarena Lee, written in 1836, almost fifty years later.
Lee's *The Life and Religious Experience of Jarena Lee, a Coloured Lady, Giving an Account of Her Call to Preach the Gospel* was followed by a series of
published and unpublished black women's spiritual autobiographies:

1. See "Petition of an African Slave to the Legislature of Massachusetts," in
*The American Museum, or Repository of Ancient and Modern Fugitive Pieces, Prose and
Poetical, 1787,* 538–40; Frances Smith Foster, *Written by Herself: Literary Production
by African American Women, 1746–1892,* 44–45; and Joanne Braxton, *Black Women
Writing Autobiography: A Tradition within a Tradition,* 2.

1

spanning the years between 1830 and 1864, Rebecca Cox Jackson kept a journal that was not published until 1981; Zilpha Elaw published her *Memoirs* in 1846; in 1851 Sojourner Truth published her *Narrative* with the aid of Olive Gilbert, a white amanuensis; Julia Foote's *A Brand Plucked from the Fire* appeared in 1879; a short autobiography entitled *Elizabeth, a Colored Minister of the Gospel, Born in Slavery* was published in 1889; Amanda Smith published her *Story of the Lord's Dealings with Mrs. Amanda Smith the Colored Evangelist* in 1893; the spiritual autobiography of Virginia Broughton appeared in 1907. I have included Rebecca Cox Jackson's writings in my study, because, although they were unpublished until 1981, and could not have influenced the writings of any of the other black women, I suggest that the themes, tropes, and modes of discourse found in her work are, nevertheless, those of a black woman signifying upon hegemonic discourses of her day. It is startling to see how her work compares with those of her published sisters, each of the parties writing, in this case, without knowledge of the others. William Andrews includes Virginia Broughton in his list of five women autobiographers writing from Reconstruction to 1920.[2] According to Andrews's calculation, Broughton was the only female spiritual autobiographer to write between 1899 and 1920. Thus, although my study primarily concerns itself with nineteenth-century evangelists, I have included Broughton among them as a bridging writer between the earlier evangelical women and the twentieth-century novelists Hurston, Walker, Morrison, and Bambara.

The autobiographies of the nineteenth-century black women evangelists—Lee, Elaw, Jackson, Truth, Foote, Smith, Elizabeth, and Broughton—along with the petition of their strongly African-identified precursor, Belinda, have never been examined collectively, as a genre changing considerably throughout the nineteenth century and giving rise to contemporary African American women's literary forms.[3] That is the contribution I propose to make here. Through

2. William Andrews, "The Politics of African-American Ministerial Autobiography from Reconstruction to the 1920s," in *African-American Christianity: Essays in History*, 131.

3. In 1789 Maria Stewart's *Meditations from the Pen of Mrs. Maria W. Stewart* also appeared. The Schomburg Library of Nineteenth-Century Black Women

close readings of primary texts, I examine the ways in which the evangelists employ discourses produced by socioeconomic determinants
such as race, gender, and class to create a complex black female
narrative economy with its own unique figurations and forms. We
may ask, for example, how black women's ideas of womanhood,
their troubled quest for community, their tropes of trial, or their
valorization of orality over literacy develop and change over time. This
evolving black female spiritual narrative economy is indicative of an
important line in the ongoing traditions of black women's writing, one
that has only relatively recently begun to be reclaimed and validated.
I join in this reclaiming, because, in the words of Barbara Christian:
"Literary criticism is promotion as well as understanding, a response
to the writer to whom there is often no response, to folk who need the
writing as much as they need anything. I know, from literary history,
that writing disappears unless there is a response to it."[4]

The task of reclaiming is, now, as necessary as ever, because African
American women's contestation for a self-defined subjective voice in
the face of virulent, silencing racism and sexism continues even as we
enter the twenty-first century in America. The citation of contemporary names, such as Judge Maxine Thomas, Tawana Brawley, or Anita
Hill, gives rise to the disturbing question of why black women, when
depicted at all by American media, are still so often and oddly spec-
tacularized as truth-distorting, failed, silenced, humiliated. Yet black
women have resisted reifying narratives about them in a history, both
written and oral, fictional and autobiographical, as old as slavery itself
in America. Wahneema Lubiano argues that hegemonic systems of
power do not need to effect reification and devaluation of oppressed
subjects "via conspirational agreement of arrangement"; rather, that
devaluation continues because public and private institutions such as
media, churches, schools, families, and civic organizations continuously reiterate "particular narratives and not others." Such "consistently reinforced" narratives serve to reproduce what is constituted

---

Writers classifies this work as "spiritual narrative," but it seems to be primarily a
compilation of the speeches and meditations of Stewart rather than a sustained
autobiography. For this reason, I have omitted the *Meditations* from my study.

4. Barbara Christian, "The Race for Theory," 78.

as reality in certain predetermined ways. In this manner, Lubiano concludes, the black woman has been demonized as abnormal, problematic, inscribed within the contemporary narrative economy of either welfare queen or betraying black-lady overachiever—both figures about which Daniel Moynihan warns us in *The Moynihan Report and the Politics of Controversy: A Transaction Social Science and Public Policy Report*.[5] Thus, it becomes crucial not only to understand how black women constitute their own narratives in a contemporary framework, but also to examine the ways in which current womanist strategies of resistance have evolved out of past forms. I use "womanist" in the way that Alice Walker has coined that word—"From *womanish*. . . . Usually referring to outrageous, audacious, courageous or *wilful* behaviour. . . . A woman who loves other women, sexually and/or nonsexually. Appreciates and prefers women's culture, women's emotional flexibility . . . and women's strength . . . . Committed to survival and wholeness of entire people, male *and* female."[6]

Several key critics, among them Joanne Braxton, Frances Smith Foster, Jean Humez, Phebe Davidson, Alice Walker, and William Andrews, have pointed out the initial necessity for *all* early women writers to adopt spiritual forms of writing in an attempt to use God's authority for their own purposes of female self-expression. However, it seems to me that in African American women's autobiography, black women's use of spiritual forms was much more than an expedient necessity; it was a way of maintaining African American traditions of being and telling (such as orality in the form of the preacherly text, or the performance of a kind of "blues") that are still of vital importance to many African Americans today. In my study I have included Belinda among the black women evangelists, because in the eighteenth century— many years before her autobiographer-sisters—it was she who first stood as a claimant, in the white-male public domain, for distinctly African spiritual modes of vision and for the sacred rights of herself,

5. Wahneema Lubiano, "Black Ladies, Welfare Queens, and State Minstrels: Ideological War by Narrative Means," in *Race-ing Justice, En-gendering Power: Essays on Anita Hill, Clarence Thomas, and the Construction of Social Reality*, ed. Toni Morrison, 329–33.
6. Alice Walker, *In Search of Our Mothers' Gardens: Womanist Prose*, xi.

a black woman, and her indigent daughter. I will be exploring how this scene of a black woman (and sometimes her child or children) facing a jury of her oppressors (whites and sometimes black men) is replayed in the spiritual writings of later black women, becoming a trope that contemporary writers such as Hurston, Morrison, Walker, or Bambara also use.

I suggest that around 1861, when Harriet Jacobs published *Incidents in the Life of a Slave Girl,* black women's autobiographies diverged along two distinct paths. Critics and theorists such as Joanne Braxton, Frances Smith Foster, and Hazel Carby have traced one direction, concentrating on later works (such as those by Nella Larsen, Frances Harper, or Pauline Hopkins) that, like Jacobs's pivotal text, became generally more secular and conformed more readily to the literary conventions for sentimental Euro-American female writing of the time. As Claudia Tate observes, late nineteenth-century and early twentieth-century sentimental texts—for example, Hopkins's *Contending Forces* (1900), Amelia Johnson's *Clarence and Corinne* (1890); and Emma Dunham Kelley's *Megda* (1891)—are preoccupied with marriage as the idealization of the formation of the family unit and a sense of bourgeois class principles concerning conduct, domesticity, and economic consumption. Such preoccupations subverted popular (white) assumptions about race and class, demonstrating in essence that blackness did not, by definition, mean poverty or danger. Nineteenth-century Victorian society viewed material comfort as indicative of a virtuous life. In such a context, then, black women writers' preoccupation with "fine clothing and expensive household articles becomes the semiotics of an emergent bourgeois-capitalism in which black people are full participants," and in which black women "construct, deconstruct, and reconstruct Victorian gender conventions in order to designate black female subjectivity as a most potent force in the advancement of the race." [7] However, Houston Baker points out that these writers—in spite of what he terms their

7. Claudia Tate, "Allegories of Black Female Desire; or Rereading Nineteenth-Century Sentimental Narratives of Black Female Authority," in *Changing Our Own Words: Essays on Criticism, Theory, and Writing by Black Women,* ed. Cheryl A. Wall, 106–7.

"provocative dancings at the very borders of social and sexual taboo" and their dreams of nonracist and "nonracial utopias"—cater in the form and content of their narratives, to a "white public opinion" with white sentimental sensibilities. Such an audience, Baker argues, can "never be effectively *moved* to more than sentimental tolerance. And that very tolerance disappears if the mothers' southern texts are summoned figuratively to view."[8] I present the texts of the evangelist women as some of the mothers' texts that cater much less in form and/or content to white sentimental opinion—and so fall out of material circulation as texts in the largely white, hegemonic public reading domain.

But the spirit of these black evangelist women retains the seeds that would sprout in the "eruptions of funk" of other black women writers. As Baker notes, "eruptions of funk" (the term is Susan Willis's) serve to disrupt an "American (male) grammar of white mythology." It depicts what Hortense Spillers terms "figurations of the flesh" and what Baker himself calls "theory." It is a form of black expressivity, "a powerful black figurative negotiation of a blackmothered past," a negotiation lacking in the texts of the "Northern-departed daughters."[9] The African remnants of form and content we discern in the novels of Zora Neale Hurston or Toni Morrison are more easily found in the petition of Belinda or the evangelical autobiographies of Julia Foote (1879), Rebecca Cox Jackson (1843–1864), or Sojourner Truth (1850) than in the secular, sentimental autobiographies of Harriet Jacobs (1861), Elizabeth Keckley (1868), or Kate Drumgoold (1896). Baker and others have argued that the texts of the "Northern-departed daughters" are lacking in the very spirit that I argue is retained by many of the evangelists.[10] Strangely, while Baker, in his insightful text *Workings of the Spirit,* acknowledges the crucial importance of the spiritual to African

8. Houston A. Baker, Jr., *Workings of the Spirit: The Poetics of Afro-American Women's Writing,* 36. See also Dickson D. Bruce, Jr., *Black American Writing from the Nadir: The Evolution of a Literary Tradition 1877–1915,* 13.

9. Baker, *Workings of the Spirit,* 36.

10. See also Bruce, *Black American Writing,* 4–5; Paula Giddings, *When and Where I Enter: The Impact of Black Women on Race and Sex in America,* 49–55; Ann Allen Shockley, *Afro-American Women Writers 1746–1933: An Anthology and Critical Guide,* 111.

American literature, he does not examine these first writings by black evangelical women, which paved the way for black American women's autobiographies and novels to come.

Henry Louis Gates, Jr., has demonstrated how the most prominent of the early black male autobiographers, such as Hammon (1760), Gronniosaw (1770), Marrant (1785), Equiano (1789), or Jea (1815), wrote themselves predominantly in accordance with the European expectation that equated civility with literacy and Christianity.[11] Gates examines the manner in which these early black male slave narratives created the framework for later literary works. Negotiating the expression of the African voice in Western letters, the earlier writers developed the trope of the "talking book," often employing it to "signify" or comment upon each other's works. The act of signifyin(g) is strongly rooted in the oral African American tradition. I want to extend the work Gates has begun by exploring the roots of a distinct African American *women's* tradition. For example, Gates uses only one female text, that of Rebecca Cox Jackson, to examine differing male and female representations of the phenomenon of the "talking book" and the ensuing issues of orality versus literacy that arose for early African American men and women. I argue that, while most black men rejected it, many of the early black women evangelists embraced orality in their writings—something that no critic has yet addressed at length. I contend that Zora Neale Hurston's use of free indirect discourse in *Their Eyes Were Watching God* evolved not only out of a tradition of black male encounters with the "speakerly text" as Gates posits, but also out of distinctly female experiences of the preacherly, and of orality versus literacy, arising from black women's spiritual autobiographical forms.

I use Hurston as a pivotal writer, a crucial connection between the early black women evangelists and contemporary black women writers, because her work clearly signifies upon the texts of the early religious women. In *Conversions and Visions in the Writings of African-American Women,* Kimberly Rae Connor has attempted a similar strategy: Connor examines three black women's narratives—the spiritual

11. Henry Louis Gates, Jr., *The Signifyin(g) Monkey: A Theory of African-American Literary Criticism,* 139–69.

autobiographies of evangelists Sojourner Truth and Rebecca Cox Jackson, and the secular autobiography of Harriet Jacobs—loosely terming all the women "converts" and visionaries, precursors of Hurston's Janie in *Their Eyes Were Watching God*. But such a conflation of the writings of spiritual and secular women seems to leave a number of crucial issues unaddressed. For example, how do Truth and Jackson operate as African American visionaries in a manner that the secular Jacobs cannot? How does Janie reject the Christianity of her African American community and her black evangelist foremothers for much more African forms of spirituality? While Connor acknowledges the existence of "the tension that is created between expressing individual personality and satisfying requirements of communal experience," she fails to pursue some extremely complex issues of community that have affected the writing of black evangelist women.[12] For example, does Janie's black friend Pheoby belong to the same "community" as the white abolitionist women? Connor believes that she does, but this seems to me to be a dangerous conflation. As I will demonstrate later, the white women editors who orchestrated the publication of Harriet Jacobs's *Incidents in the Life of a Slave Girl* were often self-serving and insensitive, and it is highly doubtful whether the version of Jacobs's story that they relayed "back to the community" (which community?) is the one Jacobs herself would have printed. The vexed issue of editing and literary performance for black writers is one that Connor does not examine but that I will investigate in my discussion of Rebecca Cox Jackson's text.

Phebe Davidson explores the "suggestive phrasing," "imbedded subtext," subtle metaphor, and other forms of subversive rhetoric employed by two black evangelists, Jarena Lee and Amanda Smith, but she compares and likens these strategies to those employed by white women autobiographers, rather than presenting us with a vivid sense of the many complex ways in which the structure and rhetoric employed by a variety of African American women *differ* from those employed by their white female counterparts. I suggest that while only some nineteenth-century white women's autobiographies emerge out

12. Kimberly Rae Connor, *Conversions and Visions in the Writings of African-American Women*, 174.

of Western enthusiastic religious traditions, *all* of the nineteenth-century black female spiritual autobiographies currently extant come from those traditions. Clement Hawes cites an extensive summary of characteristics of enthusiastic—or what he terms "manic"—rhetoric from the seventeenth to the nineteenth century: (1) preoccupation with themes of socioeconomic resentment; (2) use of socially "levelling" lists of hierarchies and catalogues; (3) excessive, often blasphemous wordplay; (4) the blending and thus the "levelling" of incongruous genres; (5) justification of symbolic transgression, especially in the context of lay preaching, as a prophetic behaviour; (6) imagery of self-fortification against persecution and martyrdom; (7) preoccupation with themes of praise and gratitude, often based on the Psalmic tradition; (8) excessive use of allusion and echo; (9) hyperbole; (10) extreme disjunctiveness.[13] In its critiques of hegemonic systems of power and stratification, enthusiastic discourse was almost always suppressed by social and religious institutions. Hawes's study is partly an examination of the ways in which the propagators of enthusiastic rhetoric have been pathologized by institutions in an attempt to (often physically) arrest and contain them. As a rhetoric of oppositional discourse, enthusiasm appears in a variety of forms in all of the black women's texts. But this prevailing tendency toward the Western enthusiastic mode is encouraged and uniquely colored by a tradition of African expressivity. Such expressivity is especially powerful in Belinda's *Petition,* Julia Foote's *A Brand Plucked from the Fire: An Autobiographical Sketch by Mrs. Julia A. J. Foote,* Sojourner Truth's *Narrative,* and Rebecca Cox Jackson's journals. Truth, for example, writing out of the space of the (African American) abject, the voiceless, the void of the unspoken, writes a form of the blues. The blues are an expressive medium that James Cone traces back to its African roots:

> As with the spirituals, the Africanism of the blues is related to the *functional* character of West African music. And this is one of the essential ingredients of black music which distinguishes it from Western music and connects it with its African heritage. "The fact that American Negro

13. Clement Hawes, *Mania and Literary Style: The Rhetoric of Enthusiasm from the Ranters to Christopher Smart,* 10–11.

music, like the African, is at the core of daily life explains the immemorial African quality of all Negro *folk* music in this country, if not of the Negro in exile everywhere."[14]

In traditional black American culture, the blues singer voices the hard experiences of her life so that she may confront and overcome them. Thus, Truth's autobiography and narrative strategy become a kind of blues in the order of performance/testimony. Indeed it seems to me that the evangelists may all be seen as blues "bad" women—to use Bernard Bell's description of Shug Avery in Alice Walker's *Color Purple*—cut from a more pious cloth than their secular singing sisters.[15] We may wonder if the same circumstances that influenced many black blues women to embark upon itinerant careers of tent shows and theater performances also influenced evangelist women. Harrison notes that famous blues singer Ida Cox, born in Knoxville, Tennessee, in 1889, started traveling with the Rabbit Foot Minstrels at the early age of fourteen—a career that reflects a pattern characteristic of many classic blues singers. The evangelists also "performed" under tents in camp meetings. Poverty forced many black women performers to the streets to find a living through music, even though the black community, in its classification of a "proper" life for young women, saw theater, music, and performance as sinful callings for "nice young ladies."[16]

Many regarded evangelists as lewd, greedy, and self-serving, and either lesbians or out to "pick up" men. As Betty Overton observes in her study of fictional depictions of black women preachers, black literature presents a "half-view" of these women—a view "characterized by an attitude that women do not belong in the pulpit and that they earn their suffering and problems by their daring to take on this role." The women are presented as caricatures of "the worst that is in religious ministry," becoming "normal" only after leaving that

14. James Cone, *The Spirituals and the Blues: An Interpretation*, 98.

15. Bernard Bell, *The Afro-American Novel and Its Tradition*, 264.

16. Daphne Duval Harrison, "Black Women in the Blues Tradition," in *The Afro-American Woman: Struggles and Images,* ed. Sharon Harley and Rosalyn Terborg-Penn, 58–63.

ministry. Overton examines novels by Claude Brown (*Manchild in the Promised Land*); Kristin Hunter (*The Soul Brothers and Sister Lou*); Langston Hughes (*Tambourines to Glory*); James Baldwin (*The Amen Corner* and *Just above My Head*); and Ann Shockley (*Say Jesus and Come to Me*) as works that "collectively present a rather negative picture of the black woman preacher."[17] My work will examine for the first time what black preacher women as a group in America had to say for *themselves*. Harrison quotes Alberta Hunter: "'To me, the blues are almost religious . . . almost sacred—when we sing the blues, we're singing out of our own hearts . . . our feelings. . . . Maybe we're hurt and just can't answer back.' "[18]

As women of God, the blues "bad" preacher women challenge hegemonic systems of race and gender. Consequentially, they are read out of churches and threatened with violence. They are "unnatural" women. The "unnatural woman" is the black woman preacher, lit-igator, speaker in the public domain who challenges the tenets of "true (natural) womanhood"—the Sojourners, Elaws, Broughtons, Janies, Shugs, and Pilates of black women's writing. How do these women, through (per)formance of self in tropes and narrative strate-gies in their autobiographies bring the very notion of what is "natural" in white/male terms into question? By "(per)formance" I mean a profound self-fashioning that demystifies and challenges the "perfor-mance" of black womanhood prescribed and/or described as "natu-ral" by hegemonic discourses. As Neil Evernden suggests in *The Social Creation of Nature*, if there is nature, then we as a society speak of things "belonging to nature" or of the "natural." If some things are "natural," we then speak of others as "unnatural"—there are some things that may exist that are "beyond or against nature." Evernden quotes C. S. Lewis's playful definition of the unnatural: "'anything which has changed from its sort or kind may be described as *unnatural*, provided that the change is one the speaker deplores. Behaviour is *unnatural* . . . not simply when it is held to be a departure from that which a man's *nature* would lead to of itself, but when it is a departure

17. Betty Overton, "Black Women Preachers: A Literary View," 158–65.
18. Harrison, "Black Women in the Blues Tradition," 63.

for the worse.' " The unnatural, Evernden encourages us to notice, is a "pejorative term."[19]

Joanne Braxton examines the development of black women's spiritual autobiography using the writings of Jarena Lee and Rebecca Cox Jackson as representative works. She also briefly examines the career of Sojourner Truth, which she (mistakenly, it seems to me) terms a "secular narrative." While Braxton chronicles the autobiographers' quest "for personal power and their assertion of the literary self . . . the problem of attaining freedom and literacy . . . expressed in dreams, premonitions, and visions," she does not conduct a close examination of their writings, or of the writings of the numerous other female spiritual autobiographers that constitute a complex genre complicated by issues of editing, performance, sexuality, historicity, community, class, and denominational affiliation. I will undertake that examination here.[20]

Frances Smith Foster also focuses on the writings of Jarena Lee. She tentatively suggests that African influences might explain "certain stylistic features" of early African American writing, and refers to the "praise-songs" mentioned by Lee, but she does not pursue such influences or features or examine how they might have been modified over time or within religious denominations.[21] For example, how do the formal and rhetorical devices employed by Rebecca Cox Jackson, initially an African Methodist and finally a Shaker, writing around 1843, differ from those used by southerner Virginia Broughton, a Baptist missionary writing in 1907?

The evangelists preached and wrote in a unique manner that complicated a number of autobiographical modes. Significantly, they favored neither the individualistic "moi, moi seul" favored by most white and many black male American autobiographers (for example, Britton Hammon, John Jea, or Frederick Douglass) nor the imposed domestic solitude in which the first white American female autobiog-

---

19. Neil Evernden, *The Social Creation of Nature*, 21.
20. Braxton, *Black Women Writing Autobiography*, 49–72.
21. Foster, *Written by Herself*, 56–76.

raphers most often found themselves.[22] Against great obstacles, many African American evangelist women struggled long and hard to come to terms with the ideal expressed in West African autobiography, of coexistence within the community or group—of autobiography as "autophylography . . . a portrait of nous, nous ensemble." James Olney argues that, unlike the individualism of typically Western auto-biographies in which the writer makes a "claim of absolute uniqueness and imagines that his experience is unrepeated and unrepeatable," African "autophylography" emphasises both the life shared by the group in the present moment and the shared life lived "countless times before, shaped by the ritual stages of birth and naming, initiation, marriage, parenthood, eldership, and death that have given form to the life of [the] people for as far back as the legendary, mythic memory of the people extends."[23] In this schema, memory is not a personal phenomenon, but a collective one. Thus, we witness in the personal narratives of Belinda, Julia Foote, and Sojourner Truth narrative strategies such as the recounting of communal tribal ritual, sermonality (communal preacher-congregation interaction), and collective storytelling, respectively. These narratives prefigure the communal telling and/or remembering played out in Zora Neale Hurston's *Their Eyes Were Watching God,* Alice Walker's *The Color Purple,* Toni Cade Bambara's *The Salt Eaters,* or Toni Morrison's *Paradise.* But for the early black American women evangelists, "nous, nous ensemble" is complicated also. The sense of the too-womanish black woman dwelling "like a speckled bird" (a biblical metaphor used by both Elaw and Elizabeth to describe themselves) among various communities, black and white, in a long, difficult, and often frustrated search for belonging, becomes a recurring and troubling theme, echoed in the works of many contemporary black women.

I have already mentioned that the sentimental autobiography of Harriet Jacobs was accepted by nineteenth-century readers, while the

---

22. Phebe Davidson, *Religious Impulse in Selected Autobiographies of American Women (c. 1630–1893),* 65.

23. James Olney, "The Value of Autobiography for Comparative Studies: African vs. Western Autobiography," in *African American Autobiography: A Collection of Critical Essays,* ed. William Andrews, 218.

narratives of the evangelists were not. Aside from its popularity as
a sentimental autobiography/novel, I suggest that the work might
have appealed to its readers as a kind of pornographic text. William
Andrews observes that abolitionist editors wanted slave narratives to
titillate audiences, and we may wonder if that is exactly what Jacobs's
narrative accomplishes.[24] I suggest that her text about black women's
sexuality became immensely marketable *because* of its prurient theme,
recognizable to a nineteenth-century community of readers (well
acquainted, for example, with Sara Baartman, the famed "Hottentot Venus") who saw black women as inextricably entangled in hy-
persexuality. I ask if Jacobs's text functions, even as it protests the
sexualization of black women, as a kind of pornography in the sense
Judith Butler suggests—that Jacobs's words, appropriated by eager
readers, are made to signify the *opposite* of what Jacobs intends them
to mean.[25] Black women writing in the nineteenth century struggled
to be heard on their own terms, but it seems that how and what their
writing signified was often dependent on audiences whose narrative
economies about the lives of black women differed drastically from the
narratives by the women themselves. If the women were recognized
at all, it may not have been in the manner that they intended (as may
be the case of Jacobs). Lacking any material that could be misread
as pornography, and refusing to employ the sentimental form and
content of so many nineteenth-century women's texts, the majority
of the black female evangelists' works were ignored and bypassed on
the literary market and simply fell out of circulation. In the history
of black women in America, this theme of speech, recognizability,
and silence has been an ongoing one—one that I will explore in my
examination of (per)formance as trope and narrative strategy in black
women's texts. What are the gains and sacrifices involved in this per-
former/audience transaction? How and to whom do the black women
evangelists strive to make themselves recognizable? Recognizability—
or *non*recognizability, as such—is how the words of some come not to
be heard at all, or to be distorted altogether.

24. William Andrews, *To Tell a Free Story: The First Century of Afro-American
Autobiography, 1760–1865*, 62.
25. Judith Butler, *Excitable Speech: A Politics of the Performative*, 82–86.

Further, how do the black women's writings function as (per)form-ances of black female selfhood, negotiating the delicate balance be-tween maintaining themselves as subjects acquiescent to white and/or male expectations and performing insurrectionary acts of resubjecti-fication? How do they exhibit what Darlene Hine terms the "culture of dissemblance" in which, to counteract negative social and sexual images of their womanhood, black women develop "the appearance of openness and disclosure but actually [shield] the truth of their inner lives and selves from their oppressors"?[26] Are there ways in which the black women evangelists say one thing and mean another, as Hine has suggested? How does the text perform? What does it say, and what does it actually accomplish? Are the two the same? How do the evangelists write of their experiences of womanhood, both spiritual and physical? How do physical exhibition, stripping and selling the body, and castration become tropes of power as well as of subjugation and fear? For example, Zilpha Elaw likens herself to the "Ethopian eunuch," yet oddly, she does not display any fearful psychological effects of castration but goes on her way "rejoicing." How does Elaw's "inward man" present a unique mode of fearless resistance and power?

The manner in which the unrecognizable, unnatural, "unspeak-able" texts of the evangelists become speakable is perhaps a gradual process of what Butler calls "resignification" or "social iterability"—so that what is unintelligible or illegitimate to nineteenth-century discourses of, say, true womanhood, becomes intelligible and legit-imate to contemporary readers.[27] Butler's "resignification" resem-bles Gates's "signifyin(g)," in that both speech acts seek not only to counter, but often to alter the meaning of speech. Signifyin(g) differs from resignification in that signifyin(g) is a social and socially accepted act with roots deeply embedded in African and African American communities. Not only that, but signifyin(g) is a game, a public performance in the fun-loving sense of the word, a chance to humorously demonstrate one's verbal prowess at the expense of an-other. Gates has also used signifyin(g) to refer to the loving exchanges

26. Darlene Hine, "Rape and the Inner Lives of Black Women in the Middle West: Preliminary Thoughts on the Culture of Dissemblance," 912.
27. Butler, *Excitable Speech*, 152.

that occur between black artists. In the case of black women writers, signifyin(g) becomes a transference of the seeds of the mothers' gardens, or a "saving of the text" (as Nanny tells Janie in *Their Eyes Were Watching God*), for the late twentieth-century daughters. Thus, the "resignificatory" autobiographies of Truth (1850) and other black evangelist women are "signified" upon by Zora Neale Hurston, whose signification in *Their Eyes* is echoed by Alice Walker in *The Color Purple* and so on, until what was unintelligible has become intelligible.

How, over time and across religious denominations, African American women spiritual autobiographers combine the variety of discourses available to them with African influences, and African American expressive strategies will be the subject of my investigation. The evangelists employ sermonizing structures, narrative style, tropes, orality, and what Karla Holloway terms "revision, remembrance, and recursion" in ways that differ from formal strategies used by their black male, white female, or black female "club" counterparts.[28] In my examination of the writings of Belinda and eight spiritual autobiographers—Jarena Lee, Zilpha Elaw, Rebecca Cox Jackson, Julia Foote, Sojourner Truth, Elizabeth, Amanda Smith, and Virginia Broughton—I explore the tensions in the texts between the manner in which each text carries the seeds of the mothers' gardens and the manner in which it exhibits the traits of the "Northern-departed daughters." I investigate how, across times and denominations, tropes of the body, music, literacy, trial, performance, and the "unnatural" are reflected in self-conscious narrative performances of communal telling, sermonality, and song. I have used the texts of several black male and white female autobiographers (John Jea, Richard Allen, Daniel Payne, Frederick Douglass, and Harriet Livermore among them) for the purposes of comparison. For example, Douglass's secular narrative grew out of the genre of the spiritual autobiography, and critics such as Gates and Braxton demonstrate how Douglass signifies upon and secularizes important spiritual moments in earlier religious texts. The question of why the black evangelist women clung to an "outdated" spiritual genre while more popular black writers, such as

---

28. Karla Holloway, *Moorings and Metaphors: Figures of Culture and Gender in Black Women's Literature*, 13.

Douglass and Harriet Jacobs, were turning to the secular mode is an important one. What did the living of a deeply spiritual life and the writing of a spiritual text mean to these women in terms of preserving an African American worldview that valorised the immanent power of the divine? Lincoln and Mamiya note: "The core values of black culture like freedom, justice, equality, an African heritage, and racial parity . . . are raised to ultimate levels and legitimated by the black sacred cosmos. . . . The close relationship between the black sacred cosmos and black culture has often been missed by social analysts who impose sacred/secular distinctions too easily upon the phenomena of black culture."[29]

In chapter 1 I examine the manner in which "Belinda, an African" uses the petition as a means by which to record a life story markedly characterized by its privileging of Africentric modes of spiritual being. Chapter 2 deals with Jarena Lee (African Methodist Episcopalian, 1836) and Zilpha Elaw (affiliated with white Methodist church, 1846) as African Americans articulating their existence in a strongly Christian framework. Chapter 3 deals with Sojourner Truth (nondenominational, 1850) and her strongly (per)formative text. In my study of Rebecca Cox Jackson (Shaker, text written between 1830 and 1864) in chapter 4, I investigate how editorial processes change the conversion stories of black evangelist women such as Jackson, altering the very sense of who she is as an African American. I have used some of Jackson's manuscripts as well as information about the prepublication editing process for Harriet Jacobs's *Incidents in the Life of a Slave Girl* to extrapolate and tentatively suggest what the process might have been like for other black women such as Truth. Chapter 5 examines the autobiography of Julia Foote (AME Zion, 1879) as a political, preacherly text. In Chapter 6 I investigate the autobiographies of Amanda Smith (AME, 1889), Elizabeth (nondenominational, 1889), and Virginia Broughton (Baptist, 1907)—the "Northern-departed daughters." My discussion of Zora Neale Hurston in chapter 7 focuses on Hurston's role in connecting early black women evangelist writers and black women writing today. The mothers have laid the groundwork for

29. C. Eric Lincoln and Lawrence H. Mamiya, *The Black Church in the African American Experience*, 7.

several important themes and tropes still visible in the works of the daughters—for example, the privileging of orality over literacy, the image of the "unnatural" blues bad woman as performer and priestess, the vexed issue of the strong black woman's quest to be both individual and member of her community (whatever community that may turn out to be), the black woman's (per)formance of self and text, and the black woman on trial. In chapter 8, I turn to the works of the daughters: Alice Walker's *The Color Purple,* Toni Morrison's *Beloved* and *Paradise,* and Toni Cade Bambara's *The Salt Eaters.*

The gardens of the mothers were never completely abandoned. While critics have traced a line of development from Jarena Lee and one or two other evangelists to Harriet Jacobs and the sentimental writers of the late nineteenth and early twentieth centuries, to Zora Neale Hurston in the Harlem Renaissance, the words and writings of the evangelists have remained largely forgotten, silenced. It is time to revive them, to see how the mothers kept the traditions of *their* mothers alive. As Alice Walker has written: "We are a people. A people do not throw their geniuses away. And if they are thrown away, it is our duty as artists and as witnesses for the future to collect them again for the sake of our children, and, if necessary, bone by bone."[30] The remainder of this text is a response to that admonition.

30. Walker, *In Search of Our Mothers' Gardens,* 92.

# ONE

## *The Cruelty of Men Whose Faces Were Like the Moon*

Petition of An African Slave, to the Legislature of
Massachusetts. To the honourable the [*sic*] senate and
house of representatives, in general court assembled: The
petition of Belinda, an African, Humbly shews. . . .

THESE ARE SOME of the first known words ciphered in the public
domain by an African woman in America.[1] They were published
by a Philadelphia magazine in 1787, five years after the aged and
penurious Belinda began resolutely petitioning a Boston court for a
judgment against her master concerning money owed her. I do not
write "African *American* woman" at this juncture, for the petitioner,
whose African name we do not know—this woman called "Belinda"—
identifies herself in no uncertain terms as "an African," although it is
in the legal discourse of the Legislature of Massachusetts that she
begins her litigation. Speaking out of the silence in black writing
in English up until the eighteenth century, Belinda—the earliest
known black woman in America whose life story survives (albeit in
the form of a legal petition) among those of a number of eighteenth-
century black male autobiographers—attests to the power of the
doubly marginalised black female voice to find expression through
whatever means are available.

Nonautobiographical writings of other black women have emerged
from the eighteenth century—the highly British-imitative, mainly

---

1. Belinda, "Petition of an African Slave, to the Legislature of Massachusetts,"
in *The American Museum or Repository of Ancient and Modern Fugitive Pieces, Prose and
Poetical,* vol. 1, no. 6: 538–40, hereinafter cited as B in the text.

occasional verse of Phillis Wheatly (*Poems on Various Subjects, Religious and Moral,* 1733) is extant, as well as a poem by Lucy Terry Prince entitled "Bars Fight" (1746), detailing an Indian massacre of a predominantly white settlement. But except for Belinda's petition, nothing by a black woman has so far come to light that we may call autobiography—that is, in the words of William Andrews, a sustained taking "one's own life (or some major portion of it) seriously enough to find in it a significance that makes reconstructing that life valuable to another." Belinda's petition before the Massachusetts Legislature would certainly qualify as autobiography under this definition. However, problems arise when we examine Andrews's next criterion; in his valuable analysis of the first century of African American autobiography, he chooses to admit all forms of first-person prose narratives written or told on recollection by African Americans from 1760 to 1865. This includes spiritual autobiographies, criminal confessions, captivity narratives, travel accounts, interviews, and memoirs. Because of the problems of origin, composition, editing, and manuscript control that complicate the investigation of early African American autobiography, Andrews is careful not to treat as autobiography anything that does not "[emanate] from the consciousness of the black man himself"; therefore, he argues, his primary criterion is "any work . . . written in the first person singular."[2] Such a criterion would exclude Belinda's third-person (black woman's) narrative.

I would argue, however, that the self-effacing slave narratives or criminal confessions supposedly taken down verbatim are at least as problematic as third-person accounts written at the behest of a slave—such as Belinda's petition. The complicated issues of voice, origin, editing, composition, and manuscript control exist with all early African American autobiographies—not only those written by white amanuenses, but even those written by blacks themselves. The question of performance creeps into all autobiography and certainly into all black writing that has passed through any form of white-controlled editorship. Thus, to ignore the third-person petition of Belinda because it seems more "biographical" than "autobiographical" is to ignore the life-writing of a black woman who found a way,

2. Andrews, *To Tell a Free Story,* 16–19.

over nearly insurmountable obstacles, of getting her voice heard at all. The injunction of Gwendolyn Etter-Lewis concerning early African American women's writing is relevant here:

> [M]ost early autobiographies of African American women can be found in this gray area, this middle ground between subject (autobiography) and object (biography). These women arrived at autobiography through a mongrel form—the slave narrative, many of which were "as told to" or ghost-written accounts. Dismissal of these texts because of their collaborative authorship would have permanently lost to obscurity crucial aspects of American history and culture.[3]

It is impossible to believe that Belinda was not a present and powerful agent in the formation of her petition, or that the petition emanates principally from any consciousness other than her own, when we consider that the petition is the result of actual conditions that prompted a black woman identifiable only as "Belinda" to take legal action in alleviating her situation, and that the petition is a bold valorization of African epistemological and ontological belief systems.

Documents show that Belinda petitioned the legislature not once, but several times. Kaplan and Kaplan observe:

> The General Court quickly responded to Belinda's plea, granting her an annual pension of some fifteen pounds out of the expropriated rents and profits of her former master. But this pension came to a halt after the first year. Time passed; despite her many requests for relief, she "never could obtain any more. . . ." During the spring of 1787, she again memorialized the legislature. . . . In June, the sympathetic editor of a Philadelphia journal printed her original petition. In November, the Court granted the old woman another year's pension. How long "Belinda an african" and her "more infirm daughter" plodded along in Boston is not known.[4]

3. Gwendolyn Etter-Lewis, *My Soul Is My Own: Oral Narratives of African American Women in the Professions*, 161.

4. Sidney Kaplan and Emma Nogrady Kaplan, *The Black Presence in the Era of the American Revolution*, 244.

The Kaplans suggest that Belinda's amanuensis might have been another African American. In light of the strong Africentricity of the work, this seems entirely possible. But white or black, she or he has not been identified, and it is difficult to say how much of the petition is of his or her design and how much of it is Belinda's. We can only surmise that Belinda was a driving force behind the creation of her own petition and examine how her text negotiates dialogue with the prevailing discourses of its day. In the case of early black male autobiographers, Gates and Andrews point out that the general movement in their writing was toward assimilation—a desire to appear as European as possible in a world that saw blackness as negativity or "absence." In these early men's writings questions go unanswered, and large gaps and silences appear, because, as Andrews notes: "the thematic sub-structure [is] generally defined according to the semantic fields and constitutive rules of white institutions and discourse. As a result, much early black autobiography traffics in ignorance about the actual choices black people had in America and about the meaning of those choices from a black perspective."[5] Using the "fields" and "rules" handed down to her by dominant power structures, a black woman might have found it necessary, as the earliest black male autobiographers did, to use prevailing white notions of what a black person should be—that is, a diligent student of European manners and mores.

But Belinda rejects all such notions and defines herself. Silence about the harsh realities of black existence in America does not inform her narrative. Neither does she maintain a European value system. Instead, her petition is constructed around a powerful African point of reference that does not present a suitably Christianized, literate, and Westernized black consciousness, in accordance with prevailing expectations for blacks but, rather, demonstrates a stubborn oppositionality to prevailing Western discourses. Belinda, seeking to have her grievances heard, turns to the petition as a means of resistance, and so finds a palimpsest for the mapping of a resistant African self in Western letters.

5. Andrews, *To Tell a Free Story*, 42.

By 1782, the petition had been used by blacks in America for some time, as a means of seeking redress for injustices committed by whites against them. Kaplan and Kaplan trace the beginnings of black petitioning to New England, 1773–1774, when five petitions—albeit cautiously worded—reflected a mood among blacks there of anger, exasperation, and the desire for equal treatment under the law. In these petitions we see references to black Americans as "Lover[s] of True Liberty" and "The Sons of Africa." Here we have no Hammon, Marrant, Equiano, or Gronniosaw—black men describing themselves in terms of black "absence"; rather there is a statement of blackness as presence—and *contentious* presence into the bargain. This blackness challenges whites to honor the spirit of their soon-to-be-legislated Declaration of Independence, to abandon a hypocrisy that prevents them from extending the tenets of the rights of freedom to blacks as well as whites. One petition, signed on May 25, 1774, by "a Grate Number of Blackes of the Province" and submitted to the new governor of Massachusetts reads in part:

> we are a freeborn Pepel and have never forfeited this Blessing by aney compact or agreement whatever. But we were unjustly dragged by the cruel hand of power from our dearest frinds and sum of us stolen from the bosoms of our tender Parents and from a Populous Pleasant and plentiful country and Brought hither to be made slaves for Life in a Christian land.[6]

It is this language that informs the petition of Belinda to the Massachusetts Legislature eight years later, in 1782. Strikingly similar references to a happy native country, as well as mentions of "tender parent[s]" and "the cruelty" of white men (B, 539) suggest that Belinda borrows a mode of discourse as yet unexamined in the research of early African American autobiographical forms. This is a discourse of active resistance, and as such, it situates itself against the more assimilative writings of black men such as Gronniosw, Marrant, Hammon, and Equiano.

6. Kaplan and Kaplan, *Black Presence,* 13.

Yet, even among black petitions, Belinda's is singular in that it is written and signed with the mark not of a man, or a number of male petitioners, but of a lone woman. Also, it goes further than other petitions in its refusal to subscribe to any Western sociomoral codes whatever. Black male autobiographers and petitioners honor the Christian God, quote scripture as a means of asserting themselves as equal to whites in a common spiritual brotherhood, or declare themselves law-abiding Christians. Such declarations are a means of attaining credibility with Christian whites. But Belinda asserts that it is a plurality of male and female Nature spirits, "the great Orisa, who made all things," and the "dishonoured deity" (B, 539), presumably Oludumare, whom she worshiped as a child in Africa. Oludumare is the One God of Ifa, a religion of the Yoruba people of West Africa. The Orisa, Oludumare's ambassadors, are the link between Heaven and Earth.[7] Belinda's assertion, when combined with a metaphorical allusion to her master that suggests a condemnation of Christianity and its followers, can only be read as an exceedingly bold gesture on the part of this black woman, standing as she does before the great white presence of the Legislature of Massachusetts: "What did it avail her that the walls of her lord were hung with splendor, and that the dust trodden under foot in her native country, crowded his gates with sordid worshippers! The law rendered her incapable of receiving property" (B, 539–40). The reference to her white master as "lord," the obvious Christian suggestiveness of this word, and the implicit conflation of Christian worship with gold-lust all create a "savage" indictment of hypocritical Western religious systems that claim to worship God but instead worship men and wealth. The hypocritical nature of Belinda's master is even further exposed as she recounts the manner in which he goes off to fight a war (presumably the American Revolution) "in the cause of freedom . . . in a land, where lawless dominion sits enthroned, pouring blood and vengeance on all who dare to be free" (B, 540).

As eagerly as the narratives of Hammon, Marrant, Gronniosaw, and Equiano embrace Christianity and the trappings of whiteness,

7. Philip John Neimark, *The Way of the Orisa*, 58.

Belinda rejects them. Hers is a refusal of white American standards of morality, a refusal similar to that of disillusioned and alienated male autobiographer Venture Smith, who, after failed attempts to succeed in the world of white men, stands bereft of friendship, agency, or religious conviction. Earlier than Smith's creation in 1798 of "an idealized African point of reference for defining morality," Belinda asserted her own Africentricity.[8] But Belinda differs markedly from Smith in that her final stance is not one of disillusioned alienation: "Vanity of vanities, all is vanity," Smith laments at the end of his narrative, after bitterly commenting on the futility of engaging in legal struggles with white men: "But Captain Hart was a *white gentleman,* and I a *poor African,* therefore, it was *all right,* and good enough for *the black dog* [italics in original]."[9] In contrast, Belinda's last words suggest hope and a readiness to continue the struggle: "she prays that such allowance will be made her . . . as will prevent her, and her more infirm daughter, from misery in the greatest extreme . . . *and she will ever pray* [italics mine]" (B, 540). These words offer a double meaning; while Belinda assures her readers that she will "ever" continue to petition the court, she will also petition God. But, in light of her earlier comments, we have our suspicions that her God is definitely not the God of the Legislature of Massachusetts. This fighting spirit is apparent throughout Belinda's narrative. We see it nowhere else so pronounced in eighteenth-century black autobiography; what we do see in the eighteenth century are black male writers for the most part addressing European and white-American debates about race, intellect, literacy, and the admissibility of Africans into the category delineating "human" subject.

I would like to examine some of the integral ways in which Belinda's text differs from the texts of black men writing in the eighteenth century. If Belinda does not use the literary trope of the talking book, as so many of her male counterparts did, she is certainly aware of the issues of orality, literacy, and humanity with which black male autobiographers grappled. However, unlike them, Belinda *critiques* literacy,

8. Andrews, *To Tell a Free Story,* 51–52.
9. Venture Smith, *A Narrative of the Life and Adventures of Venture, a Native of Africa . . . ,* 30.

as black women autobiographers such as Jarena Lee (1833), Sojourner Truth (1850), and Julia Foote (1879) would do after her. Like the nineteenth-century John Jea, and the eighteenth-century Gronnoisaw and Equiano, Belinda positions herself in two time frames: as both the present narrator and the young, ignorant "savage." But, while the men trace a process of becoming from "savage"-object (a lowly link in the ontological chain of being, to whom another object, the text, refuses to speak) to "civilized"-subject (now occupying the same chain link as white men and perfectly able to read the text), Belinda changes very little from the savage she once was in her narration. Refusing the equations of "savage"-object and "civilized"-subject, Belinda maintains an equation of her own, ever remaining the *"savage"-subject* of her own life and narrative, intent on deriving her sense of existence from "the land where she received her being" (B, 539). Her descriptions of her early, ignorant perceptions of things alien and/or Western—the white men with "faces . . . like the moon," the "floating world" of the slave ship, the "sporting monsters of the deep"— are not framed comically as are those of Equiano, Gronniosaw, or Jea. There is no attempt to hold up the young naive black self as the object of condescending authorial and readerly amusement, no sense of the funny pathos of a young savage cut off from the white civilized world by his color and his ignorance, as in Gronniosaw, who writes:

[My master] used to read prayers in public to the ship's crew every Sabbath day; and when I first saw him read, I was never so surprised in my life, as when I saw the book talk to my master, for I thought it did, as I observed him to look upon it, and move his lips. I wished it would do so with me . . . when nobody saw me, I opened it, and put my ear down close upon it, in great hopes that it would say something to me; but I was very sorry, and greatly disappointed, when I found that it would not speak. This thought immediately presented itself to me, that every body and every thing despised me because I was black.[10]

10. James Albert Ukawsaw Gronniosaw, *Narrative of the Most Remarkable Particulars in the Life of James Albert Ukawsaw Gronniosaw, an African Prince*, 16.

Instead, Belinda asserts that a series of novelties (ship, sea creatures, the meeting of the sea and the horizon) "strove, but in vain, to divert her attention from three hundred Africans in chains, suffering the most excruciating torment; and some of them rejoicing that the pangs of death came like a balm to their wounds" (B, 539). Belinda does not let us overlook the fact that, for her, the issue is not one of becoming literate or "civilized" but of remaining identified with her African sisters and brothers and refusing to forget the monstrous circumstances that have brought her before a white reading public in the first place. Just as Gronniosaw, Equiano, and Jea bring their scenes of naive comedy hard up against the scene of reading, in which the young slave encounters the "talking book" and realizes the necessity of leaving savagery behind, Belinda's scene of naïveté also immediately precedes a passage about the learning of Western language. However, learning the "sounds" of this new language are enough for the illiterate Belinda; she is not enamored of the language, as her male counterparts are. Her learning to speak English exacerbates rather than erases her sense of oppression and isolation as she learns the true extent of her powerlessness in this new world: "Once more her eyes were blest with a continent: but alas! how unlike the land where she received her being! Here all things appeared unpropitious. She learned to catch the ideas, marked by the sounds of language, only to know that her doom was slavery, from which death alone was to emancipate her" (B, 539). Belinda's petition is evidence, of course, that she does not remain completely powerless but learns to use English language in ways that subvert and criticize her oppressors. Belinda becomes her own "talking book," intent upon conveying orally her African history and experience, as well as her knowledge of the hypocrisy of American legal systems, through the language and conventions of Western tradition. One hundred years later, her attitude is reflected in that of Sojourner Truth, another black woman whose stubborn illiteracy did not prevent her from producing an autobiography, or from taking her grievances to court on numerous occasions—and winning.

Belinda's lack of concern with attaining literacy is extended to her attitudes toward gold. The gold chain given Gronniosaw by his mother becomes a symbol of savage greed that he happily casts off.

This gesture, suggests Henry Louis Gates, Jr., is a symbolic signification upon an Ashanti creation myth that Willem Bosman recounts in *A New and Accurate Description of the Coast of Guinea* (London, 1705). In the myth, God presents the greedy African with a choice between the gift of gold, and the gift of Western letters. Observes Gates, "The African, much to his regret, elected gold and was doomed by his avarice to be a slave. As a footnote to Bosman's first edition tells us, the African's avarice was an eternal curse, and his punishment was the doom of never mastering the Western arts and letters."[11] Gronniosaw casts off the gold chain given him by his ancestor in order to adopt Western letters and Western ways of being; Marrant encourages the savage Indian chief to give up *his* gold chain; Equiano longs to gain power over the objects that seem to invest his master with power, one of which is a watch (which Gates presumes to be gold); and finally John Jea turns the gold chain into metaphorical chains of sin from which he as spiritual aspirant must free himself. Only Ottobah Cuguano, writing in Britain in 1787, explicitly locates greed in the desire not of Africans and other savages, but of Europeans in their avaricious and unscrupulous quest for land and riches.

Like Cuguano's narrative, Belinda's petition stands in direct opposition to the Ashanti myth. If Willem Bosman recounts a story that paints Africans as both stupid and greedy, and most black male autobiographers portray themselves as needing to relinquish such innate greed, Belinda's story reverses such attitudes. As a child, she did not realize that "*Europeans* [italics mine] placed their happiness in the yellow dust, which she carelessly marked with her infant footsteps" or that this "dust trodden under foot in her native country" crowded her master's gates with "sordid worshippers" (B, 539, 540). Belinda disrupts European perceptions of "the greedy savage African" by presenting us with an oppositional story of her own. Her text indicates that she was a worshiper of the Orisa; as such, she most likely belonged to the Yoruba people, who, from Belinda's account, obviously lay no claim to "savage" gold-lust. The wealth of Belinda's Africa is marked in her estimation by "mountains, covered with spicy forests—the vallies, loaded with the richest fruits, spontaneously produced—joined to

11. Gates, *Signifyin(g) Monkey,* 141.

that happy temperature of air, which excludes excess." The idyllic picture of Africans living in contented moderation is disrupted in the next breath by the advent of the true savages—Sangolike men "whose faces were like the moon, and whose bows and arrows were like the thunder and the lightning of the clouds." In Ifa religion individual humans are governed by their own Orisa; one bears the characteristics of one's presiding nature spirit. Sango, one of the Orisa, is the spirit of thunder and lightning. An Orisa of "quick and vociferous temper," he is best known for his warriorlike nature and his ability as a strategist. Neimark comments, "Sangos using their energy in a nonproductive manner can wreak havoc."[12] Belinda characterizes the invading white men as children of Sango—interestingly, a sky god, like the God of Christianity. She juxtaposes the savagery and gold-lust of the invading Europeans against African familial kinship, and devotion to God: "[E]ven when she, in a sacred grove, with each hand in that of a tender parent, was paying her devotion to the great Orisa, who made all things, an armed band of white men, driving many of her countrymen in chains, rushed into the hallowed shades!" (B, 539).

While Gronniosaw, Marrant, and Jea associate the shedding of gold chains with the shedding of the chains of savage greed and the adoption of white Christianity, Belinda (like the British Cuguano) creates a new relationship between the three elements Christianity, chains, and gold-lust. Belinda draws attention to the actuality of the situation, to the eighteenth-century reality of the relationship between chains and black people. She suggests that for Africans, gold signifies nothing; it possesses none of the symbolic exchange value it accrues in the West, but lies undifferentiated from the dust under the feet of blacks intent upon worshipping their own gods.

In the passage describing her experience in America, Belinda again presents us with the reality of the relation between Christianity, gold, and chains. As I have already mentioned, she conflates whites' worship of the Christian "lord" with their worship of slave-owning aristocrats and the gold that such aristocrats accrue from slavery. Belinda, herself legally chained chattel, can only stand by and observe the scene of this hypocrisy: "What did it avail her that the walls of her lord

12. Neimark, *The Way of the Orisa*, 105.

were hung with splendour . . . The laws rendered her incapable of receiving property." Although "never had she a moment at her own disposal [having been] compelled to ignoble servitude for the benefit of [her master]," none of his wealth belongs to her. But Belinda, having exposed the reality of the relationship between Africans, gold, chains, and religion, sets out to change that reality, and does. In the final analysis, her petition is a performative act that breaks the legal chains keeping her from accessing her master's wealth; and all the while, she vows that she "will ever pray," petitioning not only the court, but also, implicitly, her own African God for deliverance from the injustices of her oppressors.

To read Belinda's petition is to read a captivity narrative of sorts. However, it is unlike the captivity narratives of Briton Hammon or John Marrant, who, situating themselves as honorary whites, imitate the conventions of a white literary form very popular in the seventeenth and eighteenth centuries. In the conventional captivity narrative, white men and women recount their horrific experiences as hostages at the hands of savage Indian tribes. Hammon, who after his title page, never once refers to the fact that he is a black man calls his Indian captors "those barbarous and inhuman Savages," and repeatedly thanks God's providence for his deliverance.[13] Marrant brings Christianity to the benighted Cherokee and avoids death at their cruel hands. Belinda, however, is no emissary of Christian white men. Her tale certainly adopts the discourse and form of a captivity narrative, detailing an idyllic scenario of peaceful existence that is violated by marauding savages who tear innocent children from their parents' bosoms and loving husbands from their wives. But in a profound reversal, those living in "complete felicity" upon the bounteous land are not European settlers, but Africans, and Belinda's savages are white men.

The astuteness with which Belinda "learned to catch the ideas" of her day is not to be underestimated. She is obviously able to enter into and comment upon a number of dominant eighteenth-century discourses that vilify blackness—discourses that equate civilization with

13. Briton Hammon, *A Narrative of the Uncommon Sufferings, and Surprizing Deliverance of Briton Hammon, a Negro Man . . .* , 6.

whiteness, Christianity, and literacy and that attempt to rescue blacks from the "chains" of savagery and gold lust. Illiteracy does not prevent Belinda from entering into these discourses, for she comes before the Massachusetts Legislature with nothing but her voice to present her case and an amanuensis to translate her African experience into Western letters on a page. Standing defiantly outside of Euro-American ontological and epistemological systems, she challenges them with a fierce oppositional Africanness that would not be seen again in black women's writing for many years.

## TWO

# *Jarena Lee and Zilpha Elaw*
## The Beginnings of African American
## Women's Christian Autobiography

FORTY-NINE YEARS AFTER the 1787 publication of Belinda's petition in a Philadelphia journal, the autobiography of Jarena Lee appeared. Lee's twenty-odd-page narrative is the second known attempt by a black woman in America to record the story of her life in writing. It is entitled *The Life and Religious Experience of Jarena Lee, a Coloured Lady, Giving an Account of Her Call to Preach the Gospel.* Ten years after Lee, another black woman would publish her autobiography—the *Memoirs of the Life, Religious Experience, Ministerial Travels and Labours of Mrs. Zilpha Elaw, an American Female of Colour* appeared in London. Until recently, Elaw's text has received relatively brief analysis. Frances Smith Foster, Joanne Braxton, and William Andrews devote about two pages each to Elaw in their texts *Written by Herself, Black Women Writing Autobiography,* and *To Tell a Free Story,* respectively.

Who edited Lee's manuscript is unknown, but we do know that she paid five dollars for the service, and that three years after the 1833 revision, Lee had one thousand copies of her autobiography printed at a cost of thirty-eight dollars. As Sojourner Truth would do almost three decades later, Lee sold her book at various camp meetings, Methodist quarterly meetings, and even "in the public streets."[1] In 1839 Lee had another thousand copies of her *Life* printed, and in 1844 she sought the support and financial backing of the AME

---

1. Jarena Lee, *The Religious Experience and Journal of Mrs. Jarena Lee* (1849 ed.), 97–127; parenthetical references in text, hereinafter appearing as L, are to Lee in *Sisters of the Spirit,* ed. William Andrews.

Church for an expanded version of her work. However, the AME book committee refused Lee, claiming that her manuscript was "written in such a manner that it is impossible to decipher much of the meaning contained in it."[2] But disregarding the church's injunction that traveling preachers publish books or pamphlets only with formal church approval, in 1849, Lee financed another edition of her *Life*. I examine the 1836 version of Lee's autobiography here. It is about twenty-seven pages, much shorter and more concise than the 1849 version, which gives an exhaustive account of her engagements and travels. After the publication of her 1849 autobiography, Lee (then about sixty-six years old) falls into obscurity and silence, her activities unknown.

We may observe a somewhat similar pattern of independence in the trajectory of Zilpha Elaw's writing career: supporting herself, she traveled the countryside, preaching under no particular denomination. Unlike Lee, who sought out the AME Church, Elaw found herself occupying an uneasy position of liminality between black and white communities, which perhaps accounts for her description of herself as a "speckled bird" in her text. She was self-consciously concerned that, in the words of a white Quaker advisor, her "'deportment . . . be prudently conducted,'" since she was "situated . . . in connexion with two distinct communities, so opposite in condition, so contrasted in intelligence, and so antipodal in their feelings and prejudices."[3] She sailed for England in 1840, and she preached there until 1845, when she made plans to return to America. She was then about fifty-five. Her autobiography was "Published by the Authoress, and Sold by T. Dudley, 19, Charter-House Lane; and Mr. B. Taylor, 19, Montague-St. Spitalfields" (E, title page) in 1846. However, it is not known if she actually did return to America and, if she did, what her activities were thereafter.

Writing a half century after Belinda, Lee and Elaw situate themselves within the parameters of a polite, Westernized, Christian iden-

---

2. William Andrews, *Sisters of the Spirit: Three Black Women's Autobiographies of the Nineteenth Century*, 6.

3. Zilpha Elaw, "Memoirs of the Life, Religious Experience, Ministerial Travels and Labours of Mrs. Zilpha Elaw, an American Female of Colour," in *Sisters of the Spirit*, ed. William Andrews, 59, 93, hereinafter cited as E in the text.

tity. Thus, their autobiographies follow the formula of the early American Puritan spiritual narrative and the autobiographical examples of famous Methodist figures such as the white English Methodist George Whitefield ("A Short Account of God's Dealings with George Whitefield from His Infancy to His Ordination, 1714–1736, 1740"; and "A Further Account of God's Dealings with George Whitefield from the Time of His Ordination to His Embarking for Georgia, June, 1736–December, 1737 [Age 21–22]," 1744). Kathleen M. Swaim outlines the formula for traditional Puritan spiritual autobiography: an initial account of the horrible, sinful state of the narrator's soul before conversion; the call of God; the struggle with Satan before conversion; the conversion, generally brought about through the reading of some holy book; the struggle with temptation, despair and doubt after conversion; one last terrific bout with Satan; the promise of glory ever after.[4]

The spiritual autobiographies of Lee and Elaw are much more assimilative in their commentaries on religion, race, and slavery than Belinda's petition. Elaw's, for example, often reads like a white lady's travelogue:

> I returned to Huddersfield on the 11th of July, where I remained a few weeks; it is delightfully situated; being entirely surrounded with majestic hills, with several streams of water running through it, which conduces much to the prosperity of its manufacturing enterprise. There are in this town four places of worship belonging to the Episcopalians. . . . The houses are neat, and chiefly built of stone; there are several bridges, watering places and baths. It has a large market; and appears to be situated in a fruitful soil, abounding with fruit trees; the gardens are extensive and many of them tastefully laid out; and the approaches to it are by railway and good high roads. (E, 153)

Unlike Belinda, these women are increasingly concerned with the impact of their testimony upon a readership of predominantly white

---

4. Kathleen M. Swaim, "'Come and Hear': Women's Puritan Evidences," in *American Women's Autobiography: Fea(s)ts of Memory*, ed. Margo Culley, 32–38.

people. If Belinda represents a powerful African sensibility, the auto-biographies of Lee and Elaw display the African American "double-consciousness" of which W. E. B. Du Bois would later speak in *Souls of Black Folk*—that conflicting sense of Africanness and Americanness that characterizes the existence of blacks in America. For on the surface, the women present themselves merely as ignorant sinners who join the fold of believers, becoming pious preachers of God's word. In their autobiographies civil liberty for American blacks seems to become subsumed under the Christian ideal of liberty from sin, and all men and women become equal before the legislature of a Christian God. On the other hand, they never forget the sociopolitical impli-cations of what it means to be a black woman in nineteenth-century America—as Elaw tells God: "thou knowest we have many things to endure which others do not" (E, 89). That sense of their Africanness emerges in a certain carefully guarded "black expressivity"—the term Houston Baker employs in his discussion of black artistic style. It is an expressivity in which "the spirit comes through; the vernacular resounds in brilliant coalescence with the formally literary."[5] In a number of subtle tricksterlike reversals, Lee frustrates white demands for reliable black autobiographical fact-reporting; she also questions the shifting nature of biblical "truth" (even as she claims truth's stability), challenging the validity of patriarchally interpreted biblical meaning concerning women. William Andrews posits that we do not see such mischievous strategies in black (male) autobiographers until about 1855, nineteen years later than Lee. William Wells Brown (1855) is the first writer whose formal strategies Andrews finds "trickster-like"—Brown's lying, delightfully glib alter ego "Sanford" continually undermines Brown's insistence that "slavery makes its victims lying and mean."[6] In a similar manner of veiled resistance, Zilpha Elaw's autobiography, while appearing to be an exercise in "whiteface" and borrowed masculinity, demonstrates an oblique indictment of racial injustice toward blacks in both Britain and America; a sense of self not as black female (sexual) object but as subversive eunuch-subject; a privileging of the expressiveness of black song over the ornateness

5. Baker, *Workings of the Spirit*, 40.
6. Andrews, *To Tell a Free Story*, 147–65.

of the very white literary language she herself employs; and a reversal of the prevailing European-over-African relation by one that valorises the African and demotes Europeans from their presumed position of power.

Both Lee and Elaw demonstrate in their autobiographies a universalizing and depoliticizing trend common in black spiritual life-writing of the nineteenth century, in which "the conventional image of the pilgrim for Christ usurps the persona of the righteously indignant African."[7] Elaw claims early that her text is a spiritual one, portraying not the "features of my outward person" but the "lineaments of my inward man, as inscribed by the Holy Ghost" (E, 51); and Lee posits that her story is that of the progress of the inveterate liar and "wretched sinner" (L, 27) from a state of ignorance and guilt to one of Truth in Christ, and spiritual salvation. There is no Belinda here, no one who speaks of the power of the Orisa or the savage cruelty of hypocritical white men. Yet, although she links herself in a universal "holy communion" (E, 51) with her British readership, Elaw nevertheless opens her dedication to them in a highly didactic style that recalls the Apostles' addresses to their flocks of early Christians; and after advising them in the way they should go, she bids farewell: "And now, dear brethren, I commend you to God and the word of His grace, which is able to build you up, and give you an inheritance among all those who are sanctified" (E, 52). Positioning herself as teacher and her flock of British "Brethren" as student-aspirants, Elaw seeks a certain consubstantiation with whites on a spiritual level; but she is hardly the nineteenth-century African hopeful, traveling to the "Old World" to be trained and civilized in European ways. In a text that often resembles a nineteenth-century travelogue to some strange, exotic and heathen land, *Elaw* is the traveler abroad in a Britain needing civilization, presenting herself as educator, the ambassador of God to the (white) spiritually disinherited heathen there.

Similarly, writing of her first attempt to attend a (white) church, Lee levels a veiled criticism of the racism existing there: "it appeared that there was a wall between me and a communion with that people,

7. Ibid., 48.

which was higher than I could possibly see over, and seemed to make this impression upon my mind, *this is not the people for you*" (L, 28). But later, upon attending the African Methodist church: "I had come to the conclusion, that this is the people to which my heart unites . . . I embraced the opportunity. Three weeks from that day, my soul was gloriously converted to God" (L, 29). It is through such brief, implicit references only that she examines issues of race and racism.

In dealing with other issues, Lee is much less subtle; for example, she uses the discourse of white feminism in no uncertain terms, to critique the sexism she encounters in the African Methodist Episcopalian Zion church. Her references in her 1836 narrative to the sexism she encounters on her spiritual quest create an oppositional feminist discourse that is much bolder than her textual challenges to nineteenth-century racist ideologies. The fact that Lee is much more explicit in her condemnation of gender oppression seems to suggest that, in 1836, discourses of feminism—as threatening as they may have been to the male power structure—were more acceptable than abolitionist sentiments. Frances Smith Foster observes that Lee's aggressive rhetorical arguments supporting women as preachers in the church demonstrate a pattern common in women's spiritual autobiography—"the citation of arguments for women's ministries, arguments which by their very repetition become almost characteristic of this literature."[8] In Lee's 1849 expanded narrative, she is more explicit concerning issues of racism and her support of abolitionism— which, again, seems to support the historical fact that by midcentury, the issue of slavery had become a central one; laws and social conditions regulating the lives of blacks had become much more repressive, and black writers in anger and frustration had become bolder in their expressions of self and their condemnations of the peculiar institution.

Foster has also observed Lee's rejection of the criteria of the cult of true womanhood. These criteria would require Lee to assume social and physical characteristics generally reserved for white women. Lee challenges such dictates, however, by referring to herself as a

---

8. Foster, *Written by Herself,* 72–73.

"coloured lady," a concept that would seem to most readers a contradiction in terms. The drawing of Lee that appears on the frontispiece
of her autobiography depicts such contradiction—and, I would suggest, a certain double-consciousness—for although Lee is a black
woman, she is presented with narrow features and thin lips. Under-
neath her white bonnet, we may see what appears to be straight black
hair. Confounding white expectations of black women's "place," Lee
wears a white shawl and sits at a desk with books and paper before
her. In her right hand (on which there appears a ring on her fourth
finger), she holds a quill pen.

The tenets of true womanhood would dictate that Lee remain at
the hearthside with her sickly son, but Lee is not to be found there.
Maternal love and/or quiet modesty do not define Lee, who, like
Belinda and black preacher women after them both, transgresses
various laws that decree that, as a woman, she be silent, passive, and
compromising. As foremothers of the "cult of the unnatural woman"
Belinda, Lee, and Elaw enter the public domain of men, breaking the
prescribed, demure silence of "natural" femininity, performing acts
and uttering statements unthinkable for those who inscribe themselves within the tenets of "true womanhood." Leaving her son with
family, Lee travels up and down the country, preaching the word of
God to black and white communities alike, in the simple language of
God's "poor coloured female instrument" (L, 37).

But the language of Lee's autobiography is deceptively simple. Lee
challenges what is natural, holy, or accepted with the unnatural, un-
holy, and unaccepted in a kind of metalanguage that confounds lying
and truth, fiction and fact—and altogether disrupts the supposedly
simple relationship between signifier and signified. That linguistic
relationship was valorised in the spiritual and literary contexts in
which Jarena Lee found herself—Christianity demanded truthfulness,
as did white editors (often abolitionists) who demanded that black
autobiographers tell the truth in a manner that was "objective" and
unemotional.

Lee was probably familiar with other spiritual autobiographies
and slave narratives, such as those of black writers John Marrant
(1785), Solomon Bayley (1825), and AME church founder and bishop
Richard Allen (1833). Lee came into contact with Allen on a number

of occasions. Initially, when she approached him to request recognition as a preacher, Allen refused her; later he endorsed Lee not as a preacher, but in the lesser role of a traveling exhorter. Lee makes several mentions of her interactions with Allen in both her 1836 and 1849 autobiographies. In the later text she also refers to a biography of a black preacher entitled *The Essence of John Steward,* describing Steward as "a Colored man, with his miraculous call to the ministry" (L, 69). Lee was certainly aware of herself as part of a black spiritual literary tradition. She might have also been aware of the new trend in American literature of her day—the development of the eyewitness slave narrative. The first publications in this genre—for example, the narratives of Rev. Richard Allen (1833), Charles Ball (1836), Moses Roper (1837), or James Williams (1838)—are strangely lacking in authorial emotion, for in order to provide curious white readers with the "truth" about slavery, white editors instructed black narrators to be as factual and objective as possible in the presentation of information and to omit the expression of feeling and sentiment altogether. In these early slave narratives, the reader is assured that the narrator has offered nothing less than a dutiful rendition of the facts, that the written word as signifier represents as faithfully as possible the events signified, and that the language of the text is free of the vagaries of expressive emotion.

But on many occasions in her autobiography, Lee examines the shifting nature of writing, language, and meaning. Early in her text, Lee shows she is well aware that the language of texts can deceive, damage, and dehumanize. At the moment that Satan tempts her to drown herself in a brook, she writes:

> At the time I had a book in my hand; it was on a Sabbath morning, about ten o'clock; to [the brook] I resorted where on coming to the water I sat down on the bank, and on my looking into it; it was suggested, that drowning would be an easy death. It seemed as if some one was speaking to me, saying put your head under, it will not distress you.
> (L, 28)

Lee's conflation of "book" with "brook" suggests that "looking into it" (the book? the brook?) can be a dangerous affair. Like the brook, this talking book is an ever-shifting, treacherous concourse of language, which has the power to spiritually and physically obliterate her. Lee's autobiography was written in 1836—*after* the time when Henry Louis Gates, Jr., claims the trope of the talking book disappeared. For Jarena Lee, unlike her black male literary predecessors, literacy is *not* analogous with civility. Already literate, she is still a "wretched sinner," painfully aware of the socioeconomic discrepancies still existing between her work-shirking, lying black servant-self and her exacting white mistress. She is still plagued by suicidal tendencies. Like her black religious sisters, Lee does not believe in the power of literacy to civilize and redeem; she must continually discriminate between texts that are detrimental or conducive to her well-being.

After the b(r)ook incident, a well-meaning mistress took the Bible away from a troubled young Lee and gave her a novel to read instead. Realizing she had been given a fictional text, Lee "refused to read [it]" (L, 28). Later, in her discussion of the biblical account of an eternal Hell "where all liars, who repent not, shall have their portion" (L, 31), she points out the inability of humans, constrained by their limited understanding of "time," to truly comprehend the meaning of the biblical concept of the "bottomless pit":

> This [biblical] language is too strong and expressive to be applied to any state of suffering in *time*. Were it to be thus applied, the reality could no where be found in human life; the consequence would be, that *this* scripture would be found a false testimony. But when made to apply to an endless state of perdition, in eternity, beyond the bounds of human life, then this language is found not to exceed our views of a state of eternal damnation. (L, 31)

If a discrepancy exists between heavenly and earthly understanding of language, such a discrepancy is also evident between early church notions of the word *preach* and contemporary patriarchal notions. Lee argues that since Mary Magdalene's first announcement of the Resurrection of Christ, women have preached and continue to preach. Indeed, Mary, an uneducated woman who did not need a scriptural text from which to preach, is no different from the first disciples, also uneducated, unread men:

> But some will say, that Mary did not expound the Scripture, therefore, she did not preach, in the proper sense of the term. To this I reply, it may be that the term *preach*, in those primitive times, did not mean exactly what it is now *made* to mean; perhaps it was a great deal more simple then, than it is now:—if it were not, the unlearned fishermen could not have preached the gospel at all, as they had no learning. (L, 36–37)

Later in her spiritual development she calls the Sabbath "seventh-day," since, "after my conversion I preferred the plain language of the Quakers" (L, 47). Once again, Lee draws attention to the fact that language and signifiers do not automatically define the signified but are affected by factors such as historicity, gender, race, or religious affiliation.

Phebe Davidson observes that by pointedly rejecting fiction (as represented by the novel) in her autobiography, Lee posits her own textual sense of self as nonfictional, as completely real. Davidson goes on to assert that for Lee, "language, as vivified by religion, is real/nonfictional . . . by virtue of its religious function; but, paradoxically . . . it is subject to the judgment and control, the use, of one such as herself, not merely 'a coloured lady,' but a human being for whom the saviour died and who shares the inspiration and experience of her predecessors—even the Apostle Paul."[9] I have already argued, however, that there is an undercurrent in Lee's text that problematizes language and reality and conflates the fictional with the nonfictional (spiritual) in the very manner that Lee ostensibly denounces.

Lee claims God's authority in order to speak truth or give language its proper meaning. She encourages us to believe her as she expounds on what "preaching" is "*made* to mean," as opposed to what she tells us it really signifies. As an instrument of God, she asks her readers to rest assured that she, a black Christian female autobiographer, has complied with readers' demands that she give the truthful facts only. But in her narrative Lee disappoints her readers' demands for factuality, objectivity, and truthfulness. Her narrative begins with a reference to lying, and throughout the remainder of her story, although Lee claims

9. Davidson, *Religious Impulse in Selected Autobiographies of American Women (c. 1630–1983); Uses of the Spirit*, 173.

to be commissioned by God as she boldly interprets biblical passages, her own dreams, and other people's words, the language of her text encourages us to question the veracity of her claims. Lee writes:

> My parents being wholly ignorant of the knowledge of God, had not therefore instructed me in any degree in this great matter. Not long after the commencement of my attendance on this lady [Mrs. Sharp], she had bid me do something respecting my work, which in a little while after, she asked me if I had done, when I replied, Yes—but this was not true. (L, 27)

bell hooks has commented upon the significance of lying for a race of people who has survived in North America largely thanks to this habit. As I have mentioned above, the black slave narrative was at once suspect as a lie in the eyes of defensive southern and ignorant northern whites, and white abolitionists took extreme precautions in tutoring their black proteges on the art of objective fact-relaying. Thus, for Lee to open her autobiography by telling her reader that she was once an inveterate liar seems an invitation for distrust—a distrust she then must set about dispelling:

> At this awful point, in my early history, the spirit of God moved in power through my conscience, and told me I was a wretched sinner. On this account so great was the impression, and so strong were the feelings of guilt, that I promised in my heart that I would not tell another lie. But notwithstanding this promise my heart grew harder, after a while, yet the spirit of the Lord never entirely forsook me. (L, 27)

Who, indeed, would believe Lee's story as she wavers been self-doubt and certainty throughout the entire process of her conviction, justification, and sanctification? This is the challenge that Lee initially sets us—to believe in the power of God to convert (black) liars. Yet throughout her spiritual struggle, Lee is continuously plagued by the fear that Satan might be deluding her:

> Satan well knew that if he could succeed in making me disbelieve my conversion, that he would catch me either on the ground of complete

despair, or on the ground of infidelity. For if all I had passed through
was to go for nothing, and was but a fiction, the mere ravings of a
disordered mind, then I would naturally be led to believe that there is
nothing in religion at all. (L, 34)

Her abundant use of phrases like "there seemed to be" "there seemed
to sound" "I felt I was led" "I thought I distinctly heard" work to
undermine our sense of sureness about this spiritual pilgrim (L, 43,
35). Is she indeed chosen of God? Or, like the dangerous Nat Turner,
is she simply a deluded fanatic presenting us with "the mere ravings"
of her own "disordered mind" (L, 34)? The immense popularity of
Turner's 1831 *Confessions* (written only five years before Lee's work) is
evidenced by the fact that its white editor, Thomas Gray, printed and
sold fifty thousand copies. Gray, concerned with demonstrating the
demonic fanaticism of a black insurrectionist allows Turner to present
his story freely—*after* Gray instructs readers that they are to discount
this slave narrator's veracity on the grounds of his insanity and that
they are to regard Turner's notions of himself as God's messenger
as the misguided products of a " 'dark, bewildered, and overwrought
mind.' "[10] If we compare Turner's narrative with that of Rev. Richard
Allen, written only two years later, we are struck by Allen's self-imposed
standards of impeccable behaviour throughout his narrative. Allen is
so concerned to impress upon whites the evidence of his trustworthy
manhood that the title page of his text carries a reassuring biblical
injunction by which the reader may assess him: "Mark the perfect
man, and behold the upright: for the end of that man is peace.—
Ps. Xxxvii, 37." The reader may only wonder at the actual emotions
of this flawless man of peace, for he never reveals what they are. What
he does tell us is that he is willing to work hard, relinquish grudges,
and love the very country of his enslavement with a fierce patriotic
pride. Thus, like its narrator, the narrative of this perfect black man
can be nothing less than perfectly truthful.

Preoccupied with the telling of truth until the end of *her* narrative—
albeit in a manner completely different from that of her contempo-

10. Andrews, *To Tell a Free Story,* 73.

rary Allen, and perhaps, disturbingly reminiscent of her other contemporary Turner—Lee writes in her penultimate sentence: "But let
it be remarked that I have never found that Spirit to lead me contrary
to the Scriptures of truth, as I understand them" (L, 48). Yet the
niggling question still remains—in what manner *does* a "poor female
coloured instrument," plagued by self-doubt, and once a hardened
liar, understand scripture? For nineteenth-century readers, grappling
with fears of black insurrection, with issues of truth-telling in black
autobiography, and with reservations about women's ability to speak
sensibly in public at all, the question would have been a disturbing one.

If Lee presents us with a before-and-after picture of herself as sinner-
made-saint/captive-made-free, in which the black slave narrator is
always at pains to dissociate the good latter from the benighted former,
we may rest assured that she has left her lying days behind. But before
we reach the end of her first page, Lee presents us with a "Psalm"
(because she capitalizes the word, we are led to presume the reference
is biblical) that sounds suspiciously as though half of it is of her own
making:

> At the reading of the Psalms, a ray of renewed conviction darted into
> my soul. These were the words, composing the first verse of the Psalms
> for the service:
>> Lord, I am vile, conceived in sin,
>> Born unholy and unclean,
>> Sprung from man, whose guilty fall
>> Corrupts the race, and taints us all. (L, 27)

Phebe Davidson has commented on Lee's manipulation of biblical
text for racial purposes, arguing that while Lee's text and sermons
are most ostensibly concerned with issues of a spiritual nature, there
seems to be a "carefully embedded subtext" that deals with the much
more volatile issues of race and racism:

> In the first Psalm quoted by Lee, the word "race" pertains, apparently,
> to the human race; yet the word and the quotations do not stand
> sole and separate from the rest of the text in the mind of the reader.

> Although Lee has said nothing overt of race in her narrative up to
> this point, she has announced herself as "a coloured lady" in its title,
> and has found herself moved toward salvation by the quoted lines
> of a psalm. . . . In her search for spiritual community, she persists in
> suggestive phrasing.[11]

There is no psalm that reads like Lee's excerpt. The psalm that begins similarly to Lee's is 51:5–6, which reads: "Surely I have been a sinner from birth, / Sinful from the time my mother conceived me." However, the next lines deal not with the corruption of "the race" but with God's desire for truth: "Surely you desire truth in the inner places; / You teach me wisdom in the inmost place." What are we to make of Lee's "suggestive phrasing," her manipulation of biblical text? In light of the fact that Lee, as black objective "eye" and as Christian pilgrim, is expected by her readership to replicate the facts and tell the truth, her discrepancy is of interest here. Is it simply a slip of the pen or a bit of negligence on the part of someone too lazy to go and check her biblical references? Because of the onus (both imagined and real) on Lee to prove her rehabilitation from lazy, lying black servant to Christian preacher, and to define her story as God's truth, we must ask if her suggestive phrasing is nothing other than a manipulation of facts—executed to create a kind of "fiction" of Lee's own making. Our suspicions are heightened when, in a later passage in which Lee attempts to describe her sanctification, she likens herself to Saint Paul, and refers inaccurately to an incident recorded in 2 Corinthians (12:2–4). Foster notes that Lee "found an archetypal model" in Paul/Saul and "not only described a conversion experience strikingly similar in both incident and language to Saul's but also made direct comparison between her life and his.[12] Lee writes: "There is no language that can describe it, except that which was heard by St. Paul, when he was caught up to the third heaven, and heard words which it was not lawful to utter" (L, 34). In actual fact, it is not Saint Paul, but a friend of his, who experiences the "third heaven," and the reason that Paul tells us about his friend rather than himself, is that he refuses

11. Davidson, *Religious Impulse,* 173.
12. Foster, *Written by Herself,* 62.

to boast about his strengths; he prefers to boast about his weaknesses only. The actual passage reads

> I must go on boasting. Although there is nothing to be gained, I will go on to visions and revelations from the Lord. I know a man in Christ who fourteen years ago was caught up to the third heaven. . . . And I know that this man . . . was caught up to Paradise. He heard inexpressible things, things that man is not permitted to tell. I will boast about a man like that, but I will not boast about myself, except about my weaknesses. Even if I should choose to boast, I would not be a fool, because I would be speaking the truth. But I refrain, so no one will think more of me than is warranted by what I do or say.[13]

Lee not only "boasts" about her own sanctification but twists the truth in that boasting in order to align herself more directly with Saint Paul. Again, it is difficult to believe that a woman intent on proving to sceptical readers her worthiness and ability to preach the Bible would err twice in quoting that Bible within the parameters of a small, twenty-seven–page pamphlet. I would suggest that Lee's discrepancies come from a desire on her part to manipulate the truth for her own convenience—in the first case, to engage in a "suggestive phrasing" that combines her sense of her own sinfulness with her search for a black community or "race" with which to unite in Christian worship. In the second instance of fact-tampering, Lee establishes her spiritual authority by associating her sanctification with the conversion of Saint Paul. She is unable to find the appropriate language to describe the incident, but, attempting to maintain her comparison with Saint Paul, she conflates two incidents: Paul's conversion, and Paul's recollection of a friend's inability to express words he heard while caught up to the "third heaven." Again, Lee engages in some inaccurate but suggestive phrasing in order to drive home a powerful message of her own.

Such phrasing belies her assertions that she is telling us nothing but the pristine truth as a converted Christian and black autobiographer. For while Lee writes outwardly as a truth-teller, her suggestive phrasing

13. 2. Cor. 12:1–6.

and her comments on the nature of language betray another Lee—a knowledgeable black female trickster of sorts who understands the shifting nature of (white/ patriarchal) "Truth," and knows that all reality—including her own—is a kind of fiction, constructed by the language and the memory that define and order it. The line between truth and fiction in this black woman's autobiography becomes a shifting and problematic one.

While Jarena Lee openly challenges patriarchal notions of biblical "Truth" concerning women and continuously undermines white belief in her capacity as a black woman for "truth-telling," Elaw is more oblique in this regard. We do not often doubt the veracity of Elaw's claims because, unlike Lee, her tone is self-assured and erudite. Indeed, early in her text, she carefully warns us about the deceptiveness of the written word: "Take heed what you read: as a tree of knowledge, both of good and evil, is the press; it ofttimes teems with rabid poisons, putting darkness for light, and light for darkness" (E, 52). But this does not dispel the fact that her very text contains its own contradictions, which demonstrate the self-preserving double-speak that blacks (men and women)—and women (white and black)—have used in order to survive their tenuous and problematic position within the confusing and contradictory parameters of a racist, patriarchal America. Elaw's description of the Quaker family she worked for as a girl is a telling example of her tendency to avoid the truth. At the age of twelve, after the death of her mother, Elaw writes that her father, "having placed my younger sister under the care of her aunt, then consigned me to the care of Pierson and Rebecca Mitchel" (E, 53). Here we are presented with a misleading parallel, for we only gradually come to realize that "care" provided by a family relation is not the same as the "care" of the Mitchels, "those kind benefactors under whom my dear father had placed me" (E, 53). Elaw works as a servant girl for the Mitchels; she later refers to Mrs. Mitchel as "my mistress" (E, 58). We also realize that her initial description of them as caring, kindly benefactors may have been less than truthful—may have been, quite possibly, the attempt of a black autobiographer to solicit white approval as a "good nigger" in the first lines of her text. For Elaw later reveals: "I *sometimes* met with very severe rebukes from my mistress, and I endured her reproofs without the exhibition of my former resentments and saucy replies [emphasis mine]" (E, 58). We begin to wonder about the nature of her relationship with the Mitchels. The following passage provides us with even greater insight:

> Prior to my experience of the life and power of godliness, my mistress *frequently* charged me with pertness and insolent behaviour; but after I had imbibed somewhat of the meekness and gentleness of Jesus, and had been instructed by his religion not to answer again when chided, then she *frequently* charged me with sullenness and mopishness. This treatment often sent me to the throne of grace, to seek the sympathy of Him who is touched with the feeling of our infirmities. I now felt, bitterly, the loss of my dear mother [emphasis mine]. (E, 59)

Mrs. Mitchel, it would seem, falls somewhat short of the initial description we have of her as "kindly benefactor." In similar oscillations, Elaw urges women to be "dependant on and subject to man" (E, 61) in one breath, and in another openly recounts the manner in which she disobeyed the injunctions of her own husband: "[My husband] advised me to decline the work [of preaching] altogether, and proceed no further. I was very sorry to see him so much grieved about it; but my heavenly Father had informed me that he had a great work for me to do; I could not therefore descend down to the counsel of flesh and blood, but adhered faithfully to my commission" (E, 84).[14]

Other instances of contradiction involve Elaw's praise of the simplicity of an oral, heavenly, songlike language, in spite of her frequent use of a belabored and pretentiously erudite literary style. Elaw's language certainly suggests a linguistic attempt at whiteface. She begins her address to her "Dear Brethren and Friends" in the following manner: "After sojourning in your hospitable land, and peregrinating among you during these last five years; in the course of which period, it

14. I borrow this term from Sidonie Smith, for whom "oscillations in . . . posture" in women's writing are a result of the female writer's tenuous and problematic position "within the complexities and contradictions of patriarchal ideologies of gender" and, I might add, race ("Resisting the Gaze of Embodiment: Women's Autobiography in the Nineteenth Century," 85).

has been my happiness to enjoy much spiritual intercourse with many of you . . . I feel a strong desire again to cross the pathless bosom of the foaming Atlantic and rejoin my dear friends in the occidental land of my nativity" (E, 51). Stilted, formulaic, eighteenth-century descriptions of nature in which the sky becomes a "broad canopy above," and the fish of the ocean are "finny tribes pouring out by thousands" or "the great leviathan" suggest Elaw's desire to demonstrate her erudition (E, 139). However, Elaw's attempt to master the "master's" literary style is puzzlingly countered by her rejection of that style in favor of simple language couched in song. She is exposed to this pure language at her sister's deathbed—a kind of song "doubtless in use among the holy angels," that "seems to be a matter of gracious promise on the part of Jehovah, on behalf of his redeemed people. Zephaniah iii.9" (E, 74). The tiny Book of Zephaniah, to which Elaw merely alludes in passing, deals in its entirety with God's wrath upon "the city of oppressors." God promises to deliver Israel: "Sing, O Daughter of Zion; / shout aloud, O Israel! / Be glad and rejoice with your heart . . . I will deal with all who oppressed you."[15] Israel has been a common metaphor for blacks in their literary explorations of their condition as an enslaved people in America. Thus, Elaw's reference to a pure language of song, laid upon the palimpsest of God's dealings with those who oppress his chosen people, seems to me a powerful assertion of an oral, black Christian spirituality on the part of Elaw. Her oblique strategy here, and her engagement in fervent song at other moments in the text—such as the pivotal transcendent moment of her conversion—suggests the "black expressivity" to which Houston Baker has referred. Baker uses the autobiography of Frederick Douglass as an example: Douglass's remembrance of black musical expressivity in his narrative is "the unifying affective bond between a spirited and singing text and the written autobiography of . . . Douglass."[16] Elaw remembers and privileges the "singing text" on many occasions. At the bedside of her sister, in a passage that demonstrates her obvious knowledge of rhetoric, Elaw notes how death may cause the dying to

15. Zeph. 3:1, 3:14–19
16. Baker, *Workings of the Spirit*, 40.

break forth and sing with a melodious and heavenly voice, several verses in a language unknown to mortals. A pure language, unalloyed by the fulsome compliment, the hyperbole, the tautology and circumlocution, the insinuation, double meaning and vagueness, the weakness and poverty, the impurity, bombast, and other defects, with which all human languages are clogged, seems to be essential for the associations of glorified spirits and the elevated devotion of heaven. (E, 74)

Yet, ironically, throughout her text, and even in the above passage, Elaw uses the very language she condemns, in a double-consciousness we do not see in the early petition of Belinda, "an African." This poignant passage also describes the manner in which Elaw receives her call to preach the word of God (significantly, from her sister): "she . . . informed me, that she had seen Jesus, and had been in the society of angels; and that an angel came to her, and bade her tell Zilpha that she must preach the gospel; and also, that I must go to a lady named Fisher, a Quakeress, and she would tell me further what I should do" (E, 73). In the actual description of the death of her sister, variations of the word *sing* are repeated seven times:

she then began singing, and appeared to sing several verses; but the language in which she sung was too wonderful for me, and I could not understand it. We all sat or stood around her with great astonishment, for her voice was as clear, musical and strong, as if nothing had ailed her; and when she had finished her song of praise, (for it was indeed a song of praise, and the place was full of glory,) she addressed herself to me . . . The next day . . . she asked me if that hymn which she had sung on the previous night was not beautiful; adding, "Ah, Zilpha! angels gave it me to sing . . ." She continued in this happy frame of mind until her soul fell asleep in Jesus. (E, 73–74)

Elaw's narrative is interspersed with further references to song such as the following: "It is like heaven descended upon an earthly soil, when all unite to: 'Praise God, from whom all blessings flow' " (E, 64). In a revelatory moment in which Elaw realises that she has been resisting the direction of God, she says, "[The pastor] gave forth the following lines to be sung—'Jesus, the hindrance show, / Which I have feared to see; / And let me now consent to know, / What keeps me back from Thee.' While singing these lines, I was led to discover that I had not obeyed the call of the Lord, by refusing to go to Mr. Budinot's as I had been directed" (E, 69).

Early in her autobiography, Elaw alludes to the importance of song in her spiritual wholeness. Comparing the happy, song-filled atmosphere of her parents' home with that of the morose white Quaker household she later serves, she writes that "in my father's house" family prayers were said and "the praises of God" sung both morning and night. However, "the persons with whom I now resided were Quakers, and their religious exercises, if they observed any, were performed in the secret silence of the mind . . . I soon gave way to the evil propensities of an unregenerate heart" (E, 54). In the moment of revelation, however, Christ finds the young black servant girl in the songless white household fervently engaged in religious song. In the space of three paragraphs, Elaw draws attention to her singing three times: "one evening, whilst singing one of the songs of Zion, I distinctly saw the Lord Jesus approach me with open arms. . . . I was singing the following lines. . . . As I was milking the cow and singing, I turned my head, and saw a tall figure approaching" (E, 56). In this moment, Elaw is no longer silent in a white household of silence; she is no longer the obedient servant girl. Instead, she becomes the teller of miraculous and incredible tales: "[T]he beast of the stall gave forth her evidence to the reality of the heavenly appearance; for she turned her head and looked round as I did; and when she saw, she bowed her knees and cowered down upon the ground. I was overwhelmed with astonishment at the sight, but the thing was certain and beyond all doubt" (E, 56–57). She is a disruptor of silence, a transgressor of the proprieties of white mistress/black servant relations, the recalcitrant female—in other words, a woman who stands outside of "true woman-hood," an unnatural woman, a monster. Like Lee, Elaw abandons her child in order to preach, unconcerned about the duties of mother-hood: "Thus I left my child . . . not knowing whither I should go. From Philadelphia I started for New York; and on my journey passed within three hundred yards of my own home, yet did not call there. . . . I was absent from home seven months" (E, 90). Tropes of monstrosity—in the form of her body as male and castrated, and in the forms of

illness and "speckled[ness]"—function in Elaw's text in a manner that
Susan Gubar describes as common to women writers of the nineteenth
century (E, 59). These writers, "who feared their attempts at the
pen were presumptuous, castrating, or even monstrous, engaged in a
variety of strategies to deal with their anxiety about authorship."[17] But
if Elaw's monstrosity signals her dis-ease as woman preacher/writer
in a nineteenth-century white male discursive field that would label
her a monster, we must question why it is that she can go on her way
rejoicing "with the blooming prospects of a better inheritance"; why
it is that, although illness becomes an important trope in her text,
Elaw's figurative castration is juxtaposed *against* illness—becoming,
indeed, a sign of spiritual *wellness,* a "regenerat[ion]," a cause for
great celebration (E, 51).

In the very first paragraph of her autobiography, Elaw presents her
readers with a

> contour portrait of my regenerated constitution—exhibiting, as did the
> bride of Solomon, comeliness with blackness . . . and, as did the apostle
> Paul, riches with poverty, and power in weakness . . . a representation
> not, indeed of the features of my outward person, drawn and coloured
> by the skill of the pencilling artist, but of the lineaments of my inward
> man, as inscribed by the Holy Ghost, and according to my poor ability,
> copied off for your edification. (E, 51)

Perhaps, in her portrayal of herself Elaw adopts the very persona of
the male writer. But how are we to read this claim to spiritual *castrated*
"manhood?" Is it perhaps a tortured representation of Elaw's own
feelings of lack as a (black) woman writing? Painfully conscious of
her physical embodiment as a black woman in a society that degrades
black female embodiment, does Elaw attempt to displace that female
physicality completely? As Katherine Fishburn observes, in a white Victorian literary discourse where "elaborate metaphoric displacements"
substituted for (white) women's embodiment, black women were,

---

17. Susan Gubar, " 'The Blank Page' and the Issues of Female Creativity," in *The
New Feminist Criticism: Essays on Women, Literature, and Theory,* ed. Elaine Showalter,
295.

conversely, overembodied. Thus, we see in nineteenth-century genteel black women's writing, especially writing in the postbellum era,
a tendency to hide "the black body from view because they no longer
felt they could trust their (white) readers."[18] Fishburn posits that this
"narrative distrust" has its origins in Harriet Jacobs's autobiography,
*Incidents in the Life of a Slave Girl,* and other less well known black
female narratives. We may suspect that Elaw effects such a conceal-
ment; but in spite of her insistence that her "inward man" is "not . . .
of the features of my outward person," she nevertheless presents a
paradoxical physical spirituality defined by bodily characteristics of
"comeliness" and "blackness" (E, 51). As such, her spiritual "contour
portrait" becomes a fleshly, black-expressive representation, signifying
not merely a disembodied, colorless, spiritual consubstantiation of her
black self with white readers, but rather the very physical fact of Elaw's
existence in America as a black woman.

But we are still faced with Elaw's presentation of herself as "man,"
more precisely as "eunuch." The first indication we receive that Elaw's
"inward man" does not possess the same endowments as other men occurs in her description of her conversion—her powerful recognition,
as a teenager, of Christ (E, 51). Elaw writes that, after the incident,

> the peace of God which passeth understanding was communicated to
> my heart; and joy in the Holy Ghost, to a degree, at the last, unutter-
> able by my tongue and indescribable by my pen; it was beyond my
> comprehension; but, from that happy hour, my soul was set at glorious
> liberty; and, like the Ethiopic eunuch, I went on my way rejoicing in
> the blooming prospects of a better inheritance with the saints in light.
> (E, 57)

It would seem that this is the exact moment at which Elaw's previously
"unregenerate" constitution becomes "regenerated"—she alludes to
herself as eunuch thereafter on a number of occasions. It is helpful
to examine the details of Elaw's life before her regeneration. Until
the age of twelve, Elaw lived with her two siblings and her "religious

18. Katherine Fishburn, *The Problem of Embodiment in Early African American
Narrative,* 93–6.

parents," who praised God with song (E, 53). On the death of her mother, however, her father consigned her to the care of the Mitchels, for whom Elaw worked as a servant. It is in this songless white Quaker household that Elaw loses her early sense of religion, becomes "unregenerate," and experiences a disturbing sense of aloneness borne out of "the singularity with which I was treated" (E, 54, 59). Here she "dwelt as a speckled bird." Only later, while still in the "care" of the Mitchels, does Elaw rediscover Jesus on her own, becoming the "regenerated" eunuch of the above-quoted passage, who goes on his way singing and rejoicing. Thus, it would seem that the disruption in Elaw's young life, which takes her from the soulful happiness of a religious and whole black-family existence to a strange, silent, white environment, is a rupture or illness healed by the advent of Jesus. But the idea of this healed rupture is problematized by the paradoxical fact that the metaphor for this healed spirit is a black man, castrated. Andrews has noted that paradox in the slave narrative is a common figuration, reflecting the systemic oppression of blacks in America; white liberty and equality as expounded in the Declaration of Independence take on their opposite meanings for African Americans since blacks live in an America where "freedom" for the white man means "slavery" for the black, where white wealth is black poverty, and white hope is black despair.[19] Elaw uses paradox in a similar manner. Disfigurement and regeneration are tropes that she introduces early. In her dedication she presents her readers with her "regenerated constitution" and exhorts them to "[shun], carefully, the destructive vices which so deplorably abound in and disfigure the Christian community" (E, 51). But in the spirit of paradox that suffuses Elaw's text, her "regenerated constitution" is a castrated man. Perhaps Elaw's inward man rejoices *because* of his lack of that commodity deemed indispensable by patriarchal standards. We must remember that one of the first things Elaw reminds her readers of is the paradox inherent in scripture: that in Christ she has found "comeliness with blackness . . . riches with poverty . . . power in weakness" (E, 51). Throughout her text, Elaw urges her readers to renounce their love of all those qualities extolled

19. Andrews, *To Tell a Free Story*, 12.

by prevailing white American standards—all the "current traditions and prejudices"; whiteness, riches, and social standing are the evils that "disfigure the Christian community" (E, 52, 51). She further admonishes: "abhor the pride of respectability"; "renounce the love of money" as well as "the pride of a white skin [that] is a bauble of great value with many" (E, 52, 85). Only by rejecting prevailing notions of power can the Christian be whole: "Cautiously, diligently, and habitually observe and obey the directions and statutes of Christ and his apostles, that your foundation may be built not upon the sands of current traditions and prejudices, but upon the prophets and apostles, Jesus Christ being the chief cornerstone" (E, 52). Lack in prevailing discourse, then, becomes wholeness, "perfect and entire" in the subversive discourse of Elaw. Elaw draws her readers' attention to lack. But it is that very lack—lack of whiteness, lack of riches, lack of social position—represented by the shocking physical lack of the phallus that facilitates her ability to go on her way rejoicing in Christ.

Hortense Spillers observes that in Alice Walker's "The Child Who Favored Daughter" and Ralph Ellison's *Invisible Man* castration is a specter that haunts both African American men and women. Spillers argues that Freudian and Lacanian theories of incest and phallic signification apply to African American existence merely by accident—black family relations are so skewed by slavery that in the writing of Walker and Ellison we see a suspension of the incest taboo, because undifferentiated black father/daughter/son/brother/sister/mother relations are strewn in a horizontal manner across the social landscape rather than in the (white) lawful vertical configurations. In such a skewed horizontal display, the paternal connection is shrouded in uncertainty; children are abducted, lost, or otherwise separated from their mothers; and castration becomes a metaphor for spiritual mutilation, social confusion, and disempowerment. Daughters are impregnated and physically abused by fathers, and fathers are emasculated in their relations with the master's house. For example, Trueblood, the consummate storyteller of *Invisible Man,* impregnates his hapless daughter and becomes the "whore/gal" of his whitemale listeners, entertaining them compulsively with sexually titillating stories of the experience. In these stories, he "disappears into an endless progression of enclosures that replicate the vaginal/uterine structure in which he has every right to fear that he will get lost and, quite correctly, fall bereft of his penal powers. . . . [This becomes] a symptom of an inverted castration complex."[20] And in Alice Walker's "The Child Who Favored Daughter," the daughter, assuming monstrous proportions because she dares to write her own desire, symbolically suffers her castrated breasts to be tossed to dogs by an impotent black father who can not use his phallic "gun" against white men but only against a black woman. For black Americans, then, castration and the castration complex is a condition that pertains not only to daughters as symbolic accident of birth or to sons as fear of paternal reprisal, but to all African American men and women as symbol—and all too often actual *fact*—of a brutal, sustained, and systematic familial rupture and racial degradation enacted on the bodies of black persons.

Yet the newly regenerated Elaw, castrated as she is, needs no phallus to go on her way rejoicing. Her "inward man" subverts expectation, ecstatic in spite of the fact that he lacks the thing that for men is most valued. Elaw, then, defies a triple brutalization: the violence patriarchy perpetuates in its aggressive valorisation of phallic hegemony over all women black and white; the shame of the sexual brutalization experienced by *black* women under slavery—who, Baker argues, transmute that shame into a genteel, whiteface approval of white patriarchy; and the castrating emasculation (both in a literal and a figurative sense) that African men in America have resisted since their involuntary arrival on these shores.[21]

The disfigured body of the castrato, then, becomes for Elaw a trope of spiritual power and resistance in the face of a racism and sexism that threatens to spiritually and physically annihilate her. From the bold defiance of Belinda, to the subtle and manipulative strategies of Lee, to Elaw's representation (in white Western erudition) of lack and absence as indicative of the ultimate presence of the power of the Spirit, the mothers' gardens have been tended by a strange and (to the

20. Hortense Spillers, "'The Permanent Obliquity of an In(pha)llibly Straight': In the Time of the Daughters and the Fathers," in *Changing Our Own Words: Essays on Criticism, Theory and Writing by Black Women,* ed. Cheryl A. Wall, 134.
21. Baker, *Workings of the Spirit,* 30.

readerly white sensibilities of the cult of true womanhood) terrifying trinity indeed. The African Orisa-worshipper, the dubiously rehabil- itated trickster-liar, and the eunuch all stand before us, inhabiting a different space than that of their more genteel black sisters. Four years after Elaw published her *Memoirs* in 1846, Sojourner Truth's *Narrative* appeared. Truth, consummate performer before the jury of her read- ership, is a new addition to this cult of unnatural (black) womanhood. She privileges black female presence and dignified embodiment over hyperembodiment and absence in a manner that makes her the best- known of the black female evangelists.

# THREE

# Sojourner Truth
# and the Embodiment of the
# Blues-Bad-Preacher-Woman Text

WRITING IN THE LATE twentieth century about Erma Brodber's contemporary analysis of the (non)position of Jamaican women in Jamaican male culture, Ashcroft, Griffiths, and Tiffin note: "Texts—the
'fairy tales' of Europe—have not only subjectified Jamaican women,
but through cultural interpellation effected the erasure of the black
female body within Jamaican male culture. Hence the black 'Prince
Charming' of Brodber's fable can *sense* his female counterpart, but
when he looks for her he can see "no/body."[1] To white (and black
male) minds across the African diaspora, black females may indeed
be "no/body"—in both the literal and figurative sense of the word as
Brodber's fable suggests. This situation is not limited to the twentieth
century or Jamaica in particular; it is also highly operative in mid-
nineteenth-century America, the time during which the first black
female spiritual autobiographers were writing. But in the nineteenth
century, if she is no/body, the black woman is also *all* body, in the
sense that she represents the epitome of that which is uncivilized,
animal, grossly indelicate, unworthy of artistic representation in any
other capacity than obeisant (and very often sexualized) servant. In
fact, she is sometimes so reified that *parts* of her body are to be found
in various exhibitions and museums—the sexual parts of the famed
"Hottentot Venus," Saartjie Baartman, remain on display at the Musée
de l'homme in Paris, even to this day—evidence of the manner in

1. Bill Ashcroft et al., *The Post-Colonial Studies Reader,* 250. Brodber's short essay
is entitled "Sleeping's Beauty and Prince Charming."

58

which black women were regarded by Europeans in the nineteenth century, and indeed, perhaps also in the twentieth. Thus, the black woman becomes no/body who, if she is found at all in the pages of polite texts, or in the display rooms of exhibitions of the fine arts, is bereft of the privilege of dignified personhood. Indeed, black women fought an objectifying embodiment in which they were degraded and often hypersexualized. As Hammonds observes: "[The] always already colonized black female body has so much sexual potential that it has none at all." And in a number of themes that emerge in the history of black women's sexuality, one is "the construction of the black female as the embodiment of sex" over against the "attendant invisibility of black women as the unvoiced, unseen everything that is not white."[2] I want to examine, then, how nineteenth-century black female evangelists strove to become "some/body" in the face of an erasure so profound that it simultaneously embodied and disembodied them in a discourse of contradiction that is common when white people conceive of black women.

Sojourner Truth's *Narrative,* first published in 1850, presents the self-portrait of a black female preacher, feminist, and abolitionist for whom the public—and textual—performance of self as "some/body" becomes a delicate and tricky negotiation of the contradictory discourses surrounding black women in mid-nineteenth-century America. Some of the most prominent of these discourses for Truth are black women as absence, such as in the sculptures of Hiram Powers or Erastus Dow Palmer; black women as hypersexualized objects; and black women as romanticized servants, strong and wise in the sense that "noble savages" are. Where Truth finally positions herself as consummate performer in her public and textual negotiation of these conflicting representations is the question I investigate here. While, indeed, all autobiographies are performances of self, Truth's narrative becomes a *meta*performance; its strategies of interruption and inconsistency expose the complex and problematic realities of what it means to be a black woman speaking in a white/male American public domain. Truth creates a self out of the very discourses of

2. Evelynn Hammonds, "Black (W)holes and the Geometry of Black Female Sexuality," 126–45.

contradiction that threaten to simultaneously embody and disembody her—she demystifies the "naturalness" of such discourses, playing, in her own self-(per)formance, upon that contradictory black female self constructed by white Americans; she becomes elusive, "unnatural," tricksterlike.

For artists such as Hiram Powers and Erastus Dow Palmer, the brutalized bodies of black women, displaced by figures of seductive and captive white women, become the invisible ground upon which the artists replicate a complex and prevalent nineteenth-century white American discourse. That discourse in effect *condones* the enslavement of Africans, in its presentation of white male terror of "Other" (dark-skinned) peoples, in its fixation on the preservation of white masculinity, and in its creation of the white male self as heroic protector of threatened white womanhood. Powers's sculpture *The Greek Slave* was mounted at various exhibitions across America and Britain during the nineteenth century, including London's famous "Great Exhibition," the 1851 World Fair at which fugitive slaves Henry and Ellen Craft were paraded, arm in arm with American abolitionists—the year after Truth's narrative was first published. Albert Boime quotes Freeman Henry Morris Murray as observing that *The Greek Slave* "excited much public attention," and according to J. Carson Webster, the work was "the most famous statue, for Americans, of that time."[3]

Early in his career, Powers secured a name for himself through the commissioned busts he completed of such famous politicians as John Quincy Adams, Daniel Webster, and Andrew Jackson (then the American president). Later sculptures such as *America, Franklin, Jefferson, California,* and *The Last of the Tribes* reflect Powers's concern with the moral, political, and ideological development of America as a fledgling nation grappling with its own (white) self-definition, often in relation to blacks and/or native peoples as those in need of European direction. Thus, the fact that he created and exhibited his *Greek Slave* at the height of the raging African-slave debates in America is no coincidence but seems instead to be Powers's commentary on an American situation that commanded attention on

3. See Albert Boime, *The Art of Exclusion: Representing Blacks in the Nineteenth Century,* 156; and J. Carson Webster, *Erastus D. Palmer,* 100.

an international level. Indeed, his *Slave* reflected the "widespread interest in the themes of bondage of one form or another" that prevailed in the mid-nineteenth century.[4] Other sculptures (to name only a few) such as American Erastus Dow Palmer's *The White Captive* (1859) and *Peace in Bondage* (1863), William Wetmore Story's famous *Libyan Sibyl* (1868), John Quincy Adams Ward's *Freedman* (1863), or staggeringly successful novels such as Harriet Beecher Stowe's *Uncle Tom's Cabin* (1852) attest to this nineteenth-century preoccupation.

Hiram Powers's obsession with his theme, as well as numerous personal requests for the statue from wealthy friends, drove him to produce six replicas of the *Slave* between 1843 and 1869. The statue portrays a white woman, standing upright with her hand resting on a support. The support is covered by a piece of Greek drapery. Powers himself describes the impetus behind his work:

> I remembered reading of an account of the atrocities committed by the Turks on the Greeks during the Greek revolution, which were finally put an end to by the destruction of the Turkish fleet by Admiral Corington and the Russian Naval Commander, whose name I do not now remember. During the struggle the Turks took many prisoners—male and female, and among the latter were beautiful girls, who were sold in the slave markets of Turkey and even Egypt. These were Christian women and it is not difficult to imagine the distress and even despair of the sufferers while exposed to be sold to the highest bidder. But as there should be a moral in every work of art, I have given to the expression of the *Greek Slave* what trust there could still be in a Divine Providence for a future state of existence, with utter despair for the present mingled with somewhat of scorn for all around her. She is too deeply concerned to be aware of her nakedness. It is not her person but her spirit that stands exposed, and she bears it all as Christians only can.[5]

The "Greek Revolution" of which Powers speaks culminated in the July 6, 1770, Battle of Chesme. This revolution seems to be part of

---

4. Donald Martin Reynolds, *Hiram Powers and His Ideal Sculpture*, 216.
5. Ibid., 141.

a concerted European effort, dubbed "the Greek Scheme," in which Russia's Catherine the Great and Austria's Joseph II joined forces in an attempt to drive the Turks out of Europe.

The *Slave* became the subject of many poems, including a sonnet by Elizabeth Barrett Browning, "Hiram Powers' 'Greek Slave,' " in which the statue, a representation of "Ideal beauty," confronts "man's crimes in different lands / With man's ideal sense." Browning entreats the "fair stone" to "strike and shame the strong / By thunders of white silence, overthrown."[6] While it may be argued that, in using a white woman to portray the appalling reality of millions of black women in America, Powers sought to both shock by defamiliarisation and to ask rhetorically, "What if this were your sister?" we are nevertheless faced with several disturbing concerns. These concerns are substantiated when we acknowledge what seems to be Powers's reluctance to be seen as an abolitionist at all in his creation of another sculpture, *Liberty/America*. Debating how the sculpture will be represented, Powers writes that he would fashion chains under the feet if he were sure such an addition would not be interpreted as bearing some relation to slavery in America. Finally, Powers concludes: "*America* is done— all but the chains under the left foot. Do not start! They are not manacles—no allusion to the "Peculiar Institution" but simply an emblem of despotism or tyranny."[7]

In his description of the *Slave,* Powers's conflation of white womanhood with Christianity, Europeanness, and the metaphysical Ideal, is set against his conflation of darkness with that which is heathen, non-European and "atrocious"; neither conflation can be overlooked here. What we see in his rendition of *The Greek Slave* is the first conflation—white womanhood represents Christianity and so on. The second conflation (that of darkness with the heathen, etc.) has no existence before the spectator who stands looking at *The Greek Slave;* if we suppose that Powers condemns the white American institution of slavery, especially the enslavement of black women, we must acknowledge that he erases the black female slave altogether.

6. Elizabeth Barrett Browning, "Hiram Powers' 'Greek Slave,' " in *The Norton Anthology of Literature by Women,* ed. Sandra M. Gilbert and Susan Gubar, 390.
7. Reynolds, *Hiram Powers,* 179.

Her presence is signified only by a thunderous "white silence," to use the term of Barrett Browning, as if the black woman herself were too crude a subject to represent the horror felt by whites upon witnessing the "Ideal beauty" of the spirit bound in chains. The fact that the *Slave* is "too deeply concerned" about a future, otherworldly, Christian state of existence to care about her nakedness presents further troublesome contradictions—the reality of the slave market, for instance, would reveal something far from the image Powers offers us of a spotless, unscarred, well-groomed, and serenely preoccupied pubescent woman bound by rather delicate-looking leather thongs and reposing in a leisurely and thoughtful manner upon a piece of Greek fabric. The woman gazes demurely downward, away from the spectator, and, rather accidentally it seems (for, after all, she is unconcerned about her nakedness), she covers her pubes with her hand, drawing the spectator's attention to this place immediately. Thus *The Greek Slave* is titillating but inaccessible to the spectator— again a complete denial of the reality of black female enslavement; the *Slave* stands in an eternal moment of Christian reverie, obviously untouched by the "atrocities" waiting to be committed against her by "heathens," for as Powers asserts: "It is not her person but her spirit that stands exposed, and she bears it all as Christians only can." (We must wonder if Powers's turn of phrase "bears it all" is an unconscious pun here.) Of course, it is Christianity that will save the slave. While the consciences of white slaveowners may have been pricked somewhat by Powers, another part of his message—if indeed, his sculpture is meant as an indictment of slavery at all—is that the slave must forbear. For in Christianity, political activism, rage, and shame are unnecessary—one need only abandon one's heathen beliefs and be washed clean and white by the salvation of the Lord.

But Powers's concern that he not be seen as indicting the "peculiar institution" in his creation of *Liberty/America* seems an indication that, in sculpting *The Greek Slave,* he was not criticising slavery either. What, then, *was* he doing? Nowhere in Powers's notes or correspondences do we read that the *Slave* was a commentary on American slavery. Instead, we read that Powers was concerned to convey the plight of European women taken hostage by marauding (dark-skinned) Turks.

*The White Captive* of Erastus Dow Palmer, sculpted in 1859 at the

height of political tensions over slavery, two years before the onset of
the American Civil War, has nothing to do with American slavery at
all, either. What it did represent, according to Palmer, was his finest
work—a nude, young, white pioneer woman in bondage. Palmer
compared it to another of his works, *Indian Girl* (1855), in which
a young Native American woman examines a crucifix, saying that the
one sculpture demonstrated the influence of the "savage" upon Christianity, and the other the influence of Christianity upon the "savage."
One critic, Henry T. Tuckerman rapsodized: "In this statue the artist
has illustrated one of those tragic episodes of border life on this continent. . . . [T]he 'White Captive' shows . . . civilization, in its purest
form, dragged into the cruel sphere of barbarism, yet unsubdued in
its moral superiority. The subject is thoroughly American."⁸ The sim-
ilarities, physical and ideological, between Tuckerman's description
of Palmer's *White Captive* and Powers's description of his own *Greek
Slave* are too striking to ignore here. What both Powers and Palmer
seem intent on preserving, as debates on slavery rage all around
them, is the European ideal of Civilization, Culture, and Christianity,
represented by the figure of assailed white womanhood. The immense
popularity of both their works attests to a mood in mid-nineteenth-
century America of fear and contempt of blackness (African, Native
American, Turkish, etc.) and of black demands for freedom—without
actually speaking or representing that fear. Indeed, it is the body of a
white woman that represents what it is white men must preserve for
themselves. Thus, works such as *The White Captive* and *The Greek Slave*
impose upon the shocking actuality of black women's enslavement
their own obsession with white masculinity and maintaining a sense
of the (fearful) white male self in the face of threatening (even while
enchained) "Other" civilizations.

What black female evangelists such as Sojourner Truth attempt to
establish in the face of this erasure of their realities in the culture
of dominance is a reclaiming of their black bodies and black selves
as dignified subjects. Truth's *Narrative* presents us not only with her
text, but also with a daguerreotype of her black body, under which

---

8. Webster, *Erastus D. Palmer*, 29.

she has had printed: "I sell the shadow to support the substance." This daguerreotype depicts a black woman gazing frankly into the camera, her head covered by a bonnet and her shoulders draped by a shawl. Her hands are clasped in her lap, and she sits calmly before what looks like a fireplace, the mantle of which is decorated with ornaments. Thus, as she travels the countryside preaching abolition, women's emancipation and God's word, Truth resists objectification and erasure through the selling not of her body nude and shackled, but of representations of that body demurely dressed and located at the hearthside. Truth herself commented that she " 'used to be sold for other people's benefit, but now she sold herself for her own.' "[9] That a daguerreotype depicting Truth in her public role as roving lecturer and preacher—a much more accurate representation—is not used, suggests that Truth, astute businesswoman, offers what will sell. Her obeisance to the dictates of the cult of true womanhood (woman seated in her proper sphere by the fireplace) seems to take precedence for Truth in matters of saleswomanship. Truth actively peddles her self as commodity in a manner that is both a signification upon and an undermining of the commodification of black bodies by the slave trade. Like Ralph Ellison's Trueblood, Truth as performer creates a "cult of Sojourner."[10] Trueblood, Houston Baker argues, performs his way into a steady source of income from white philanthropists who believe his story of how he impregnated both his wife and daughter. They believe it because the story fits the preconceived notions these whites have of blacks as lascivious and sexually insatiable. For Baker, the question of the black performer's integrity becomes a crucial one: "To deliver the blues as entertainment—if one is an entertainer—is to maintain a fidelity to one's role. Again, if the performance required is that of a minstrel and one is a genuine performer, then donning the mask is an act consistent with one's stature. There are always fundamental economic questions involved in such uneasy

9. Sojourner Truth, Olive Gilbert, and Frances Titus, *Narrative of Sojourner Truth; a Bondswoman of Olden Time . . . with a History of Her Labors and Correspondence Drawn from Her "Book of Life,"* title page, hereinafter cited as TGT in the text.

10. Carlton Mabee and Susan Mabee Newhouse, *Sojourner Truth: Slave, Prophet, Legend,* 216.

Afro-American public postures."[11] As storyteller par excellence, Truth creates a marketable public persona in shrewd strategies that sometimes belie her self-selected name. Privileging presence over absence of the dignified black female self, communal telling over individual account, and the spoken vernacular over the written word, she enters the white abolition circuit to negotiate public spaces, receiving far more recognition than her black sister evangelists ever do. Truth alone of them all resists complete obscurity, her legendary name surviving well into the present time.

By standard definitions, Truth's 1850 *Narrative* qualifies as biography since it is written in the third person, and Olive Gilbert, her white amanuensis, refers to it as such. In the 1850 text, Gilbert relates the events of Truth's life up until 1850, before Truth's actual career as abolitionist and women's rights activist began. However, I have mainly used the 1878 version of the *Narrative,* compiled by Frances Titus (also white) here because I believe it may be characterized even more fully as what James Olney terms "autophylography": "a portrait of 'nous, nous ensemble.' "[12] The 1878 *Narrative* was written communally, by Truth, Olive Gilbert (her 1850 amanuensis), and Frances Titus—who, in 1878, added to the stereotyped 1850 *Narrative* "The Book of Life," a collection of articles, letters, anecdotes, and commentaries written by various white people about Truth. Although the *Narrative,* along with its compilation of testimonies, does not conform to standard definitions of "autobiography," I nevertheless include it in my study since, like Belinda's petition, it represents the attempt on the part of a black woman to recount her life story to others in a nontraditional and innovative form.

Truth's text may also be characterized as "testimony," which Ketu Katrak includes in her definition of autobiography as a form of oral self-revelation by working-class women.[13] Sometimes this self-revelation is facilitated through the process of interview, and it is

11. Houston A. Baker, Jr., *Blues, Ideology, and Afro-American Literature: A Vernacular Theory,* 194.

12. Olney, "Value of Autobiography," 218.

13. Ketu H. Katrak, "Decolonizing Culture: Toward a Theory for Post-colonial Women's Texts," in *The Post-Colonial Studies Reader,* ed. Bill Ashcroft, Gareth Griffiths, and Helen Tiffin, 258.

always set down in the presence of actual witnesses—hence the term *testimony,* a "declaration or statement made under oath or affirmation by a witness in a court, often in response to questioning to establish a fact" or a "public avowal, as of faith or of a religious experience."[14] Indeed, Truth's *Narrative* is a *testimony* of her life in both the legalistic and the spiritual sense; interviewers Gilbert and Titus act as witnesses to the claims of Truth and provide the testimonials of others who witnessed Truth in her spiritual journey from slave woman to evangelist/political activist. These testimonials are often contradictory in nature, creating in the text a virtual courtroom of evidence in which we as readers must eventually judge Truth for ourselves. Truth's *Narrative* is an embodiment of the complex relationship that existed between the illiterate Truth, her white amanuenses, and other whites who supported or derided her.

Truth presented herself to the public gaze as a simple truth-telling black woman who was most often surrounded by liberal white abolitionists eager to befriend her. Carlton Mabee notes that while her "primary focus as a reformer was on improving the condition of blacks, she lived primarily among whites and spoke primarily to whites."[15] As something of a legend in her own time, she was well known for her "Amazon[ian] form" (TGT, 133) and was dubbed, in an article written by Harriet Beecher Stowe, the "Libyan Sibyl"—to which Truth commented: " 'I don't want to hear about that old symbol; read me something that is going on now, something about this great war!' " (TGT, 174). The comment indicates that while Truth may have encouraged whites' legendizing of her, she also harboured a certain amount of contempt for such romantic reification. But the politically astute Truth, deeply and seriously concerned with assisting black soldiers and freedmen during and after the Civil War, concerned with emancipation and woman suffrage, recognized early the need to create the public persona that would be most expedient in helping her to accomplish her aims. The body that came before a predominantly white public, the body of Truth, was one carefully constructed and

14. Victoria Neufeldt and David B. Guralnik, *Webster's New World Dictionary of American English,* 1383.

15. Mabee and Newhouse, *Sojourner Truth,* 213.

presented by Truth herself, according to her negotiation of at least two considerations—Truth's own political agenda, and the expectations of whites who assisted her and/or heard her speak publicly. In order to further her political mission, Truth—like her literary daughter Zora Neale Hurston—is always the performer. As Nell Irvin Painter observes, Truth self-consciously created her public Self, having been recognized as a consummate performer for twenty years before she gave her now-famous "Ain't I a Woman" speech in Akron, Ohio. Painter argues that Truth created a persona that had a powerful appeal for educated white Americans. Truth could manipulate white notions of blackness and slavery in ways that brought her to the attention of publicists and secured her a place in the history of antislavery feminism. Indeed, I would argue that, like Ellison's Trueblood, on many occasions Truth lies in order to gain white support. Painter continues that, taking our cue from Truth, most of us as readers conclude that Sojourner "embodied some fundamental characteristic of blackness rooted in slavery, some power of race in rhetorically concentrated form."[16] Truth purposefully presents herself as the illiterate, oracular naïf. But the complexities of that presentation result in a *Narrative* rich in its own multiplicities of signification.

In comparing her with her contemporary Frederick Douglass, we may observe that Truth, in her crusade for the cause of women's rights and freedom, refused to present herself as educated and socially sophisticated in the manner of Douglass. Unlike Douglass, for whom literacy in his autobiography became obsessedly synonymous with freedom, Truth was not concerned with learning to read and write. In fact, she was quite comfortable being read to, especially by children, who would read the Bible to her as often as she wished, without any of the commentary that adults would often attempt to impose. Thus, for Truth, reading becomes not an individual but a communal task. Indeed, the very fact that she has relied upon others to produce her narrative attests to the fact that it is in community (especially with women and children) that she establishes

16. Nell Irvin Painter, "Difference, Slavery, and Memory: Sojourner Truth in Feminist Abolitionism," in *The Abolitionist Sisterhood: Women's Political Culture in Antebellum America,* ed. Jean Fagan Yellin and John C. Van Horne, 154.

a sense of selfhood—even if that community is predominantly a white one.

Douglass, whose autobiography is written with a sense of strong individualism, refused to play the role of untutored fugitive that white abolitionists felt he should present in order to conform to (white) public expectations. Throughout his career as an abolitionist, he repeatedly disagreed with his white "mentors," resolutely refusing to speak, as they encouraged him, in the black vernacular or to write in a more "objective," and less angry, less expressive style. But Esther Terry notes that Truth, in the words of Douglass " 'was a genuine specimen of the uncultured Negro . . . [who] seemed to please herself and others best when she put her ideas in the oddest forms.' " Terry suggests that men of culture, the "talented tenth," such as Douglass, might have "perceived Truth as he felt (feared) others saw him . . . an 'uncultured Negro.' "[17] Truth, if she had adopted the style of Douglass, would perhaps have allied herself with educated and relatively affluent, well-bred black club women such as Anna Julia Cooper or Ida B. Wells. But Truth, along with her evangelist sisters, occupied class positions of poverty rather than affluence. Truth is perhaps the luckiest of the female evangelists—with the help of white abolitionist friends she was able to purchase a small home; we are able to locate her whereabouts and activities until her death (we are unable to do this with the other evangelist women); and after her death, a large commemorative tombstone was erected (again, by white friends) to mark the place of her burial in Battle Creek, Michigan. That tombstone still stands today. Interestingly, however, if we compare the trajectory of Truth's life with that of her black male contemporary Douglass, we find that she died in relative poverty and obscurity. Douglass lived to become an American statesman—marshal of the District of Columbia, and minister to Haiti. He resided in a grand Victorian house, very much like one his former master might have owned. Douglass's house was

17. In his influential text *The Souls of Black Folk,* W. E. B. Du Bois speaks of the role of the "talented tenth"—that elite group of exceptionally gifted black men and women who would lead the black masses in their struggle to achieve equality with whites as full Americans. See also Esther Terry, "Sojourner Truth: The Person behind the Libyan Sibyl . . . with a Memoir by Frederick Douglass: 'What I Found at the Northhampton Association,' " 430.

furnished with Greek busts, and other European works of art. He
was paid $150 plus expenses for every one of the numerous lectures
he gave until his death. In contrast, Truth died penniless, the last
printing of her narrative an "offering . . . to the public . . . [so] that
by its sale she may be kept from want in these her last days" (TGT,
viii). This revelation comes directly upon the heels of a statement that
suggests that Truth should be granted a government pension "for her
services in the war, no less than for her labors since the war, for the
amelioration of those yet half enslaved" (TGT, viii). While Titus does
not indict the American government for its lack of responsibility in
supporting Truth, the silent insinuation cannot be missed.

The textual self-crafting or performance of Truth, who—although
she never achieved the fame of Douglass—felt it " 'her duty' to 'trip'
him in his speeches, and to 'ridicule' his efforts to elevate his cul-
tivation" is what I examine here.[18] How are we to interpret Truth's
ridiculing of the very cultural "refinement" Douglass presented as
an antidote to white expectations? Who is the minstrel here? The
refined Douglass, aspiring to Euro-civility, or the unrefined Truth
presenting the very image that whites wanted and expected of black
fugitives? This problem of performance and minstrelsy is, of course,
difficult and complex. In her presentation of her narrative, does the
illiterate Truth valorize African American ways of saying, or does she
merely reinforce damaging white stereotypes of African Americans as
uneducated naifs? Significantly, this same question would later arise
in the critical controversy surrounding Truth's literary descendant
Zora Neale Hurston in her departure from the prevailing theories
of black male writers such as Alain Locke and Richard Wright during and after the Harlem Renaissance. As we enter the twenty-first
century, however, literary criticism favors Hurston in *her* privileging
of orality over literacy, communal telling, and the black vernacular.
Truth, writing almost one hundred years earlier than Hurston, may
be regarded as a foremother of Hurston.

Distance and difference play pivotal roles in Truth's creation of herself as legend—the distance and difference of romantic exoticization.

18. Mabee and Newhouse, *Sojourner Truth*, 113.

It is what allows the white abolitionist audience to be "entertained" by a "peculiarly amusing" Truth (TGT, 202, 232). However, difference concerning more serious and uncomfortable issues of white abolitionist racism must be silenced. On few occasions do we observe Truth's discomfort with the dynamics of her relationship to the white abolitionist "community" in which she situated herself after 1850 (the date of publication of the first *Narrative*). These occasions are located in the second part of her 1878 *Narrative,* the "Book of Life." One (which I have already described) is Truth's impatient dismissal of white attempts to effect her "apotheosis" as mythical "Sibyl" in the manner that Harriet Beecher Stowe described. Another hint of Truth's dissatisfaction with white abolitionists concerns Truth's attempts to gain land, funds, and education for free blacks in Kansas. Frances Titus writes: "she says that not much encouragement is given her, except the constant adjuration to talk to the people, and 'stir 'em up,' and adds, 'why don't you stir 'em up? as tho' an old body like myself could do all the stirring' " (TGT, 234). Truth's double meaning is sharp-edged. Her signifying upon a white abolitionist system structured very much like the system of slavery it purports to destroy cannot be missed here. Indeed, if a sketch of Truth, penciled by Charles C. Burleigh, Jr., son of a prominent New England abolitionist family, is any indication, after Emancipation was actually achieved, white abolitionists *did* expect Truth to "do all the stirring"—for they largely lost interest in the cause of black people, ignoring the fact that millions of blacks were now homeless and destitute. In Burleigh's sketch, a sinewy-armed, light-skinned, and Caucasian-featured Truth bends over a washtub, stirring and scrubbing the washing therein. Two points are of interest here. One is the attempt to ennoble Truth by "whitifying" her physical features, a common nineteenth-century artistic strategy (as in the case of Hiram Powers's sculpture or William Wetmore Story's *Libyan Sibyl*). Another common strategy was the insulting representation of blacks as buffoons in cartoonlike caricature. But it is Burleigh's artistic attempt to romanticize and idealize Truth (as white, and therefore as deserving of admiration and empathy) that pertains here. The other point of interest is that Burleigh represents Truth, not at the podium where the public would have seen her, but at the washtub. His portrait, then, seems a codification of two conflicting public perceptions of black women—both of which served to simultaneously objectify and erase them. One perception is of the black woman as stereotyped Mammy figure (washing clothes at a washtub), but the other is as romanticized heroine. In the former, the black woman is "all body," fit only to perform the menial duties reserved for those of the servant class; in the latter, she becomes "no/body," a presence represented by an absence—when one looks at the artistic representation, the physical reality of the black woman's body is not to be found. Similarly, in Frances Gage's rendition of Truth's "Ain't I a Woman" speech at the Akron, Ohio, women's rights convention, Truth is portrayed not only as powerful rescuing hero and comrade of a (white) women's movement, but also as (black) servant: "She had taken us up in her strong arms and carried us safely over the slough of difficulty, turning the whole tide in our favor" (TGT, 135).

But at times, Truth herself helps to perpetuate her "super-mammy" role. At an antislavery meeting, a proslavery speaker gives an abusive and "inflammatory" speech, comparing blacks to "monkeys, baboons, and ourangoutangs." As he concludes his speech:

> Sojourner quietly drew near to the platform and whispered in the ear of the advocate of her people, "Don't dirty your hands wid dat critter; let me tend to him!" The speaker knew it was safe to trust her. "Children," said she, straightening herself to her full height, "I am one of dem monkey tribes. I was born a slave. I had de dirty work to do—de scullion work. Now I am going to 'ply to dis critter"—pointing her long, bony finger with withering scorn at the petty lawyer. "Now in de course of my time I has done a great deal of dirty scullion work, but of all de dirty work I ever done, dis is de scullionist and de dirtiest." Peering into the eyes of the auditory with just such a look as she could give, and that no one could imitate, she continued: "Now, children, don't you pity me?" She had taken the citadel by storm. The whole audience shouted applause, and the negro-haters as heartily as any. (TGT, 149)

A somewhat amused and dismissive article about Truth, written in the *New York Tribune*, portrays her as an odd, ranting personage, for whom "*war, slavery,* and the *prided fashions*" are all worthy of simultaneous condemnation: "We leave Sojourner Truth with her intuitiveness and without the letter, to battle almost alone these world-wide evils. May Heaven bless and sustain her in her humanitarian work and 'God-like mission' " the article condescendingly concludes (TGT, 245). This picture of Truth, battling "almost alone" on behalf of blacks after Emancipation is perhaps a telling encapsulation of Truth's career as a black activist among white abolitionists. In the *Narrative,* the words *entertain* and *amuse* are so often used by white abolitionists (including amanuensis Frances Titus) with reference to Truth that we can hardly overlook the vast (yet unmentioned) distances that existed between them—distances that separate a minstrel from her audience.

Truth plays minstrel on many occasions, but if the role of the minstrel is to slavishly cater to white expectations of her in her performance, she is also adept at manipulating the emotions of her audience in order to solicit the most out of them in the way of financial patronage. Thus, crafting *un*truths in order to maintain the "supermammy" image her white abolitionist audience desires, Truth belies the very veracity-announcing promise of her (also self-crafted) name. For example, her claim in her "Ain't I a Woman" speech that she bore thirteen children and lost most of them to slavery is complete fabrication—what Esther Terry and Sterling Stuckey, in their references to Truth as a blues woman, might call Sojourner's wily singing of the blues: " 'I have borne thirteen chilern and seen 'em mos' all sold off into slavery, and when I cried out with a mother's grief, none but Jesus heard—and ar'n't I a woman?' " (TGT, 134). Truth, in fact, bore only five children, Diana, Elizabeth, Sophia, Peter, and James. Of these children, James died in infancy. Peter was sold South into slavery at age five, but Truth, in an astounding demonstration of bravery and determination, retrieved him through court proceedings. Truth, upon taking leave of her former master, Mr. Dumont, eventually took Peter with her to New York City and left her daughters to live as bound servants with the Dumonts.

In another instance of fabrication, a scene recorded by a white observer recounts the manner in which Truth moves an entire assembly with her words:

Just as the meeting was about to close, Sojourner stood up. Tears were coursing down her furrowed cheeks. She said: "We has heerd a great

deal about love at home in de family. Now, children, I was a slave, and
my husband and my children was sold from me." The pathos with which
she uttered these words made a deep impression upon the meeting.
Pausing a moment, she added: "Now, husband and children is *all* gone,
and what has *'come* of de affection I had for dem? *Dat is de question before
de house!*" The people smiled amidst a baptism of tears. (TGT, 149–50)

No mention is made in the *Narrative* of the traumatic events of which
Truth speaks. In fact, the text early on relates that Truth was forced
to marry a slave named Thomas after her lover, Robert (a slave from
another plantation), was beaten and sent back to his master. When
Truth escapes from the Dumont plantation, and eventually leaves
Dumont for New York City, taking only her son Peter with her, no
mention is made at all of the husband she leaves behind. We wonder
what "affection" she had for this husband, Thomas, to whom only a
fleeting allusion is made in the text.

In another example of Truth's manipulativeness as performer,
Truth spoke alternately with a Dutch accent, in black dialect, and
in standard English—an astute selection of speech presentations that
she could use as she chose or as the occasion warranted. Indeed, in
her text her voice is recorded sometimes in an almost caricatured
dialect, sometimes in perfect standard English. We may compare this
recording of Truth's speech: " 'Chile, do n't be skeered; you are not
going to be harmed. I don't speck God's ever hearn tell on ye' "
with: "Sojourner says: 'I went in company with several ladies and
gentlemen to see the president. While waiting in the ante-room with
other visitors, a gentleman called, to whom I was introduced' " (TGT,
136, 273). Truth's performance, then, as both "super-mammy" and
as the articulate and astute political figure she was, suggests a canny
ability to "play" her audience, as a blues bad woman ready and willing
to sing the tune that would gain her both their attention and their
monetary support. As Mabee notes, Truth claimed with pride: " 'I tell
you I can't read a book, but I can read de people.' "[19]

Finally, in describing the eventual fate of Mrs. Gedney, the white
woman who derides Truth for attempting to regain custody of her

19. Ibid., 64.

son, Truth gives two astoundingly manipulative and contradictory accounts. The first derives from Olive Gilbert's rendition of the *Narrative:* "The derangement of Mrs. G. was a matter of hearsay, as Isabella saw her not after the trial"; the second is Harriet Beecher Stowe's account of how Truth told the story to her and a group of her friends: " 'Well, I went in an' tended that poor critter [Mrs. Gedney] all night. She was out of her mind—a cryin', an' callin' for her daughter; an' I held her poor ole head on my arm an' watched for her as ef she'd been my babby. An' I watched by her, an' took care on her all through her sickness after that, an' she died in my arms, poor thing!' " (TGT, 58, 164). The "truth" that Sojourner, as blues performer, imparts to Gilbert seems very different from the heartrending and infinitely more entertaining "truth" she imparts to Stowe and Stowe's husband, a man who "was wont to say of an evening, 'Come, I am dull, can't you get Sojourner up here to talk a little?' She would come up into the parlor, and sit among pictures and ornaments, in her simple stuff gown, with her heavy travelling shoes, the central object of attention both to parents and children, always ready to talk or to sing" (TGT, 165).

In the course of the *Narrative,* at least three references are made to Truth's performance as singer. Two of these attest to Truth's long-standing concern with black homelessness after Emancipation. In one scenario, she subdues with song an entire gang of ruffians who threaten to violently disrupt a camp meeting; the *Narrative* proper closes with a Civil War song composed by Truth, to be sung to the tune of "John Brown," one passage of which reads: "They will have to pay us wages, the wages of their sin; / They will have to bow their foreheads to their colored kith and kin; / They will have to give us house-room, or the roof will tumble in, / As we go marching on" (TGT, 117–19, 126). Another song, the words for which Truth wrote to the tune of "Auld Lang Syne" and recorded in the "Book of Life," begins: "I am pleading for my people— / A poor, down-trodden race, / Who dwell in freedom's boasted land / With no abiding place" (TGT, 302).

The manner in which Mrs. Stowe says that Truth introduced herself to her provides us with Stowe's first exposure to Truth's performance of the blues:

She seemed perfectly self-possessed and at her ease. . . . Her whole air
had at times a gloomy sort of drollery which impressed one strangely.

"So this is you," she said.

"Yes," I answered.

"Well, honey, de Lord bless ye! I jes' thought I'd like to come an'
have a look at ye. You's heerd o' me, I reckon?" she added.

"Yes I have. You go about lecturing, do you not?"

"Yes, honey, that's what I do. The Lord has made me a sign unto this
nation, an' I go round a-testifyin', an' showin' on em' their sins agin my
people."

So saying, she took a seat, and stooping over and crossing her arms
on her knees, she looked down on the floor, and appeared to fall into
a sort of reverie. Her great, gloomy eyes and her dark face seemed
to work with some undercurrent of feeling; she sighed deeply, and
occasionally broke out, "O Lord! O Lord! Oh, the tears, an' the groans,
an' the moans, O Lord!" (TGT, 152)

For Truth, performance is a singing of the blues in all its forms. At
least fourteen songs of Truth's own making have been preserved.
The tunes of five of her songs were those of popular melodies of
Truth's time. According to Mabee, Truth's singing style "reflected
African influences more clearly than most aspects of her life."[20] If
Truth performs as blues artist inside and outside of her text, singing
and telling "the tears an' the groans, an' the moans, O Lord!", we must
remember that the performing artist is a manipulator of information,
never merely conveying a story unadulterated, but always deciding
what will be *withheld* as well as what will be told. Amanuensis Gilbert
comments upon Truth's reticence at certain moments in the text.
In the case of Mrs. Dumont's harsh treatment of Truth, we are told
that "delicacy" prevents outspokenness, as does an awareness that
"the relation of [certain things] might inflict undeserved pain on
some living." Therefore, "the reader will not be surprised if our
narrative appear somewhat tame at this point, and may rest assured
that it is not for want of facts, as the most thrilling incidents . . . are

20. Ibid., 219.

from various motives suppressed" (TGT, 30). If we surmise that the "delicate" silence referred to here might conceal sexual relations between Mr. Dumont and Truth (a not uncommon occurrence in slave families), which Mrs. Dumont at some juncture discovered, we may compare Truth's words with those of Linda Brent, who also found it necessary to protect information of a sexually explicit nature:

> Reader, be assured this narrative is no fiction. I am aware that some of my adventures may seem incredible; but they are, nevertheless, strictly true. I have not exaggerated the wrongs inflicted by Slavery; on the contrary, my descriptions fall far short of the facts. . . . I have not written my experiences in order to attract attention to myself; on the contrary, it would have been more pleasant to me to have been silent about my own history.[21]

In the same text, Brent's white abolitionist friend and endorser L. Maria Child is concerned to rationalize the sexual content of Brent's autobiography:

> I am well aware that many will accuse me of indecorum for presenting these pages to the public; for the experiences of this intelligent and much-injured woman belong to a class which some call delicate subjects, and others indelicate. This peculiar phase of Slavery had generally been kept veiled; but the public ought to be made acquainted with its monstrous features, and I willingly take the responsibility of presenting them with the veil withdrawn. I do this for the sake of my sisters in bondage, who are suffering wrongs so foul, that our ears are too delicate to listen to them. (LB, 337–38)

I am interested in the use, in both Truth's and Brent's narratives, of the words *delicacy* and *silence*. Maria Child "willingly" takes the "responsibility" for presenting Brent's sexual history "with the veil withdrawn," but we suspect that Truth refuses to "draw the veil" that conceals the "private parts" of *her* life. Amanuensis Gilbert writes,

---

21. Linda Brent, "Incidents in the Life of a Slave Girl," in *The Classic Slave Narratives*, ed. Henry Louis Gates, Jr., 335, hereinafter cited as LB in the text.

in a chapter entitled "Gleanings": "There are some hard things that crossed Isabella's life while in slavery, that she has no desire to publish, for various reasons" (TGT, 81). The desire to conceal clearly seems to be Truth's. Truth "has no desire to publish," the "hard things" in her life, first because of the negative implications for innocent parties, and second, "because they are not all for the public ear, from their very nature." But, it is the third reason for withholding information that provides us with the most important insight into Truth, the performer: the truth would not be believed by "the uninitiated"—" 'Why, no!' [Sojourner] says, 'they'd call me a liar! they would, indeed! and I do not wish to say anything to destroy my own character for veracity, though what I say is strictly true' " (TGT, 81–82). The tongue-in-cheek irony of Truth's statement performs a number of things simultaneously: (1) her use of the word *uninitiated* creates an automatic hierarchy in which the superior "initiated" (blacks who have had experience of slavery) possess knowledge that those excluded from the club of knowers, the white "uninitiated," do not have; (2) her suggestion that she would be branded a "liar" if she told the truth about the atrocities of slavery points to the double oppression of blacks by whites, first in enslaving blacks and then in refusing to believe their stories about the horrors of that enslavement; (3) her admission that she will say nothing to "destroy [her] own character for veracity," may be read as Truth's ladylike reluctance to let crude facts tarnish her pure image— but more subversively, Truth hints at the fact that for her as performer, truth-telling does not stand in the way of the maintenance of the persona she has created for public consumption.

Truth, like Trueblood, deftly manipulates white preconceptions of blacks in order to gain credence, room, board, and financial backing. As such, Truth's and Trueblood's acts of minstrelsy become subversive strategies that seek to overturn hegemonic systems of power, even while seeming to reinforce them. Thus, what Mabee refers to as inconsistency, disturbing omission and poor organization in Truth's *Narrative,* seem to me to be more accurately described as demonstrations of Truth's power as performer.[22] Deliberate or not, they point

22. Mabee and Newhouse, *Sojourner Truth,* 52.

to a relational dynamics—both in the incidents and in the rhetoric of the text—in which Truth as illiterate and "amusing" entertainer wields more power than her audience (and perhaps many readers of her text) realize.

Truth's *Narrative* functions—in a number of striking reversals—as oppositional text as well as minstrel performance. Truth's very text, first published in 1850 (at the height of both the slavery debate and the popularity of productions such as Erastus Palmer's, Hiram Powers's, and Elizabeth Barrett Browning's) is a kind of reversal in itself; its first announcement is "A PREFACE which was intended for a postscript." In addition, the list of white names and comments that, in other slave narratives, is presented at the beginning as an endorsement of the veracity of the slave narrator appears at the end of Truth's text in the form of a number of autographs. These include signatures of such famous personages as William Lloyd Garrison, Abraham Lincoln, Susan B. Anthony, and Harriet Beecher Stowe. However, these white supporters do not endorse Truth here; instead, what we read is *her* commendation of *them* as suitable and worthy enough to be included in her "Book of Life." They are the names of those whites whose names have been noted in God's holy register: "Autographs of distinguished Persons who have befriended Sojourner Truth by words of Sympathy and Material aid," the "names of men and women . . . pure and sparkling as the shimmer of a white wing flashing through the yellow sunlight—names of those who manifested their love to God by tender compassion for the lowliest of his children" (TGT, 313, 316). Immediately after the actual autographs come a series of commendations—"Notes on the Autographs"—to which there are no names attached. Thus, in what amounts to good Christian modesty but very bad autobiographical protocol, we do not know which commendation belongs with which autograph; we cannot attach the commendation to the signer commented upon. For example: "The name of one who was dragged through the streets with a halter about his neck will be remembered . . . for the immortality attained through his sublime heroism" or "The name of one is written who only 'awaited the opportunity to enfranchise millions' " (TGT, 316). Another unidentified signer inscribes this formula in Sojourner's "Book of Life": "Equality of rights is the first of rights" (TGT, 318).

In this confounding of beginnings, endings, and accreditations Truth establishes not only a reversal, but also a circularity that Karla Holloway attributes to many contemporary black women's texts: "A decentered ethic also shifts the place of logic from one that emphasizes a binary argument (between polar opposites) to one that seems more circular, and more woman-centered. . . . Complexity, multiple presences, and cyclic rather than linear principles are definitive aspects of the works of black women writers."[23]

Truth's *Narrative,* then, in its very structure, acts as an oppositional text, subverting prevailing nineteenth-century autobiographical form, challenging the glaring absence of the black female self as perpetuated by renowned white male artists such as Hiram Powers or Erastus Dow Palmer. But, if she struggles to resist her disembodiment, she also conversely challenges the prevailing white abolitionist obsession with black *embodiment* in the form of what Houston Baker calls "the negro exhibit." Barbara McCaskill also notes the eagerness with which white abolitionists sought to display escaped slaves Henry Brown, Ellen Craft, and William Wells Brown at the World's Fair in London 1851: "William Wells Brown and his panorama must be displayed. Henry "Box" Brown and his crate must be displayed. William Craft, too, and Mrs. Craft, costumed in the masculine garments of her escape, must be displayed—both standing on an auction block." Eventually, the escaped slaves simply "strolled [through the Fair] arm-in-arm with a prominent British abolitionist of the opposite gender." McCaskill also notes that "William Wells Brown did bring, as a souvenir of sorts, London's infamous Punch illustration excoriating American enslavement. The drawing, entitled 'The Virginian Slave,' depicted a forlorn, bare-breasted Black woman chained to a post garlanded with Old Glory. Dramatically, Brown posted the drawing with New York artist Hiram Powers's 'The Greek Slave' . . . a romantic nude of a white slave and one of the Fair's most popular attractions."[24]

As Baker observes, a common feature of white abolitionist meetings was the fugitive slave, "a silent, partially naked body turning to a

23. Holloway, *Moorings,* 33.
24. Barbara McCaskill, " 'Yours Very Truly': The Fugitive as Text and Artifact," 524–27.

predominantly white audience. The silent, fugitive slave's body became an erotic sign of servitude in the social, liberational discourse of white abolitionists and their predominantly white audiences. Gasps and moans (of empathy? reassurance? relief?) followed." Baker argues that writers of slave narratives, such as Tubman, Douglass, Truth, and Jacobs refused to accept this silent exhibition of themselves "for private, indoor use," but instead, "wanted to craft and tell [their] own horrendous tale rather than serve as an illustration or mere exhibit in that society's inside tale-tellings." Thus, Frederick Douglass made a "consciously crafted decision to become a floating signifier . . . [a decision that carried] him beyond abolitionist historical containment."[25] One must ask, however, if Douglass's very description of the act of abuse is not, ironically, in itself a kind of exhibit, which Truth, in her own *Narrative* challenges.

It seems that in the narrative of Douglass, the beating of women is described in much greater detail than the beating of men, a strategy that, of course, elicits the appropriate horror in the reader. The first instance of whipping that Douglass describes involves a beautiful slave woman, Douglass's Aunt Hester, who is jealously guarded by her master when she demonstrates interest in a slave from another plantation: "Why master was so careful of her, may be safely left to conjecture. She was a woman of noble form, and of graceful proportions." The incident proceeds as follows:

> Before [master] commenced whipping Aunt Hester, he took her into the kitchen, and stripped her from neck to waist, leaving her neck, shoulders, and back, entirely naked. He then told her to cross her hands, calling her at the same time a d—d b—h. After crossing her hands, he tied them with a strong rope, and led her to a stool under a large hook in the joist . . . He made her get upon the stool and tied her hands to the hook. She now stood fair for his infernal purpose. Her arms were stretched up at their full length, so that she stood upon the ends of her toes . . . and soon the warm, red blood . . . came dripping to the floor.[26]

25. Baker, *Workings of the Spirit*, 13–14.
26. Frederick Douglass, *Narrative of the Life of Frederick Douglass, an American Slave*, 25–26.

The suggestion of the sexual titillation the sadistic master receives cannot be missed in Douglass's re-creation of what virtually amounts to a sentimental scene of ravishment. The detailed description of the stripping and the phrase "she now stood fair for his infernal purpose" establish Aunt Hester as the "fair" (?) heroine about to be despoiled by the "infernal" villain—a common scenario in the genre of the sentimental novel.

Truth's description of her own whipping, unlike Douglass's, presents no sentimental scene of ravishment, but one of ugly brutality:

> she was told to go to the barn; on going there, she found her master
> with a bundle of rods, prepared in the embers, and bound together
> with cords. When he had tied her hands together before her, he gave
> her the most cruel whipping she was ever tortured with. He whipped
> her till the flesh was deeply lacerated, and the blood streamed from her
> wounds—and the scars remain to the present. (TGT, 26)

The description of how her lover is beaten is even more gruesome: "[T]hey . . . [beat] him with the heavy ends of their canes, bruising and mangling his head and face in the most awful manner, and causing the blood, which streamed from his wounds to cover him like a slaughtered beast, constituting him a most shocking spectacle" (TGT, 35).

Truth, even before her narrative begins, counters the danger of a discourse liable to slip in spite of itself into the exhibitive mode with her daguerreotype, which, as I have already mentioned, becomes a pictorial "discourse" of its own. Unlike Harriet Jacobs, whose autobiographical story of sexual abuse at the hands of a white master was discreetly published in 1861 under the pseudonym Linda Brent, without daguerreotypes, Truth presents us with a frank camera likeness. As such, the likeness promises to offer not the passive Negro exhibit but Truth's own staring-down of white hypocrisy; again and again in the text, this black woman marches, fully clothed, into the arenas of learned white men to deflate their rhetoric with (to use the words of white abolitionist Parker Pillsbury), "a single dart" of her own rhetorical making.[27] In examining her daguerreotype, the *reader* becomes the object examined as Truth returns an unwavering stare. Significantly, in one incident in her *Narrative,* Truth executes a deliberate public "exhibition" of her own body in a manner that merits some examination. At one of her many speaking engagements, Truth is confronted by a heckler who expresses the doubt existing "in the minds of many persons present respecting the sex of the speaker." The heckler then demands that Truth "submit her breast to the inspection of some of the ladies present, that the doubt might be removed by their testimony." The white ladies are embarrassed and indignant at the suggestion. The heckler calls for a vote and "a boisterous 'Aye' was the result." What then ensues represents a powerful moment in the text:

> Sojourner told them that her breasts had suckled many a white babe, to the exclusion of her own offspring; that some of those white babies had grown to man's estate; that, although they had sucked her colored breasts, they were, in her estimation, far more manly than they (her persecutors) appeared to be; and she quietly asked them, as she disrobed her bosom, if they, too, wished to suck! . . . [S]he told them that . . . it was not to her shame that she uncovered her breast before them, but to their shame. (TGT, 138–39)

The implications of Truth's action as a *dis*erasure (a "dissing" or disrespecting of erasure) of the black woman's body are astounding here. While Hiram Power's *Greek Slave* stood exposed at the London Fair, her white nakedness a representation of a lofty spiritual transcendence and Ideal beauty, slavemasters at a political gathering attempted to shame Truth into silence by goading her to do something that they and their forefathers did to all black women and men in the slave-market—reduce them to naked pieces of chattel, whose nakedness was not a sign of the transcendent but rather of their shameful impotence before white purchasers who prodded, probed, and poked before buying. As such, the black slaves, reduced

27. Mabee and Newhouse, *Sojourner Truth,* 86.

to the sum of their parts—a strong arm, exposed genitals, a naked breast—are simultaneously all-body and nobody. What Hiram Powers does with his *Greek Slave* is to remove from the public eye the too-shameful embodiment of black women. Black women, then, as *The Slave* suggests, become simply nobody. But Truth, in her action, as it is related in the text, brings herself and her body out from under erasure, casting shame where it belongs—back upon the slaveowners. Prepared to deride the proud black woman who must lose this battle of wits by either slinking out of the meeting-hall (her womanhood left in doubt) or succumb to the humiliating demand to let "the (white) ladies" physically examine her, the white male slavemasters are shocked by Truth's response. The shame of the black woman's being at once all-body and nobody becomes *their* embarrassment, confronted as they are by things for them best left unsaid—the fact that many of them grew up on black women's milk, that black babies were deprived of their mothers and their mothers' milk so that white ones could thrive, that the request of the men is puerile and as shameful as if they were to be caught suckling at the breast of a black woman—which was indeed a reality for many white men, to which the miscegenation laws they created for their own benefit will attest. The miscegenation law stated that a black child must always follow the condition of its mother (who was almost invariably black and enslaved). This law allowed white slave owners unlimited and unencumbered access to the bodies of black slave women—indeed, it *encouraged* such access, since one's slave capital was increased by the (undoubtedly enjoyable) practice of "studding" one's own female slaves oneself.

Truth again reclaims the black female body from erasure in her "Ain't I a Woman" speech. Truth, a powerful, physically arresting, deep-voiced black woman activist who has been forced to work the fields as well as bear children, is denied the status of womanhood according to the standards of the cult that defines "true womanhood." But Truth divorces femininity (of the white variety as depicted by Hiram Powers) from womanhood, and in so doing, challenges the skewed white assumption that the black woman, because of her black-ness, her hard labor, her intrusion into the public speaking sphere of men, is both all-body and nobody: "'I have plowed and planted, and gathered into barns, and no man could head me—and ar'n't I a woman?'" she demands (TGT, 134).

If Truth wrests the task of black embodiment from the hands of white abolitionists eager to display the silent black body in the "negro exhibit," she also wrestles with her white amanuenses over this very same issue. While Gilbert and Titus attempt to assist Truth in her creation of a dignified self, they very often concentrate on the particulars of her body, in a romantic reification of Truth as the black primitive, seductive to the imagination, "picturesquely charming" (TGT, 158). Olive Gilbert closes her preface to the *Narrative* with a gesture that suggests nothing less than perfect presence, an absolute embodiment in which Truth and her narrative become one: "This is Sojourner Truth at a century old. Would you like to meet her?" (TGT, xii). The complexity of this embodiment, however, merits closer examination.

In the preface alone, we are struck by the manner in which the voices of Truth and Gilbert vie with each other in their attempts to create Truth as persona, as presence. The preface begins with a reference to the very fact that Truth is a "self-made woman." An anecdote about her reads: "Sojourner Truth once remarked, in reply to an allusion to the late Horace Greeley, 'You call him a self-made man; well, I am a self-made woman'" (TGT, v). Truth self-consciously creates herself in direct opposition to the Algeresque liberal white male individualism that a man such as Greeley represents—a man who initially supported emancipation, but afterward "opposed any special help to blacks now that they were freed."[28] But while Truth fashions herself in oppositional comparison to famous, supposedly liberal white male politicians, Olive Gilbert effects an embodiment of Truth that compares her with the forces of Nature. She likens Truth to "her lofty cousins, the Palms, which keep guard over the sacred streams where her forefathers idled away their childhood days." Indeed, Gilbert is sure that Truth's very blood "is fed by those tropical fires which had slumberingly crept through many generations, but now awaken in her veins; akin to those rivers which mysteriously

28. Ibid., 161.

disappear in the bosom of the desert, and unexpectedly burst forth in springs of pure and living water." And as Truth enters old age, her "sun of life is about to dip below the horizon; but flashes of wit and wisdom still emanate from her soul, like the rays of the natural sun as it bursts forth from a somber cloud" (TGT, vi-vii). Allusions to Truth's "idle" forefathers and "slumbering" tropical fires reflect a nineteenth-century propensity to conceive of Africa and Africans in terms of slothfulness, power unrealized, civilization yet unattained. For example, nineteenth-century artistic depictions survive in which "Africa" and "America" are represented as women in postures of sloth and happy industry, respectively.[29]

Truth, then, both in her life and in the double-voiced rhetoric of her preface, performs in opposition to white tendencies to reify and/or silence her as exotic object. The conflicting strategies that Truth and Gilbert employ in their attempts to effect Truth's dignified embodiment in the face of disembodiment and hyperembodiment point to significant characteristics of the *Narrative*—the communal manner in which its joint telling is accomplished and the problematization of that telling throughout the text.

In Hurston's *Their Eyes Were Watching God,* community—the community of two formed by Janie and Pheoby—creates what Gates calls the voice of free indirect discourse, or the speakerly text. The written standard English voice of the nameless narrator (presumably someone who heard Janie's story from Pheoby) begins to sound more and more like the quoted, oral, vernacular voice of Janie, as the voices of Janie and narrator become intertwined. I believe that it is a similar process of communality that creates what amounts to the free indirect discourse of Olive Gilbert and Sojourner Truth. The style of Truth's *Narrative* is conversational, anecdotal, tangential, and nonchronological, very much in the manner of informal verbal communication. However, if the community of Janie and Pheoby is one of black sisterhood, that of Gilbert and Truth presents problems that arise out of the racial difference existing between the latter "sisters." Kimberly Rae Connor observes that "Linda Brent and Sojourner Truth both relied

---

29. See Boime, *Art of Exclusion.*

on the goodwill and faith of abolitionists to get their stories told."
According to Connor, Pheoby, like the abolitionist scribes and editors,
"stands within a traditional role of women who take their message back
to the community."[30] But, for early black women autobiographers, the
issue of community is a difficult and vexed one, and it is this problem
that constitutes what I will call the "grammar of interruption" that
we see in Truth's *Narrative*. In chapter 4 I examine how issues of
white editing affected the self-written autobiography of Rebecca Cox
Jackson. In the *Narrative* of Truth, I want to explore a similar editing
issue—the troubled "community" of voices in the *Narrative* and how
it creates the interrupted grammar of the text.

Because Truth's narrative is actually written by white women, au-
thenticity becomes problematic in her text. Jeffrey Stewart argues,
understandably, that Truth's *Narrative* "suffers" as a result of the fact
that it was written with the help of white abolitionist Olive Gilbert.
Stewart surmises that the "unfortunate" decision to have her story told
by Gilbert may have been influenced by Sojourner's astute awareness
that because the truthfulness and reliability of black autobiographies
was often questioned, "having a white woman tell her story would lend
credibility to [Truth's] accomplishments. . . . Sojourner may have believed that Gilbert would give her story a more authoritative voice."
As Stewart sardonically observes, Truth's *Narrative* is interrupted—
"marred" —by Gilbert's "tendency to interpolate her own opinions
in the text. Rather than let her subject speak without moralizing
interjections, Gilbert seizes upon Sojourner's life story as a vehi-
cle for her own indictment of slaveowners and their justifications
for slavery . . . Sojourner's narrative thus provided Gilbert with an
opportunity to find her voice."[31] However, in considering Stewart's
indictment of Gilbert's motives for writing the narrative, we must
also consider Truth's role as performer—in the creation of both her
narrative and her public self. Thus, rather than lament the fact that
some "pure" narrative by Truth is obscured by the interference of her
white amanuensis Gilbert, we might instead examine the dynamics
that shaped Truth's performance of her public self. I suggest that

30. Connor, *Conversions and Visions*, 162.
31. Jeffrey C. Stewart, introduction to *Narrative of Sojourner Truth*, xxxix.

whatever it was that propelled Truth out of the African American community to seek white American public circles, and to negotiate a number of (often conflicting) discourses is the same force that lies behind the conflicting voices in her multi-voiced and contradictory narrative.

In the relation of Truth's *Narrative,* Olive Gilbert obviously seeks to include Truth, but we are struck by the manner in which the women struggle with each other in telling—struck by a text that, in effect, struggles with itself. While Gilbert relates the major portion of the *Narrative,* she almost never allows us to forget that Truth is at her side while Gilbert writes. For example:

> She shudders, even now, as she goes back in memory, and revisits this
> cellar, and sees its inmates, of both sexes and all ages, sleeping on
> those damp boards, like the horse, with a little straw and a blanket; and
> she wonders not at the rheumatisms and fever-sores, and palsies, that
> distorted the limbs and racked the bodies of those fellow-slaves in after-
> life. (TGT, 14)

Often, Gilbert quotes Truth's direct speech: "'And then, as I was taking leave of him,' said his daughter [Truth] in relating it, 'he raised his voice, and cried aloud like a child—Oh, how he DID cry! I HEAR it *now*—and remember it as well as if it were but yesterday.' " (TGT, 22).

But other moments in the text reveal discrepancies of opinion between Truth and Gilbert or Truth and other white witnesses in the text. For example, in "The Book of Life," compiled by Frances Titus, we compare Truth's attitude to the homeless blacks who congregate around Washington after Emancipation, with the attitudes of white abolitionists. Titus quotes a letter written by Truth to a white friend, Rowland Johnson: "'I find many of the women very ignorant in relation to house-keeping, as most of them were instructed in field labor, but not in household duties' " (TGT, 179). In contrast, Titus herself writes: "Sojourner spent more than a year at Arlington Heights [in Washington], instructing the women in domestic duties. . . . She especially deprecated their filthy habits" (TGT, 182). Similarly a newspaper article advertising a talk by Sojourner Truth on solutions to the problem of destitute free blacks in Washington reads: "'No gang of paupers should be allowed to huddle together like pigs anywhere, and be fed out of the public funds. Go and hear on the subject'" (TGT, 202). Nowhere in the representations of whites do we find the compassionate attempt that Truth makes to explain the oppressive sociopolitical conditions contributing to the "ignorance" of the freed blacks with respect to "house-keeping."

Gilbert's own ambivalence about Truth's ability to tell her story herself is evident in the following passage: "One comparatively trifling incident she wishes related, as it made a deep impression on her mind at the time—showing, as *she* thinks, how God shields the innocent, and causes them to triumph over their enemies, and also how she stood between master and mistress" (TGT, 30). Gilbert's emphasis of the word *she* suggests a difference of opinion between Truth and Gilbert on the matter of the incident's importance for each woman. In another instance, in a chapter that reveals how slaveholders fail to fulfill their promises to slaves, Gilbert presents a long narration by Truth in direct discourse (quoted speech). Here, Truth relates a story which had considerable effect upon her—the fatal beating with a stick of a slave who, after completing the harvest, insisted on going to see his wife as his master had promised. Truth did not witness the beating, only heard about it; however, the impact of the incident upon her as a black woman was still profound: "'The poor colored people all felt struck down by the blow.'" Gilbert concludes the chapter with a moralistic aside of her own: "Ah! and well they might. Yet it was but one of a long series of bloody, and other most effectual blows, struck against their liberty and their lives. But to return from our digression" (TGT, 40). We can only wonder at the complexities of a relationship in which what one woman describes as a "digression" the other experiences as a painful, horrific, and significant memory.

I have already noted Carlton Mabee's description of Gilbert's writing in the *Narrative* as "earnest and sometimes, by later standards, gushing. The book contains contradictions and disturbing omissions, and is not well organized."[32] But what these textual "flaws" suggest is the existence of converging, diverging, and struggling voices in the

---

32. Mabee and Newhouse, *Sojourner Truth,* 52.

*Narrative*—a grammar of interruption, which is evident in the very first line of the text: "The subject of this biography, SOJOURNER TRUTH, as she now calls herself—but whose name, originally, was Isabella—was born, as near as she can now calculate, between the years 1797 and 1800" (TGT, 13). If we examine the grammatical structure of this sentence the uncertainty of its voice(s) becomes immediately apparent. The core of the sentence, carrying its basic meaning and containing subject, verb and adverbial clause, is: "Sojourner Truth was born between the years 1797 and 1800." However, what Karla Holloway refers to as "recursion" in contemporary black women's texts— the repetitive, reflective, backward glance important to strategies of revision and (re)membrance—serves to (re)present Sojourner Truth three times here as: (1) "the subject of this biography," (2) "Sojourner Truth," and (3) "Isabella." In addition, the sentence is complicated by a multiplicity of interruptions: the interruption "as she now calls herself" is itself further interrupted by "—but whose name, originally, was Isabella."[33] And finally "as near as she can remember" disruptively separates the verb "was born" from its adverbial clause "between the years 1797 and 1800." What the reader is left with is a frustrating uncertainty about "the subject of this biography"; is her name Sojourner Truth, or Isabella? When exactly *was* she born? This grammatical uncertainty of voice reflects the state of existence for most slaves in nineteenth century America—one's name and birthdate were very often tenuous assignments. But the uncertainty reflects something else—a recursive naming and renaming, a multidirectionality of voice and meaning that suggest the problematics of self-fashioning. In this first sentence, we understand that to be a "self-made" woman is not a simple task; the vision and revision it entails involves a proliferation of strategies and voices.

Throughout Truth's narrative, breaks in the structure of sentences, indicating parenthetical elements, appositives, and other disruptions abound. For example, the following excerpt in which Gilbert discusses the filthy and abject accommodations of Truth's family as slaves

33. Holloway, *Moorings*, 3.

of a certain Charles Ardinburgh, demonstrates the interruption of Truth's views (as expressed by Gilbert), by a moral outburst purely Gilbert's own:

> Still, [Truth] does not attribute this cruelty—*for cruelty it certainly is, to be so unmindful of the health and comfort of any being, leaving entirely out of sight his more important part, his everlasting interests,*—so much to any innate or constitutional cruelty of the master, as to that gigantic inconsistency, that inherited habit among slaveholders, of expecting a willing and intelligent obedience from the slave, because he is a MAN [emphasis mine] (TGT, 15)

If the body of the text is marked by such interruption, however, there are also places where interruptive voices become indiscernible from one another. Often Gilbert directly quotes the speech of Truth, but at times, free indirect discourse—the adoption of spoken black dialect within the otherwise standard English of the narrator's written text—seems to suggest itself. The narrator begins to take on the speech patterns of the person about whom she narrates. Indeed, this adoption is apparent in the text's first sentence: "SOJOURNER TRUTH . . . was born as *near* [emphasis mine] as she can now calculate, between the years 1797 and 1800" (TGT, 13). We may contrast this nonstandard use of the adverb with a later sentence in which the accepted grammatical form is rendered: "Her teachings were delivered in Low Dutch . . . and . . . ran *nearly* [emphasis mine] as follows" (TGT, 17).

In another instance, referring to the thoughts of Truth (then Isabella) and Gertrude, the young daughter of Truth's master:

> Isabella thought that she had done all she well could to have [the sullied potatoes] *nice* [emphasis mine]; and became quite distressed at these appearances. . . . Gertrude . . . advanced to Isabel, and told her . . . she would get up and attend to her potatoes for her . . . and they would see if they could not have them *nice* [emphasis in original], and not have "Poppee," her word for father, and "Matty," her word for mother, and *all of 'em* [emphasis mine], scolding so terribly. (TGT, 31)

And in describing Truth's treatment at the home of her new master, Gilbert writes: "They gave her a plenty to eat, and also a plenty of whippings" (TGT, 27).

At the end of the *Narrative,* the voices of Gilbert and Truth become one; we are no longer able to discern where one ends and the other begins:

> "Never mind," says Sojourner, "what we give to the poor, we lend to the Lord." She thanked the Lord with fervor, that she had lived to hear her master say such blessed things! She recalled the lectures he used to give his slaves, on speaking the truth and being honest, and laughing, she says he taught us not to lie and steal, when he was stealing all the time himself and did not know it! Oh! how sweet to my mind was this confession! And what a confession for a master to make to a slave! A slaveholding master turned to a brother! Poor old man, may the Lord bless him, and all slaveholders partake of his spirit! (TGT, 125)

Gilbert begins this final passage by quoting the direct discourse of Truth (" 'Never mind,' says Sojourner"). But halfway through the passage, a clause that begins as indirect discourse—that is, a paraphrasing of what was said ("she says he taught")—turns into something that seems to be direct discourse but is not signaled as such by the usual quotation marks: "she says he taught us not to lie and steal." The omission of the quotation mark before the word *he* creates an intriguing problem around the word *us.* Without the missing mark, "us" becomes not Truth and the other slaves but Truth, the slaves, and Gilbert also. In this final conflation of voices, narrator and amanuensis become one. How Zora Neale Hurston and Alice Walker use this conflation of voices in a negotiation between standard English and black American vernacular, Henry Louis Gates, Jr., has examined in detail in *The Signifyin(g) Monkey.* But more than eighty years before Hurston, the joint efforts of Truth and Gilbert produced what Gates would call "free indirect discourse" in his discussion of Hurston's work.

Truth, consummate performer, embodies her self in the creation of her text, and so counters a powerful white male nineteenth-century discourse that threatens to both disembody and hyperembody African American women. But the voice of Truth becomes entangled with the voice of the white woman who narrates her story on her behalf. For critics such as Stewart and Mabee this confounding of voices becomes problematic—Truth's voice is somehow "corrupted" or "lost" in the text. Truth, however, is the double-voiced trickster—like Esu Elegbara, like Trueblood—blues performer, market-savvy businesswoman who embodies the tragedy and the comedy of her complicated situation in the very fabric of her text. Baker quotes Ralph Ellison: " '[The blues] combine the tragic and the comic in a very subtle way. . . . [But] if you are going to write fiction there is a level of consciousness which you move toward which I would think transcends the blues.' " Thus, as African American trickster-performer, Truth "can detatch [herself] from, survive, and even laugh at [her] initial experiences of otherness."[34] In so doing, Truth becomes, indeed, a "self-made" woman.

34. Baker, *Blues, Ideology,* 174, 198.

# FOUR

# *Rebecca Cox Jackson and the Black Vernacular Text*

THE ISSUE OF SELF-FASHIONING is one I want to examine further in relation to Rebecca Cox Jackson's autobiography in order to understand how the process of editing acts to alter her performance and modify her discourse. I am interested specifically in how the "contour portrait" or the "shadow" (the metaphors of Zilpha Elaw and Sojourner Truth, respectively) that Jackson created of herself was radically altered by a well-meaning editor who aimed to present a reading public with a text which that public could readily accept and digest. Jean Humez's edition of Jackson's writings has been an immensely important contribution to the field of African American women's literature, ensuring a wide dissemination of Jackson's writings and opening a path for new scholarship. It is with the intent to recover Jackson's voice more fully that I suggest a rereading of her work in its original form—as a black vernacular text. It seems to me that this text privileges "oracy" over literacy, employing its own system of spelling and grammar, and speaking with the black voice of Jackson, a voice that "looks back to an African linguistic tradition which was modified on American soil."[1]

In conjunction with my examination of Jackson, I will also look at the readily available records of the editing processes involved in Harriet Jacobs's *Incidents in the Life of a Slave Girl*, because I believe that an understanding of the manner in which one nineteenth-century black American female autobiographer (Jacobs) had to negotiate her performance of self in her work is helpful in surmising what similar

1. Geneva Smitherman, *Talkin and Testifyin: The Language of Black America*, 15.

processes (either of self-censorship, or of editing implemented by others) the evangelist women may have undergone.

I have already sought to uncover how Belinda, Lee, Elaw, and Truth dealt with issues of autobiographical performance, (white) reader expectations and self-censorship in their own life-writings. In my examination of Truth, for example, I have dealt in detail with the manner in which the "grammar of interruption" and the multivoiced or hybrid nature of Truth's text reflects its complex editorial history. We may describe Jackson's Shaker autobiography in a similar manner, since it reflects not only a Shaker mythology, but also powerful African American influences in its language and style. Diane Sasson has provided a comprehensive study of the hybridity of Jackson's work. Shaker influences may be seen in Jackson's use of certain metaphors and strategies common to Shaker autobiographies in general—for example, the emphasis on subjective spiritual experience and the gradual decline of the writer's interest in worldly or external events.

Certain Shaker motifs are apparent; for instance, the "feeling" of "gifts"—that is, divinely inspired urges or visions; the description of often female spiritual "leads" perceived in visions; manifestations of a female deity—in Jackson, a "woman clothed with the sun"; dreams of white lambs representing the Shaker community; and dreams of spotted garments. However, as Sasson comments, Jackson's use of traditional Shaker motifs often betrays Jackson's own individual twist—for instance, dreams of walled enclosures are common in Shaker narratives as representative of the security of the Shaker community, but Jackson seldom demonstrates confidence in Shaker communal protection. Instead, houses in her visions represent prisons rather than havens: "Thus, even when Jackson employs conventional images and metaphors from Shaker literature, she often molds them to convey her personal fears."[2] What Sasson refers to as Jackson's "personal fears" however, are perhaps more accurately seen as the fears born out of her experience as *African American* in a white-dominated religious community.

In a sense, editing—or, as I have just demonstrated in the case of Sasson, even interpretation—forces black women's texts into a

2. Diane Sasson, *The Shaker Spiritual Narrative*, 172.

certain conformity with prevailing hegemonic expectations and/or discourses. In the case of Harriet Jacobs, the editorial work and presumptuous attitudes of Lydia Maria Child alters not only the persona Jacobs presents in *Incidents,* but also the language and structure of her text. While Jacobs's autobiography was written and published in the nineteenth century (1861), the manuscripts of Rebecca Cox Jackson were not published until 1981—about 150 years after Jackson wrote them. Jackson's twentieth-century editor, Jean Humez, presents *Gifts of Power* in a language and style palatable to a contemporary audience. Humez is certainly more concerned about issues of editorial intrusiveness than Lydia Child seems to have been; yet, Humez's "normalization" of Jackson's numerous spelling idiosyncrasies and unconventional grammatical constructions gives us a sanitized portrait of Jackson, one in which we lose a crucial sense of Jackson the black woman writing a Shaker autobiography in nineteenth-century America.[3]

Of course, I am aware that my desire to find the "real" author behind the text seems futile by certain contemporary theoretical standards that claim that the concept of "real" author or authorial "intention" signifies a misguided attempt to classify what might more correctly be termed the "author function." But no study of black writing in America can be complete without a consideration of the strategies black writers have employed to negotiate white mainstream editorial processes, discourses, and expectations that encouraged them to say what they did not mean and mean what they did not say. Those strategies are defined by authorial class, race, and gender. I want to decipher as nearly as possible what the writer *does* mean in the case of Rebecca Jackson and Harriet Jacobs—for Jacobs, I contrast the persona she presents in actual letters she wrote to her white editors with the persona of "Linda Brent," whom we see in Jacobs's edited *Incidents in the Life of a Slave Girl.* In the case of Jackson, I will compare an excerpt from Jackson's original manuscript with the edited, standardized English text Humez gives us. In both cases, we will see behind the "white-washed" (whiteface?) text, a black woman, in part erased.

3. Jean McMahon Humez, *Gifts of Power: The Writings of Rebecca Jackson, Black Visionary, Shaker Eldress,* 66–7.

How this erasure operates in other black women's texts for which there are no handwritten manuscripts, letters, or other documents must be left to conjecture. But interestingly, the black women whom we find behind the edited texts of Jacobs and Jackson demonstrate that black expressivity that so far we have found often submerged in the writings of Belinda, Lee, Elaw, and Truth. It is an expressivity that later fictional writers such as Zora Neale Hurston, Toni Morrison, Toni Cade Bambara, and Alice Walker are much bolder about claiming in their texts. But while Hurston, Morrison, Bambara, and Walker operate in a late twentieth-century black literary discursive field that has been powerfully affected by political movements toward black power in the sixties and seventies and heightened black nationalism in the eighties and nineties, Jacobs and the other nineteenth-century writers operated in different circumstances. Thus, Morrison and Walker attempt to reclaim what Jacobs (or is it Lydia Maria Child?) rejects; similarly, Jean Humez, in the interest of presenting standard English to mainly academic readers, discards the "incorrect" spelling and grammar of Jackson at the expense of losing an important aspect of Jackson herself. Later nineteenth-century black women evangelist writers increasingly subsume aspects of themselves under cover of a genteel, "white-face" discourse—yet those subsumed aspects nevertheless continue to appear as disruptive "fissures" (Africanisms, disrupted chronology, disruptive metaphors, etc.) in the otherwise genteel text.

In order to discern how the "real" Harriet Jacobs differed from the presented "Linda Brent," I examine the editorial process involved in getting *Incidents* printed and compare letters written by Jacobs with textual excerpts from *Incidents*. Interestingly, Jean Fagan Yellin, the critic responsible for authenticating the veracity of Jacobs's narrative, comments that "the discovery of Jacobs's correspondence shows that the style of *Incidents* is completely consistent with her private letters."[4] I disagree with Yellin; it seems to me that a study of Jacobs's letters reveals a persona quite different from that presented in *Incidents in the Life of a Slave Girl*. Indeed, Yellin, in presenting Jacobs's letters,

---

4. Jean Fagan Yellin, "Text and Contexts of Harriet Jacobs' 'Incidents in the Life of a Slave Girl: Written by Herself,'" in *The Slave's Narrative*, ed. Charles T. Davis and Henry Louis Gates, Jr., 269.

offers us a version with standardized spelling—with no explanation or rationalization (unlike Rebecca Jackson's editor, Humez) for why she does so.

Jacobs's letters to white friend and editor Amy Post, Post's missives to Jacobs, and white editor Lydia Maria Child's letters to Post reveal a number of important "incidents" in their own right. After reading them, we realize that the narrative structure of Jacobs's autobiography has been significantly altered by Lydia Child. Child writes in a letter that Jacobs forwarded to Post:

> I have very little occasion to alter the language, which is wonderfully good, for one whose opportunities for education have been so limited. The events are interesting, and well told; the remarks are also good, and to the purpose. But I am copying a great deal of it, for the purpose of transposing sentences and pages, so as to bring the story into continuous *order,* and the remarks into *appropriate* places. I think you will see that this renders the story much more clear and entertaining [emphasis in original].[5]

How much language has been altered? What Child considered "continuous order" and "appropriate places" are what we read in *Incidents in the Life of a Slave Girl.* What *Jacobs* considered acceptable, we do not see. I concern myself with this because, as Susan Willis writes in "Histories, Communities and Sometimes Utopia," the narrative strategies of black women differ radically from what is deemed "appropriate" by white, mainstream standards. Black women often write in what Willis calls "the four-page formula"—that is, stories that are told anecdotally, rather than chronologically, in small segments that can easily be read by people who do not have the leisure to digest a text in one sitting but must read during short breaks or while waiting at bus stops.[6] Such anecdotes are connected in a novel-length work according to theme, not chronology. One memory triggers another in a kind of weblike

5. Dorothy Sterling, *We Are Your Sisters: Black Women in the Nineteenth Century,* 83.
6. Susan Willis, "Histories, Communities, and Sometimes Utopia," in *Feminisms: An Anthology of Literary Theory and Criticism,* ed. Robyn R. Warhol and Diane Price Herndl, 821.

effect that has little to do with "order." Is this what Jacobs's original manuscript might have been?

We are led to question the suitability of Child as an editor handling Jacobs's text when we realize the disregard with which she treated Jacobs as a person. Jacobs writes to Amy Post, being careful not to offend any party, that the death of her mistress's infant, and the subsequent urgency of the white household's demands upon her, prevented her from attending an editorial meeting with Maria Child: " 'For this reason my dear friend I could not attend to my own business as I should have done. I know that Mrs. Child will strive to do the best she can, more than I can ever repay but I ought to have been there that we could have consulted together, and compared our views. Although I know that hers are superior to mine yet we could have worked her great Ideas and my small ones together.' "[7] Why Maria Child did not schedule another meeting with Jacobs, in light of the circumstances, can only be left to conjecture. We have the presentation of Child's "great ideas" in *Incidents,* but what were Jacobs's "small" ideas? Only an examination of Jacobs's original manuscript (no longer extant) could reveal this.

Jacobs's timid insecurity among white friends, her fear of their censure and ridicule, and their disregard of her does not emerge as distinctly in her autobiography as it does in her letters to Amy Post. In these letters we see that Jacobs's friendships with whites are complex and problematic, and they sometimes allow the white women to carelessly disregard the feelings and wishes of Jacobs and the limitations under which she must operate. In fact, the limitations themselves are imposed on Jacobs by her white friends. She writes to Post of her constraints in the Willis household:

> If I was not so tied down to the baby house I would make one bold effort to see you. Patience. Perhaps it will not be always thus. I have kept Louisa [Jacobs's daughter] here this winter so that I might have my evenings to write, but poor Hatty name is so much in demand that I cannot accomplish much. If I could steal away and have two quiet

7. Sterling, *Sisters,* 83.

months to myself I would work night and day. To get this time I should
have to explain myself, and no one here accept Louisa knows that I have
even written anything to be put in print. I have not the courage to meet
the criticism and ridicule of educated people. . . . I stayed ten days to
do the Winter shoping for Mrs. Willis. Having a young baby she could
not go herself. I had the little girl portrait painted while there. I had a
long distance to go to the Artist and they refused one day to take me in
the cars. . . . Will you please try and get my Brother Daguerotype from
Miss Charlotte Murray and keep it for me. If this said Book should ever
come in existance I want to have an illustrated Edition and the whole
family in.[8]

I have quoted this long excerpt because in it a number of important questions and issues arise that drive home much more clearly
some intimations Jacobs makes in *Incidents* about her friendship with
Mrs. Bruce [Willis]—a friendship in which "[l]ove, duty, gratitude . . .
bind me to [Mrs. Bruce's] side" (HJ, 513). For example, in *Incidents*
we learn that, in spite of Jacobs's explicit wishes that she not be
purchased, but rather obtain her freedom on her own terms through
more complex and time-consuming means, Mrs. Bruce nevertheless
pays money to rescue her from her owner. "I am deeply grateful to
the generous friend who procured [my freedom]," Jacobs is hasty to
assure her readership, "but I despise the miscreant who demanded
payment for what never rightfully belonged to him or his."[9] Jacobs's
anger is directed not at her friend but, more safely, at the man who
once owned her. Jacobs only hints at some of the aspects of her relationship with Mrs. Bruce that trouble her. But in her autobiography,
she is sparing with her criticism and profuse with her praise. This
strategy does not change in the letters—the difference seems to be
that she tells Amy Post a great deal more about the restrictions of her
circumstances at the Willises than she reveals in her autobiography.
   From Jacobs's letters we must wonder, did Mrs. Willis use the
services of both Louisa (Harriet's daughter) *and* Harriet, getting, in

   8. Ibid., 80.
   9. Harriet Jacobs, "Incidents in the Life of a Slave Girl," 512, hereinafter cited
as HJ in the text.

essence, the labor of two for the price of one? Did Jacobs feel so insecure with her white friends the Willises that she could not share with them something so emotionally significant as the fact that she was trying to write her autobiography? Where are the daguerreotypes that Jacobs writes about, and why did the published text not contain them as Jacobs wished? In addition to such questions, we may observe that the persona of the genteel, northern black "lady" that we see in *Incidents* seems to contrast with the "Hatty" who emerges in Jacobs's letters. Jacobs's writing style in her letters is not as "polished" as *Incidents* presents it. For example, Jacobs omits the use of the possessive— as in "Hatty name," "my Brother Daguerotype" or "the little girl portrait." This is a speech pattern common to people of the diaspora whose ancestors came from West Africa.[10] Nonstandard spelling also appears, as in "shoping," "existance" or "couloured." Sentences seem much shorter and more unadorned than they do in *Incidents*. Jacobs's last line, "If this said Book should ever come in existance I want to have an illustrated Edition and the whole family in" suggests a kind of conversational orality ("in" instead of "into" and "in *it*") that also does not appear in *Incidents*. The autobiography is impeccable in its standard English spelling and grammatical "correctness," as Jacobs's letters are not. If one can find such a person as the "real" Jacobs, I believe that she emerges much more clearly in her letters than she does in her edited autobiography. What would Jacob's unedited, "unordered," illustrated work look like? At this juncture we can only imagine.

In Rebecca Cox Jackson's text, similar issues of spelling and grammar arise. The woman we see in the unedited manuscript is a different woman than the one portrayed by the comparatively polished text Humez presents us. Jackson's autobiography remained stored in manuscript form in Shaker archives until Humez's publication of it in 1981. What we can surmise from this late "discovery" of Jackson's text is that Jackson either never considered it valuable enough to be published or was unsuccessful in obtaining a publisher for her work. Intent upon orally spreading God's word from the Shaker community

10. Smitherman, *Talkin*, 28.

to urban black populations, she might have written down her experiences only because of the Shaker community's intense interest in her prophecies and the traditional Shaker practice of encouraging written testimonies from those who had had particularly powerful spiritual experiences. After her death, Jackson's most intimate friend, Rebecca Perot, with whom she lived and traveled for thirty-five years, relinquished Jackson's manuscripts to the guardianship of the Shakers. Alonzo G. Hollister gathered the writings into a single anthology, beginning with the incomplete narrative and adding to this smaller books in Jackson's handwriting, which he arranged chronologically. Later, he received a second, more elaborate autobiography written by Jackson. Hollister compared the two autobiographies and recorded variations and new material at the end of his original manuscript anthology. He never managed to produce a second, comprehensive draft; however, this task was accomplished (badly) by another Shaker who was not as familiar with Jackson's life, history, and friends as Hollister was, and who made many errors in transcription. Humez's published version of Jackson's work, then, derives from the original manuscripts and Hollister's compilations.

In order to derive a sense of the Jackson of the manuscripts, we may compare the following excerpts. The first is from Humez's text. It is a disturbing passage of brutalized embodiment that reflects a recurring preoccupation in Jackson—that of self-preservation in the face of threatened physical violence. Humez writes that this fear of violence must have had its roots in the escalating tensions that exploded in white mob aggression against black Philadelphians, starting around 1829 and recurring in 1834, 1835, 1842, and 1849. Humez surmises: "It is hard to see how any black person living in Philadelphia during these years could have escaped feeling terror and rage."[11] But in addition to racial violence, Jackson seems to have been plagued by fears related to her position as a preaching female. She identifies the murderer in her dream of slaughter as "a Methodist preacher and about four years after I had this dream he persecuted me in as cruel a manner as he treated my body in the dream. And he tried

---

11. Humez, *Gifts of Power*, 14.

to hedge up my way and stop my spiritual useful influence among the people and destroy my spirit life."[12] Later, this same minister along with two others "appointed what death I ought to die. One said I ought to be stoned to death, one said tarred and feathered and burnt, one said I ought to be put in a hogshead, driven full of spikes, and rolled down a hill" (RCJ, 149). Jackson's response to her fear of such violence is her attempt to gain complete control of herself physically and spiritually by means of guidance from the Spirit. For Jackson, that control seems to involve a kind of "via negativa"—a joyful embracing of *denial* of the world's enjoyments—sexual activity with her husband, food, sleep—in order to increase her spiritual "gifts." Eroticism is then sublimated in spiritual metaphor—such as Jackson's dream of Rebecca Perot "abathing herself. . . . She looked like an Angel" or her dream of Christ's entering her heart with a mantle wrapped "close around him" during a period of particularly virulent persecution for Jackson (RCJ, 225, 148). Humez's version of Jackson's "Dream of Slaughter" script reads:

**A Dream of Slaughter**

In a night or two after I had this dream, I also dreamed I was in a house, entered in at the south door. I heard a footstep quick behind me and looked at the east window and saw a man coming. I run upstairs, told the child's nurse a robber was in the house. She fled. I went to the east window, then to the west, to jump out. I found in so doing I should kill myself, so I sat down on a chair by the west window with my face to the north. He came up and came right to me. He took a lance and laid my nose open and then he cut my head on the right side, from the back to the front above my nose, and pulled the skin down over that side. Then he cut the left, did the same way, and pulled the skin down. The skin and blood covered me like a veil from my head to my lap. All my body was covered with blood. Then he took a long knife and cut my chest open in the form of the cross and took all my bowels out and laid them on the floor by my right side, and then went in search of all the rest of

---

12. Rebecca Cox Jackson [untitled autobiography], *Gifts of Power: The Writings of Rebecca Jackson, Black Visionary, Shaker Eldress,* 95, hereinafter cited as RCJ in the text.

the family. This was a family that I sewed in. When the lance was going through my nose it felt like a feather was going over my nose. I sat in silent prayer all the time saying these words in my mind, "Lord Jesus, receive my spirit." After I found he was gone I thought I would make my escape before he returned. (RCJ, 94–95)

It is only by "sit[ting] still"—again a resistance of *not*-acting as she receives the instruction and protection of God—that Jackson is able to survive this incident: "But a voice above my head told me to sit still, as though I was dead, for that was the only thing that would save me" (RCJ, 95). A second version of the above I have taken from a single-page facsimile in Humez, of Jackson's own handwritten manuscript:

**A Darm of Slopter**
In A night or two after. I had this Dram also I was in A hous entered in at the South Door I heared A footstep queck behind me I looket at the east Winder I saw a man coming I run up Sares [stairs] tould the Childs noss a robber was in the house She flad I whent to the east Winder then To the Wast to Jump out I found in So douing I Should kille my Selfe So I Set down on A chare by the West Winder With my faces to the north he com up And com rit to me he tok a lanc [lance] and layed my nous [nose] Open and then he cut my head on the right sid from The back to the frount ~~nous~~ A bov my nous and pult the Skine down over that Sid then he cut the left Sid the Same Way and puld the Skin down the Skins and the blood covered me like a Wale [veil?] from my head to my lap all my body Was covered With blood He then tok a long kniffe and cut my Chest open in the form of A croos and tok all my ~~bolles~~ Bowlles out and lad them on the floor by my rit Sid and then Whent in Such [search] of all the rest of the family this Was A family that I Sowed in When the lanc Was going throu my nowse it felt like a father [feather?] going over my nose I set in Silent Prare all the tim Saying this Wordes in my mind Lord Jesus recive my Sirit after I found He Was gon I thought I Would mak my a ~~Skett~~ Skept [escape]. (RCJ, 64)

As in the case of Jacobs's editing process, Humez has radically altered Jackson's original manuscript. Sentence structure has been changed, spelling standardized, and the text generally "cleaned-up" in a manner that erases the woman standing behind it. Jackson seems to spell her words as she would have pronounced them, thus presenting us with an opportunity to *hear* her, which Humez's standardization obliterates. The fact that Jackson was a self-educated woman struggling to put her life on paper is nowhere in *Gifts of Power* so clear as it is in the facsimile of one page of Jackson's original manuscript. That lengthy manuscript, housed in the Berkshire Athenaeum, must be examined again in detail and printed with attention to Jackson's details if we are to have what I believe would be a text truer to Jackson herself.

Yet, even in Humez's edited version of Jackson's autobiography, we become aware of Jackson's pervasive use of colloquial language and nonstandard grammatical constructions throughout her text. *Gifts of Power* demonstrates a preponderance of the black colloquial—that is to say, an aspect of the expressive vernacular—that we do not see with such frequency in the other black evangelist women's writings. For example, in the very opening of her autobiography, Jackson writes: "In the year of 1830, July, I was wakened by thunder and lightning at the break of day and the bed that had been my resting place in time of thunder for five years was now *taking away* . . . my only place of rest is *taking away* [emphasis mine]." Or "And all this time it was athundering and lightning as if the heavens and earth were acoming together." Her use of "improper" verb conjugations is also common: "we *was* all called to get something to eat [emphasis mine]." Another example is "And it began to rain, a little while after I got there, so the streets *was in one slush*" (RCJ, 72, 75, 76). The last phrase I have italicized suggests a colloquial manner of using the superlative (the standard English expression would be "the streets were in a most terrible slush"). Later, Jackson refers to the sympathetic Methodists who try to defend her against men who persecute her: "So when they found that I would not [defend myself against the persecutors], they took it in hand. They said it was a shame, a set of men ariding through the country, persecuting a poor, strange, lone woman" (RCJ, 153). The term "a set" to describe a "large number" is, again, colloquial usage.

Jackson's frequent use of the colloquial suggests an "orality in literacy" that we see in the narrative of Sojourner Truth in its fluctuations between standard English and the black vernacular. As Humez

observes: "Jackson's modern readers can hear her making connections, thinking aloud about the meaning of events." As such, her work
becomes an oral text.[13] However, if we read the original "unsanitized"
manuscript of Jackson, it is a much more powerful sense of the black
vernacular that emerges. A later black spiritual autobiographer, Julia
Foote, also incorporates oral style into a written text, in a much more
conscious and deliberate literary strategy than Jackson ever brings to
her manuscript. It is in the work of such women as Jackson, Truth,
and Foote that we see the precursors of free indirect discourse in the
Zora Neale Hurston's *Their Eyes Were Watching God.*

Humez writes: "I . . . scrupulously retained Jackson's own narrative
ordering of material as in BA [Berkshire Athenaeum] even in cases
where she probably would have changed it herself, preparing it for
publication."[14] As I have mentioned, Jackson's unordered autobiographical entries adhere to Susan Willis's "four page formula"; the
entries are fairly short and divided by subheadings—for example,
the section entitled "My Heavenly Lead Entered Her Little Temple"
is followed by a passage called "The Blind Receive Sight." In "My
Heavenly Lead" Jackson recounts a mystical experience in which she
achieves union with a divine female figure: "And as soon as I was
under, this woman entered into me, who I had followed as my heavenly
leader for over three years. . . . This was in the fall." This passage of
female spiritual empowerment seems to engender another memory
of such empowerment for Jackson. In the following passage ("The
Blind Receive Sight") she describes how "[t]he summer before" she
healed a blind old woman who recognized Jackson by her singing
voice: "My mother and her used to belong to band meeting together
when I was a child. It was my mother's voice she heard in me. . . ."
(RCJ, 133). In another instance, dreams in which Jackson bakes for
multitudes, washes quilts, journeys, and has visions—dreams she interprets as harbingers of her ministerial calling—seem to nudge her
memory backward in time to the beginning of her ministry, when she
assumed a role of leadership in initiating a small prayer group for
herself, her husband, and two sisters too shy to attend large group

13. Humez, *Gifts,* 45.
14. Ibid., 67.

meetings (RCJ, 102). In both the examples I have cited, Jackson disrupts the chronological progression of her text. Such disruptions occur frequently as she relates stories according to theme rather than chronological teleology.

Whatever Jackson's reasons for not editing, ordering, or publishing her autobiography, the fact remains that it represents a voice given scant recognition in Jackson's (and in our own) time—the voice of many black women for whom literacy and publication was (is) of little concern. As Humez observes, even if Jackson had had the opportunity to complete her autobiography and oversee the publication of the work, she would not have demonstrated the sense of literary style or form that we normally expect from a writer. Humez attributes this to the fact that Jackson was not a "professional writer," but rather a working class, religious woman who achieved literacy only in adulthood.[15] Her models for writing would have been the Bible, oral forms of religious testimony, and a few published religious testimonials and tracts. I suggest, however, that the autobiographies of other black evangelist women hardly represented the works of "professional writers" either—women such as Amanda Smith, Jarena Lee, Julia Foote or Zilpha Elaw also published their autobiographies predominantly for religious rather than literary reasons. However, their texts used more "polished" standard English style than Jackson's, which in the case of Lee, we know reflects her employment of an unidentified outside editor. This may also have been the case with the other women's autobiographies. Another explanation for the standard English of the evangelist texts might be that the women independently demonstrated a level of literacy that Jackson in her manuscripts either did not care about achieving or could not achieve. (The content and style of Elaw's autobiography, for instance, demonstrate a knowledge of literature and a pervasive orotundity for which it is doubtful an editor would have been responsible.) But at any rate, regardless of whether she was urged by others to publish her work as some black women were, Jackson did not publish. Thus, her manuscripts present us with the writings of a black woman seemingly unconcerned with standards of literacy or literary conventions of her day.

15. Ibid., 46.

In addition to Jackson's colloquialisms, her text is rich in what Zora Neale Hurston has termed "hieroglyphics" or word-pictures. Humez suggests that

> Jackson's inexperience with secular nonfictional narration only partly explains the comparative flatness of the writing that links the extraordinarily vivid and moving accounts of visionary experience. Another explanation comes to mind that seems more telling. Her lifelong, cultivated habit of excluding from her mind the distractions of external, ordinary material reality, in order the better to concentrate upon the revelations occurring within, undoubtedly took its toll on her ability, as a writer, to reconstruct that ordinary reality.[16]

If we read Jackson's abundant visionary descriptions as priestesslike states of spiritual transcendence, however, we may describe her text not by traditional literary standards as flawed in its failure to combine her "moving accounts" of the visionary with colorful glimpses of ordinary reality, but as demonstrative of a life of the spirit so intense for this black woman that all else pales in comparison. Humez surmises that Jackson acquired her storytelling from a tradition of visionary conventions, which Jackson would have known as a member of black Methodist congregations in the early nineteenth century. Indeed, at one point in her struggle to adopt Shaker ways of being, Jackson writes: "I was so buried in the depth of the tradition of my forefathers, that it did seem as if I never could be dug up." And at another junction: "Then I woke and found the burden of my people heavy upon me. . . . I cried unto the Lord and prayed this prayer, 'Oh, Lord . . . [I pray] Thou art going to make me useful to my people, either temporal or spiritual,—for temporally they are held by their white brethren in bondage . . . and spiritually they are held by their ministers, by the world, the flesh, and the devil' " (RCJ, 181–82). Although Jackson describes her African heritage in extremely negative terms here— perhaps under Shaker influence—we can hardly dismiss the fact that, as she herself admits, the impact of that heritage upon her and "her people" is a deep and lasting one.

16. Ibid., 46.

Diane Sasson echoes Humez's conviction that Jackson is steeped in black Methodist influence. That influence vies with Shaker literary strategies to produce the hybrid nature of Jackson's text. Shaker influences emerge in Jackson's use of certain metaphors and strategies common to Shaker autobiographies—for example, the Shaker emphasis on "subjective religious experience, [and] the fading away of interest in external events" (RCJ, 159). Certain Shaker motifs are apparent, for instance, the "feeling" of "gifts"—that is, a divinely inspired urge or vision; the description of often female spiritual "leads" perceived in visions; manifestations of a female deity—in Jackson, a "woman clothed with the sun," dreams of white lambs representing the Shaker community, dreams of spotted garments. However, as Sasson comments, Jackson's use of traditional Shaker motifs often betrays Jackson's own individual twist—for instance, dreams of walled enclosures are common in Shaker narratives as representative of the security of the Shaker community, but Jackson seldom expresses confidence in Shaker communal protection. Houses in her visions are often prisons rather than sanctuaries, as Jackson molds conventional Shaker images to convey her own personal fears. In describing Jackson's incredibly powerful opening passage, Sasson notes that the imagery Jackson uses is unusual in Shaker expression but may often be found in black spirituals or spiritual narratives. Sasson also observes that Jackson's powerful sense of meter and rhythm is enhanced by her use of poetic devices borrowed from folk sermons. Indeed, Jackson's narrative demonstrates the theology and language of black evangelical Protestantism more strongly than it does a Shaker influence.[17]

Jackson's (and other black evangelist women's) propensity for sermonic and lyrical/metaphorical modes of description may be seen in the following passages concerning justification. In Chapter 2 I have already examined the significance of song in Elaw's description of her conversion. The justification experience of Julia Foote reads as follows:

> The minister preached from the text: "And they *sung* as it were a new song before the throne. . . ." As the minister dwelt with great force

17. Sasson, *Shaker Spiritual Narrative,* 162–66.

and power on the first clause of the text, I beheld my lost condition
as I never had done before. Something within me kept saying, "Such
a sinner as you are can never *sing that new song.*" . . . I fell to the floor,
unconscious, and was carried home. Several remained with me all
night, *singing* and praying. I did not recognize any one, but seemed to
be walking in the dark, followed by someone who kept saying, "Such a
sinner as you are can never *sing that new song.*" . . . The voice which had
been crying in my ears ceased at once, and a ray of light flashed across
my eyes, accompanied by a sound of far distant *singing;* the light grew
brighter and brighter, and the *singing* more distinct, and soon I caught
the words: "This is the new *song—redeemed, redeemed!*" I at once sprang
from the bed where I had been lying for twenty hours, without meat
or drink, and commenced *singing: "Redeemed! Redeemed*! glory! glory!"
Such joy and peace as filled my heart, when I felt that I was *redeemed* and
could *sing the new song* [emphasis mine].[18]

Jarena Lee gives a detailed account of her sanctification:

When I rose from my knees, there seemed a voice speaking to me, as I
yet stood in a leaning posture—"Ask for *sanctification*" [emphasis mine].
When to my surprise, I recollected that I had not even thought of it in
my whole prayer. . . . But when this voice whispered in my heart, saying,
"Pray for *sanctification,*" I again bowed in the same place, at the same
time, and said, "Lord, *sanctify* [emphasis in original] my soul for Christ's
sake." That very instant, as if lightning had darted through me, I sprang
to me feet, and cried, "*The Lord has sanctified my soul!*" There was none
to hear this but the angels who stood around to witness my joy. . . . That
Satan was there, I knew; for no sooner had I cried out, "*The Lord has
sanctified my soul,*" than there seemed another voice behind me, saying,
"No, it is too great a work to be done." But another spirit said, "Bow
down for the witness—I received it—*thou art sanctified!* [Lee's emphasis]"
The first I knew of myself after that, I was standing in the yard with my
hands spread out, and looking with my face toward heaven. (L, 11)

18. Julia Foote, *A Brand Plucked from the Fire: An Autobiographical Sketch by
Mrs. Julia A. J. Foote,* 32–33, hereinafter cited as F in the text.

For Jackson, "thunder" and "lightning" become the rumbling voice of God and "streams of bright glory to my soul," respectively, operating together in a call-and-response pattern, and producing what is virtually an audiovisual effect. In repeated response to this virtual symphony of light and sound, Jackson is physically moved to leap up in ecstasy and praise. Jackson's repetition creates a sense of the sermonic and of dramatically heightened emotion:

> I was wakened by *thunder and lightning* at the break of day and the *bed which had been my resting place* in time of *thunder* for five years *was now taking away*. About five years ago I was affected by *thunder* and always after in time of *thunder and lightning* I would have to go to bed because it made me so sick. Now *my only place of rest is taking away*. . . And all this time it was a*thunder*ing *and lightning* as if the heavens and earth were acoming together . . . While these thoughts with many more rolled against my troubled breast, they covered me with shame, fear and confusion . . . My sins like a mountain reached to the skies, black as sack cloth of hair and the heavens was as brass against my prayers and everything above my head was of one solid blackness . . . And in this moment of despair the cloud bursted, the heavens was clear, and the mountain was gone . . . And the *lightning*, which was a moment ago the messenger of death, was now the messenger of peace, joy, and consolation. And I rose from my knees, ran down stairs, opened the door to let the lightning in the house, for it was like sheets of glory to my soul . . . And at every clap of *thunder* I leaped from the floor praising the God of my salvation. I opened all the windows in the house to let the *lightning* in for it was like streams of bright glory to my soul and in this happy state I praised the Lord for about an hour without ceasing [emphases mine]. (RCJ, 71–72)

We may contrast Elaw's, Foote's, Lee's and Jackson's sermonic descriptions with what Virginia Lieson Bereton cites as traditional Euro-American nineteenth-century descriptions of Protestant conversion. Bereton characterizes (mainly white) male and female nineteenth-century spiritual autobiographers as reticent in describing their conversion experiences. "As good Victorians, most nineteenth century narrators—and women in particular—shied away . . . from sensuous imagery. . . ."[19] She further suggests that the narratives employed "styl-ized" and "stock" descriptions. I quote Protestant Sara Hamilton, two other white female autobiographers, Harriet Livermore and Phoebe Palmer, as well as black AME ministers Richard Allen (1833) and Daniel Payne (1888) at length in order to effect a comparison between these recitations of a pivotal spiritual moment of conversion and those of a large percentage of the black female spiritual autobiographers. Sara Hamilton writes of her conversion:

> . . . surprising astonishment filled my soul: I beheld the Son of God expiring in agonies unknown, to gratify the malicious rage of wicked men. I thought he died to save my life, and arose again for my justifica-tion . . . I then saw that God could be just and justify him that believeth in Jesus, even such a wretch as I was. In this view, no tongue can tell the ecstasy of joy that I was the subject of; my distress left me, and I could give glory to God with all my heart. I longed to praise him with every breath; my prayer was, Lord, what wilt thou have me do? Lord, speak; for thy servant heareth.[20]

Hamilton's passage possesses little of the intensity we see in Jackson. Repetition and metaphor are absent. Jackson takes the reader to heights of transcendence that Hamilton cannot—in essence telling of the ecstasy Hamilton claims "no tongue can tell" with words.

Bereton also cites Church of Galilee believer Harriet Livermore, who belonged to an evangelical sect, as virtually all of the black women spiritual autobiographers did. Her conversion experience is more expressive than Hamilton's, but less so than the descriptions of the black evangelist women:

> I retired to my chamber and locked my door. No eye but those flames of fire which fill all Heaven with light, was upon me. I sat in the corner of the room, trying to meditate upon my situation, when a sudden impulse moved me to give myself away to Jesus. I dropped quick upon

19. Virginia Lieson Bereton, *From Sin to Salvation: Stories of Women's Conversions, 1800 to the Present*, 21.
20. Hamilton in Bereton, *Sin to Salvation*, 20.

the floor, crying, "Jesus, thou Son of David, have mercy on me." I can
recollect no more, till I stood upon my feet and walked around the
room, where all about me seemed wrapt in mystery. And as poor as
was the offering I presented, even my sinful self, Jesus took me up in
his arms of mercy. I was a volunteer in the act of giving myself up to
God . . . Feeling a solemn stillness in my mind, as I walked the room,
I could not account for the alteration, as it had so recently resem-
bled the surging waves in a violent gale. The noise of an accusing
conscience was suddenly hushed . . . The first thought that I recollect
passing through my mind, breathed perfect purity; it was like this—
O, I hope I shall never sin again . . . I believe when a soul is given to
Christ, he . . . separates the weeping sinner from the old crimes; and
heals every wound, making perfectly whole. The newborn soul is white
as snow.[21]

Livermore employs metaphor to describe the fires of hell and the
purity of the "newborn soul" but does not exhibit the sense of repetition and climactic momentum that black evangelists Jackson, Lee, or
Foote do. Livermore "dropp[s] quick upon the floor" at one juncture
only, while Jackson, "at every clap of thunder . . . leaped from the floor
praising . . . God." Livermore, throughout her autobiography, repeatedly attempted to disavow any predilections in herself toward religious
"enthusiasm"; this may explain her emotional restraint. However, the
conversion experience of evangelical Holiness leader Phoebe Palmer
reflects a similar staidness to that of Livermore and Hamilton:

When about thirteen she acknowledged herself, before the world, as
a seeker of salvation, and united herself with the people of God. One
night, about this time, after having wrestled with the Lord till about
midnight she sought the repose of her pillow. . . . She believed herself
to have fallen asleep, when, with a power that roused body and mind by
its heavenly sweetness, these words were spoken to her inmost soul—
    "See Israel's gentle shepherd stands,
    with all-engaging charms;

21. Livermore in Bereton, *Sin to Salvation*, 21.

> See how he calls the tender lambs,
> And folds them in his arms."
> The place seemed to shine with the glory of God; and she felt that
> the blessed Saviour indeed took her to the bosom of his love, and bade
> her "be of good cheer." All was light, joy, and love.[22]

The power of God in Palmer is represented as a "heavenly sweetness"—
a far cry from the intense "sheets" and "streams" of glory that flash
into Rebecca Jackson's soul. Words such as "gentle" and "tender"
characterize Palmer's experience. Interestingly, in Jackson's text, as
well as in the texts of other black female evangelists—for example
Lee, Foote, and Elaw—singing, shouting, and "leaping" or "springing"
characterize the actions of the converts, as opposed to the descriptions
of Hamilton, Livermore, and Palmer; Hamilton mentions no physical
reactions, Palmer speaks objectively about a sweet and heavenly power
that "roused body and mind," and Livermore "walked about the
room" in a "solemn stillness." The shout, a distinctly African form
of spiritual worship, is described by an unidentified eyewitness as
follows:

> all stand up in the middle of the floor, and when the "sperichil" [spir-
> itual] is struck up, begin first walking and by-and-by shuffling round,
> one after the other, in a ring. The foot is hardly taken from the floor,
> and the progression is mainly due to a jerking, hitching motion, which
> agitates the entire shouter, and soon brings out streams of perspira-
> tion. . . . Song and dance are alike extremely energetic, and often, when
> the shout lasts into the middle of the night, the monotonous thud, thud
> of feet prevents sleep within half a mile of the praise-house.[23]

22. Thomas Oden situates Palmer as an integral "missing link" between Meth-
odism and Pentecostal spirituality. While her "rationalistic tendency distinguished
her from those who emphasize[d] experience predominantly without rigorous
reflection on scripture," she nevertheless occupies an important place within the
development of revivalism in America (*Phoebe Palmer: Selected Writings*, 16, 15).
Phoebe Palmer, *The Way of Holiness, with Notes by the Way; Being a Narrative of
Religious Experience Resulting from a Determination to be a Bible Christian*, 76–77.
23. Eileen Southern, "The Religious Occasion" in *The Black Experience in Religion*, ed. C. Eric Lincoln, 61–62.

Finally, we may compare the renditions of the black women to those of their black male counterparts. Richard Allen presents a highly formulaic rendition of his conversion:

> [Around] twenty years of age . . . I was awakened and brought to see myself, poor, wretched and undone, and without the mercy of God must be lost. Shortly after, I obtained mercy through the blood of Christ, and was constrained to exhort my old companions to seek the Lord. I went rejoicing for several days and was happy in the Lord. . . . I was brought under doubts, and was tempted to believe I was deceived, and was constrained to seek the Lord afresh. I went with my head bowed down for . . . days. My sins were a heavy burden. I was tempted to believe there was no mercy for me. I cried to the Lord both night and day. One night I thought hell would be my portion. I cried unto Him who delighteth to hear the prayers of the poor sinner, and all of a sudden my dungeon shook, my chains flew off, and, glory to God, I cried. My soul was filled. I cried, enough for me—the Saviour died. Now my confidence was strengthened that the Lord, for Christ's sake, had heard my prayers and pardoned all my sins.[24]

Like Allen's account, Daniel Payne's description of his own experience is strictly formulaic and without great emotion:

> I have felt the spirit of God moving my childish heart. When I was only eight years old such was the effect of a sermon upon my young heart that I went home crying through the streets, and sought the garden and prayed. After my mother's death I was often led by the Spirit to go to the garret to bend the knee and look up into heaven, beseeching the Lord to make me a good boy. . . . My conversion took place in my eighteenth year. . . . Here I . . . gave [God] my *whole heart,* and instantly felt that peace which passeth all understanding and that joy which is unspeakable.[25]

24. Richard Allen, *The Life Experience and Gospel Labors of the Rt. Rev. Richard Allen . . . Written by Himself and Published by His Request,* 15–16.
25. Daniel A. Payne, *Recollections of Seventy Years,* 16–17, hereinafter cited as P in the text.

The black women's intense descriptions and rhetoric may reflect a religious expressivity (physical, vocal, spiritual, or textual) common also in white nineteenth-century Holiness sects that as early as the 1820s branched away from more traditional churches. As Lincoln and Mamiya observe, African Americans found in some of the more expressive (white) Christian sects a mode of worship familiar to them as Africans with their unique experience of the black sacred:

> In spite of . . . obvious obstacles to the retention and the transmission of the African's cultural heritage in the new context of the American experience, the evidence that critical elements of that heritage managed to survive and their adaptation in the New World is substantial, especially in religion. Black singing and performance practices associated with it is perhaps the most characteristic logo of the African heritage retentive in the Black Church. . . . [I]t was the spiritual romance of the camp meetings of the Awakening that first stirred the religious imagination of the black diaspora, and brought thousands of displaced African Americans and their descendants into meaningful Christian communion for the first time.[26]

How African Americans and whites influenced each other regarding religious worship has only relatively recently become the subject of study. (Influential critics as late as the 1960s thought that blacks merely mimicked what white religion they found in America). But I am interested in the fact that among the eight nineteenth-century African American female spiritual autobiographies I examine (which constitute a complete group of such works currently extant) not including Belinda's eighteenth-century legal petition, seven privilege and/or demonstrate an expressivity not evident in such a high incidence in similar bodies of black male or white works. Elizabeth is the only one of the evangelists to denounce "shouting," in spite of the fact that she admits that others have labeled her as an enthusiast. This suggests that in her modes of worship—

26. Lincoln and Mamiya, *Black Church*, 347–48.

if not in her text—she probably exhibited some of the expressivity I attribute to the other black women's autobiographies. As Jean
Humez notes, "most accounts of the Holiness movement suggest
that it, like evangelical religious experience in general in nineteenth-
century America, was from the outset a predominantly female affair,
growing even more disproportionately attractive to women as the
century advanced."[27] Periodic conflagrations of enthusiasm ranging
from seventeenth-century Britain to nineteenth-century "Great Awak-
enings" in America were denounced by the more traditional religious
as disruptive and heathenish. The history of patriarchy's response to
enthusiasm is at least as old as Plato's denouncement of inspiration
(allied with the feminine) as disruptor of reason and order (masculine) in his *Ion* and *Republic*—disciplining of such behaviour as a
threat to established social order has historically included anything
from ridicule on the part of other community members, to excommunication from the church in question, to physical intimidation—for
example, the threats of violence many of the black women evangelists
receive.

The prevalence of the enthusiastic in such an overwhelming number of the black women's spiritual texts suggests not only an adherence
to what Clement Hawes terms a (Western) religious rhetoric of rebel-
lion toward hegemonic socioeconomic and political discourses, but
also the black women's *choosing* of this form of spiritual expressivity
because of its resemblance to the religion of their African forefathers.
Black women choose the enthusiastic mode more often than their
black brothers and white sisters because they occupy two of the most
precarious positions in America: that of blackness and of femaleness.
And as such, it is of necessity that in their texts they employ, often
in a uniquely African American manner, an oppositional religious
rhetorical mode, which locates God squarely in the midst of the
oppressed classes. More than the white women or black men I have
used here (Hamilton, Livermore, Palmer, Allen, and Payne), the black
evangelist women exhibit many of the characteristics of enthusiasm in

27. Humez, *Gifts,* 5.

their autobiographies. I would suggest, however, that the black women do not fall into the category of extreme enthusiasm, where writers demonstrate excessive, blasphemous wordplay, excessive allusion and echo, or radical disjunctiveness. Hawes cites as further examples of extreme enthusiastic rhetoric: "paragogical figures of speech," "incantatory rhetoric that promotes sound over sense," the use of "esoteric" and "hieroglyphic connotations" that "completely fragment the verbal surface," and the use of acrostics and anagrams as a "path to divinity."[28] These tendencies point to a much more radical enthusiasm than that we see in the black women's texts. The highly expressive writings of the black women arise both out of an oral, communal, and communicative mode, and out of a tradition of black writing that in part attempted to demonstrate the eligibility of blacks to the (white) human family. As such, their texts, while more enthusiastic than the texts of black men or most white women, remain logical and accessible to a wide reading audience.

The language employed by Jackson in her unedited manuscripts, then, is a black vernacular, often visionary, sermonic, and enthusiastic. We do not see these elements so pronounced in published black evangelist women's works either before or after her. Indeed, subsequent to Julia Foote—writing in 1879, fifteen years after Jackson's last autobiographical entry—AME evangelist Amanda Smith (1889) and Baptist missionary Virginia Broughton (1907) produce autobiographies that demonstrate the sentimental gentility marking much black women's writing after midcentury. While she does not use the vernacular Jackson does, Foote identifies her intended readership as blacks of scant financial means—a small readership indeed, given that the rate of literacy for blacks in 1880 America was a mere 20 percent.[29] Thus, the number of blacks who could read Foote's book at all would have been none other than the proverbial "talented tenth" she seems unconcerned about addressing. Valorising vernacular practices such as shouting (a highly unpopular form of worship as far as official AME pronouncement was concerned), Foote locates herself firmly within

28. Hawes, *Mania and Literary Style,* 56–61.
29. Reynolds Farley and Walter R. Allen, *The Color Line and the Quality of Life in America,* 190.

the working class and presents virtually her entire autobiography in a sermonic folk style. Thus, she, like Jackson (and Sojourner Truth) presents a hybrid work, one in which the writer's complex search for community is reflected in the oracy *and* literacy, blackness *and* whiteness, vernacular *and* nonvernacular—indeed, the very *doubleness* of the form of the text.

# FIVE

# The Politics of Conversion
## Julia Foote and the Sermonic Text

IN A TRANCELIKE VISION, during which Jesus himself gives her a "letter . . . from God" authorizing her to preach, Julia Foote (1823–1900) receives her spiritual baptism:

> [God the Father, the Son, and the Holy Spirit] . . . looked me over from head to foot, but said nothing. . . . [Christ] then lead me . . . till we came to a place where there was a great quantity of water. . . . Christ . . . stripped me of my clothing. . . . Christ then appeared to wash me, the water feeling quite warm. During this operation, all the others stood on the bank, looking on in profound silence. When the washing was ended, the sweetest music I had ever heard greeted my ears. We walked to the shore, where an angel stood with a clean, white robe, which the Father at once put on me. In an instant I appeared to be changed into an angel. The whole company looked at me with delight, and began to make a noise which I called shouting. We all marched back with music. When we reached the tree to which the angel first led me, it hung full of fruit. . . . The Holy Ghost plucked some and gave me, and the rest helped themselves. We sat down and ate of the fruit. . . . When we had finished, we all arose and gave another shout. Then God the Father said to me: "You are now prepared, and must go where I have commanded you." I replied, "If I go, they will not believe me." Christ then appeared to write something with a golden pen and golden ink, upon golden paper. Then he rolled it up, and said to me: "Put this in your bosom, and, wherever you go, show it, and they will know that I have sent you to proclaim salvation to all." He then put it into my bosom, and they all went with me to a bright, shining gate, singing and shouting. (F, 203)

The incident marks a pivotal visionary moment in the difficult life of Foote—the moment at which Christ anoints her to preach his word publicly. But while Foote records what is a conventional experience in the life writing of men and women who embark upon a public spiritual career, she effects a distinct and transformative narrative strategy both in the visionary passage above and throughout her narrative. She subverts white (male and female) and black male Christian narrative practice to present a rather *un*conventional spiritual text. Using oral strategies of African American folk sermonizing instead of the literary conventions defining written spiritual autobiography, Foote transforms her 1879 spiritual narrative into a political and revolutionary sermon in which Foote describes how, as a rebellious young black woman, she was saved. In so doing, she engages in something Cornel West deems integral for African American survival: a reclaiming of a sense of black community, power, body, and self, a politics of conversion:

> Like alcoholism and drug addiction, nihilism is a disease of the soul. It can never be completely cured, and there is always the possibility of relapse. But there is always a chance for conversion—a chance for people to believe that there is hope for the future and a meaning to struggle. . . . Any disease of the soul must be conquered by a turning of one's soul. This turning is done by one's own affirmation of one's worth—an affirmation fuelled by the concern of others. This is why a love ethic must be at the center of a politics of conversion.[1]

In a number of rhetorical strategies Foote also reclaims the black female body from its dehumanizing objectification under both slavery and the white abolitionist gaze. As such, she produces a narrative of spiritual conversion that is—unlike either conventional spiritual autobiographies, or the largely conservative, patriarchal, bourgeois-aspiring majority of black writing (both fictional and autobiographical) in the post-Reconstruction era—a uniquely oral, African American, womanist text.

1. Cornel West, "Nihilism in Black America," in *Black Popular Culture,* ed. Michele Wallace, 43.

Foote's autobiography was written in 1879, two years after the end of Reconstruction in America. That end was signaled by the restoration of white rule in the southern states and the withdrawal of all federal troops from the South. Reconstruction marked a period of hopefulness for African Americans. Although blacks were increasingly terrorized during that time by vigilante groups such as the Ku Klux Klan (founded in 1866), they made important gains: public facilities became accessible to them as well as whites; some black men attained major political offices; and black men secured the vote (1870). But Reconstruction's end precipitated a rapid downward spiral in the social, political, and economic condition of blacks. By the 1890s the process of disfranchisement in the South had begun; during that same period segregation was instituted in virtually all facets of southern (and many facets of northern) life; racial violence, of which there had been a marked increase during Reconstruction, rose to new heights in both North and South; and racist notions of blacks as subhuman beings focused increasingly on the conviction that emancipation had given rise to a degenerate and idle class of free blacks whose rampant sexuality, criminality, and propensity for brutality and violence posed a grave threat to the fabric of white American society.

Black literary output during this time was marked by its largely assimilationist tendencies—that is, the desire on the part of black writers to demonstrate their membership as equal citizens in (white) America. As such, most black writing was produced by a black bourgeois class in the prevailing sentimental and melodramatic literary styles. That writing valorized such white Victorian tenets as gentility, true womanhood, Euro-cultural refinement and education, and a dignified conservatism—a valorization that the writers (including leading black intellectuals Frederick Douglass and AME Bishop Daniel Payne) felt would ultimately serve to produce a literature that would appeal to—and so educate—a white readership.[2]

What we see in the autobiography of Foote, however, is not the literary gentility demonstrated by her black contemporaries. As Hazel Carby demonstrates in her study of the development of novels by black

2. Bruce, *Black American Writing*, 13.

American women, the popular black sentimental heroines of Elizabeth Keckley's autobiographical *Thirty Years a Slave and Four Years in the White House* (1868), as well as those of fictional works such as Frances Harper's *Iola Leroy or Shadows Uplifted* (1892), Pauline Hopkins's *Contending Forces: A Romance Illustrative of Negro Life North and South* (1900), and Nella Larsen's *Quicksand* (1928) and *Passing* (1929), all belong to the bourgeois-aspiring genre of the mulatto woman bound to uplift herself and/or her race. Carby argues that in novels dating from the postbellum era well into the first half of the twentieth century, the mulatta figure served as a trope for the exploration of troubled black/white relations. The mulatta "was a recognition of the difference between and separateness of the two races at the same time as it was a product of a sexual relationship between white and black."[3] We must note, however, that, Carby's rationale aside, popular submission guidelines for black writers of the day reflect an internalized societal colorism that refused to legitimize black-skinned African Americans in fictional texts: "The heroine should always be beautiful and desirable, sincere and virtuous. . . . [She] should be of the brown-skin type."[4] Although they often critique the hypocrisy of a white society that sets different standards for white and black women, these works largely adopt the formula of the white sentimental novel, and the precepts of the cult of true (white) womanhood: chivalrous, manly heroes; chaste, fair, and beautiful belles; evil, dark, lascivious villains; a happy, domestic ending at the hearthside or the tragic death of the heroine and/or her dreams. For example, while Harriet Jacobs, in *Incidents in the Life of a Slave Girl* (1861), defends her decision to take a white lover in order to protect herself against her master's sexual advances, she also feels the need to apologize to her white readership for her fallen virtue: "The remembrance fills me with sorrow and shame . . . I will not try to screen myself . . . I know I did wrong" (HJ, 384–86). The dream of Jacobs's life is to possess a home and hearth of her own, where she is surrounded by her children—even though, because of slavery and racism, that dream "is not yet realized" (HJ, 513). Thus,

3. Hazel Carby, *Reconstructing Womanhood: The Emergence of the Afro-American Woman Novelist,* 89–90.
4. Gates, *Signifyin(g) Monkey,* 179–80.

Jacobs criticizes not so much the tenets of white American society (for women: a valorisation of motherhood, hearth, children, and home) as the white hypocrisy that denies her access to those tenets, denies her the opportunity to live the life of polite bourgeois gentility available to all hardworking and industrious (white) Americans.

Foote, however, writing at the height of the American Victorian era, rejects its cult of true womanhood, and writes against discourses of the sentimental novel and black elite racial uplift, replacing them with a black womanist discourse of her own. Foote never dreams of cooking and sewing for her children beside a warm hearth as Harriet Jacobs does. Piety and purity, the first two tenets of the "cult of true womanhood," might be virtues to which Foote aspires.[5] But submissiveness and domesticity, the final two tenets, she rejects. For it is not the dream of Foote's life to have a home and hearth of her own as many other black women after Emancipation might have desired. Giddings describes the dilemma of black women as that in which their desire for assimilation required them to be "ladies"— a position that carried a certain class-consciousness. She cites the exhortations of Maria Stewart to her nineteenth-century black sisters that in adherence with the Victorian ethic, black women had an important part to play in the moral and intellectual development of African Americans. Stewart advised that it was important for black women to excel in " 'good house-wifery, knowing that prudence and economy are the road to wealth.' " The role of mothers was integral. Indeed, only through adherence to the tenets of true womanhood could black women exercise suitable moral influence in their families. Giddings also observes that, while slavery produced a proliferation of matrifocal famlies, Emancipation produced a new determination on the part of black men to establish patriarchal authority in their families.[6] Yet, Julia Foote, by her own volition, has no permanent home, no children. She is not the victimized sentimental heroine nor is she intent upon honouring, obeying, and otherwise empowering the manhood of a strong, providing husband. When, in exasperation,

5. Barbara Welter, "The Cult of True Womanhood: 1820–1860," in *Dimity Convictions: The American Woman in the Nineteenth Century*, 21.

6. Giddings, *When and Where I Enter*, 50–62.

George Foote leaves her to go to the sea, Julia is torn between appearing appropriately distressed at the departure of her husband and expressing her feelings of exhilaration at her newfound freedom. How she reconciles this difficulty is to very subtly legitimize her exhilaration with biblical text. Foote's strategy is a complex one that is much more powerful than it first appears. Hers is an indirect "signifying" upon (both white and new black bourgeois) societal injunctions for women to cleave to husband, family, and children. What Foote does is reject those injunctions completely, but in a manner unnoticed by the reader unless she or he further pursues the biblical text that Foote offers. On the surface, Foote appears to struggle between the desire to condemn her husband for abandoning her and the Christian duty to exercise wifely patience and forbearance: "The day my husband went on ship-board was one of close trial and great inward temptation. It was difficult for me to mark the exact line between disapprobation and Christian forbearance and patient love. How I longed for wisdom to meet everything in a spirit of meekness and fear, that I might not be surprised into evil or hindered from improving all things to the glory of God" (F, 197). It is the Bible that solves Foote's dilemma: "While under this apparent cloud, I took the Bible to my closet, asking Divine aid. As I opened the book, my eyes fell on these words: 'For thy Maker is thine husband' [Isa. 54–5]. I then read the fifty-fourth chapter of Isaiah over and over again. It seemed to me that I had never seen it before. I went forth glorifying God" (F, 197). The passage from Isaiah, which she reads "over and over again" but from which she quotes only one line, begins as follows:

"Sing, O barren woman,
you who never bore a child;
burst into song, shout for joy,
 . . . because more are the children of
the desolate woman
than of her who has a husband," says the Lord.

In a well-calculated maneuver that she repeatedly uses, Foote speaks loudest when she plays the silent and prudent woman ruled by "a spirit of meekness and fear" while cleverly employing biblical references to argue for her. Such a strategy is a mode of "signifying"—the speaker's apparent meaning is not to be taken merely at face value; it points to a subtle, unspoken meaning, nevertheless understood by everyone present.[7] Foote, then, signifies silently and/or indirectly upon the tenets of the cult of true womanhood. (What "true" woman would burst into rapturous song at her own inability to keep a husband and bear children?) Foote's seemingly silent voice literally becomes one with the biblical text as she uses its authority to convince her readers.

Foote rejects not only the "true womanhood" aspired to by many postbellum black women, but also any semblance of politeness and gentility when discussing the terrible past of slavery. We may contrast her bluntness with the attitudes of Amanda Smith, who wrote her autobiography in 1893; Virginia Broughton, in 1907; or AME Bishop Daniel Payne, in 1888. Smith, whose prose style is genteel and ladylike, describes her parents' owners as "good," "kind," and "proud of [her parents] for [their] faithfulness" (S, 17). Broughton refers to the South as "the fair South Land" and to whites only in terms of their kindly benevolence toward blacks.[8] Payne, in the same polite manner as Smith and Broughton, paints America as "a vast empire of freemen" where, in the place of "nomadic savages" has sprung up "a forest of flourishing villages, towns, and cities, the abode of civilized men and devout Christians" (P, 246–47). Foote, on the other hand, writing in a postbellum era that encouraged African Americans to downplay their humiliations under slavery and to aspire to genteel, bourgeois ideals, describes an incident in which her mother's master whips her for refusing "to submit herself to him" (the sexual connotation cannot be missed). Her mother's mistress rips the slave's blood-congealed garment from her back, "which took the skin with it, leaving her back all raw and sore" (F, 166). Foote describes the manner in which her mother was shunted from one cruel master to another until "she found a *comparatively* kind master and mistress in Mr. and Mrs. Cheeseman, who kept a public house [emphasis mine]" (F, 166). The implications of this statement are revealing. Unlike the genteel

7. Smitherman, *Talkin,* 119–20.

8. Virginia Broughton, "Twenty Year's Experience of a Missionary," in *Spiritual Narratives,* ed. Henry Louis Gates, Jr., 7, hereinafter cited as VB in the text.

Smith, Foote does not refer to her mother's new masters as "good" or "very kind" but rather as "comparatively kind." In light of previous treatment received, "comparatively kind" makes the benevolence of the new masters questionable, to say the least. Foote refuses to adopt an attitude of refinement and gentility but maintains an accusatory tone. Emancipation has neither erased her memory of the atrocities of slavery nor allowed *her* family access to higher status or the cult of true womanhood; Foote's sister, the first child of her parents, is now, in 1879, "more than seventy years old, and an invalid, dependent upon the bounty of her poor relatives" (F, 166).

Thus, it is not the culture of Du Bois's "talented tenth" that Foote privileges, but that of black people without access to financial means and/or education: "My object has been to testify more extensively to the sufficiency of the blood of Jesus Christ to save from all sin. Many have not the means of purchasing large and expensive works on this important Bible theme" (F, 163). Indeed, at a time when black contemporaries such as Daniel Payne, Frederick Douglass, Ida B. Wells, Maria Stewart, Frances Harper, Pauline Hopkins, or Julia Cooper have abandoned the oral, and many also the spiritual, in favor of literary, intellectual, and political pursuits of a more temporal nature, the tenacity with which Foote clings to an oral, sermonic, spiritual mode of writing places her outside the black elite intellectual circle.

Foote's encounter with learning and literacy most explicitly demonstrates her distrust of these markers of gentility in the new black bourgeoisie. In his study of the development of the talking book trope, Henry Louis Gates, Jr., observes that this trope gives way in later nineteenth-century male autobiographies to a more literal "scene of instruction in terms of reading and writing." Gates suggests that "an angel teaches the [male] slave how to read and thus escape the clutches of the devil that keeps the slave in chains. Equiano's angel was a young white boy; Frederick Douglass's guardian angel was the white woman married to his master. Many of the post–1830 slave narrators' guardian angels were also white women or children."[9] However, the white man who teaches Julia Foote to read is no angel. In 1879, Foote

9. Gates, *Signifyin(g) Monkey,* 166.

describes her disillusionment when this man who teaches her to read the Bible is hanged for the senseless and brutal killing of a woman: "Never shall I forget the execution of my first school teacher. The remembrance of this scene left such an impression upon my mind that I could not sleep for many a night" (F, 173). The moment of literacy for Foote is also the moment of the shattering of girlhood trust—a moment of intense disillusionment. Thus, Foote questions the undiscriminating acceptance of white hegemonic systems of education, social training and religious instruction. Instead, she privileges a spirituality based in nonbourgeois, nonwhite traditions—one rooted in African American forms.

How Foote turns the traditional discourse of white spiritual autobiography into an African American sermonic folk orality is an accomplishment that requires some examination. Foote indeed adopts the genre of spiritual autobiography, following the traditional formula used by white Methodists such as George Whitefield; or the narratives of such black Methodist preachers as George White, founder of the New York AME church or Richard Allen.[10] However, Foote alters the discourse of spiritual autobiography in two important ways. First, her extensive use of song turns her narrative into something more than traditional English autobiographical prose, and second, her adoption of African American sermonic techniques turns her readership into a congregation with whom she maintains an ongoing sermonic call-and-response dialogue throughout her text. The final three chapters of the text are really two parting sermons, "A Word to My Christian Sisters" and "Love Not the World," and a song, "Holy Is the Lamb" that Foote composed herself. In Foote's thirty-chapter, sixty-eight–page autobiography, what I term "lined" verses (the use of hymn excerpts to comment upon the text) are used a total of fourteen times; her closing

10. See "A Short Account of God's Dealings with George Whitefield from His Infancy to His Ordination, 1714–1736," and "A Further Account of God's Dealings with George Whitefield from the Time of His Ordination to His Embarking for Georgia, June, 1736–December, 1737 (Age 21–22)" in *George Whitefield's Journals*; *A Brief Account of the Life, Experience, Travels, and Gospel Labours of George White, an African; Written by Himself, and Revised by a Friend*; *The Life Experience and Gospel Labors of the Rt. Rev. Richard Allen . . . Written by Himself and Published by His Request.*

hymn is a fifteenth instance of such musical commentary (a total of a 22 percent occurrence of song in her text). By contrast, white autobiographer George Whitefield's sixty-page, two-part autobiography of his early life and ordination contains only two songs, one at the end of each part (3 percent); black autobiographer George White quotes excerpts from four hymns in thirty-four pages (about 12 percent); and Richard Allen (also black), four in seventy-four (5 percent). White preacher Harriet Livermore cites fifty-two verses in an 1826 epistolary autobiography of two hundred and seventy-eight pages (19 percent) written in the form of "Twelve Letters." The daily journals of George Whitefield and white Holiness evangelist Phoebe Palmer (as opposed to their autobiographies) contain a great many excerpts from songs and psalms. However, journal entries written on a daily basis, ostensibly for one's private contemplative purposes, "for personal use or pleasure, with little or no thought of publication," differ from the public autobiographical act.[11] In the specific case of Foote, the sermonic, oratorical nature of her autobiography combined with her numerous hymn excerpts create a congregational atmosphere that is not found in the autobiographies of Whitefield, Palmer, Livermore, White, or Allen.

Foote's work is written primarily in the narrative prose mode in which she uses her life as exemplum to illustrate a number of biblical themes—God's saving of sinners (she has been "a brand plucked from the fire"); drunkards as excluded from the Kingdom (she was once a "drunkard"); obedience to parental authority (her father taught her to celebrate in Christ); obedience to God's authority (that may override parental authority); women's calling to "labour . . . in the Gospel" (Foote herself was called); Christ's stripping the sinner and washing her clean (Foote was called by Christ in this way), and so on. However, in the telling of her prose narrative, Foote privileges hymn-shouting and uses black-church musicality at a time when a great number of her black sisters strove for the right to be "ladies" and bookish intellectuals in a white bourgeois society. Foote's liberal use of music and song throughout her autobiography—in other words, "lining," reflects a

11. M. H. Abrams, *A Glossary of Literary Terms*, 15.

practice that began when early white Puritan deacons read out a
line to be sung back by illiterate congregations. African Americans,
long versed in West African call-and-response storytelling patterns,
also practised this type of worship, using their own unique modes
of singing and responding. The practice was gradually abandoned
by eighteenth-century white Methodists, because the congregation
often "'stole the show' with their virtuoso projections of the hymn
lines," but in black churches the practice remained, was built upon,
and thrived.[12] Indeed, black members of the "Amen Corner" did not
merely wait to parrot back a line given by the minister but sang their
own enraptured lines in response to whatever it was he might be
preaching upon. It is important to note that lining is used to encourage the efforts of the minister in a climactic building of ministerial
and congregational emotion. Thus, lining and call-and-response are
used in a supportive manner, and the service becomes a kind of
buoying up of both preacher and black worshippers, a reenergizing
that allows them all to return fortified to a society in which they must
face opposition on a daily basis.

Foote's entire autobiography reads like a long sermon or perhaps a
series of sermons in which Foote as preacher encourages her "congregation" to join her in lining, shouting, call-and-response, and dialogic
patterns. Foote accomplishes this oral scenario in her written text by
either recalling lines of a song she remembers that she or somebody
else sang or by simply providing hymn lines in a kind of script that
might be acted out as if she indeed were preaching to a receptive and
verbally responsive congregation. Unlike her signifying through use
of biblical quotations, her lining is meant not to oppose or insult, but
to enhance and support.

Foote's first use of lining occurs as a particularly powerful, black-
familial memory recall in the second chapter of her autobiography,
"Religious Impression—Learning the Alphabet." When Julia was eight
years old, two kindly ministers from the white Methodist church to
which her parents belonged called at the Foote house. One of the
ministers asked Julia if she prayed, to which she tremblingly replied

12. Henry H. Mitchell, *The Recovery of Preaching*, 133.

that she did, "and began to say the only prayer I knew, 'Now I lay me down to sleep.' " Julia was terrified by the minister. Later, a white woman who came to the Foote house to sew taught Julia to say the Lord's Prayer, something that filled the young girl with great joy: "It has always seemed to me that I was converted at this time." Julia, inspired by the family worship and song led by her father, then desired to learn to read the Bible. Interestingly, lining is not used to support the anecdote of how a kind white benefactress teaches a fearful young Julia to pray the uplifting "Our Father." And while her feelings of joy and celebration are certainly initiated with the learning of the "Our Father," the actual lining supports the climactic "great delight" the girl experiences in "family worship" led by her earthly father, the black man who teaches her the initial fragmentary rudiments of reading and writing: "I took great delight in this worship, and began to have a desire to learn to read the Bible." The daybreak song sung by her father counters the falling, petitionary, and death-focused nighttime prayer "Now I Lay Me Down to Sleep." As Foote observes: "When my father had family worship, which was every Sunday morning, he used to sing, 'Lord, in the morning thou shalt hear / My voice ascending high' " (F, 169), a song Foote lines from a Methodist hymnal.[13] Thus, the prayer to her heavenly Father gives way to the image of black family worship and an actual citation of song led by her beloved black father on earth. In turn, these lines sung by the father, who praises the Father, inform the rest of the chapter—an exhortation to children to read the Scriptures and obey and learn the ways of God from earthly parents.

The second type of lining occurs as Foote praises God for saving her from the snares of anger and despair. Oppressed by a societal racism that makes it well-nigh impossible to get an education in spite of her greatest efforts, the young Foote "was brought into great distress of mind; the enemy of souls thrust sore at me; but I was saved from falling into his snares—saved in the hour of trial from my impetuous spirit, by the angel of the Lord standing in the gap, staying me in

13. Andrews cites *The Methodist Harmonist* and *Hymnal of the Methodist Church with Tunes* as texts to which Foote, Lee, and Elaw would have had access. Andrews, *Sisters of the Spirit*, 243, n. 2.

my course" (F, 184–85). This testimony is immediately followed by two lines from a song: "Oh, bless the name of Jesus! he maketh the rebel a priest and king; / He hath bought me and taught me the new song to sing" (F, 185). The insertion of this hymn of praise into the text seems a kind of script-writing in which Foote provides us with a hymn that might well be heard today from the amen corner at such an emotional preaching juncture—a song of praise and thanks to God for converting the young black youth from gangsta to Gospel preacha at a critical moment in her development.

A final example of lining seems to recreate a congregational scene in which a worshipper, succumbing to the preacher's gentle encouragement, suddenly becomes sanctified in the Lord. Foote writes: "Why not yield, believe, and be sanctified now—while reading? . . . Say: "Here, Lord, I will, I do believe; thou has said now—now let it be— now apply the blood of Jesus to my waiting, longing soul" (F, 234). This invocation is immediately followed by the lines: "Hallelujah! 'tis done! / I believe on the son; / I am saved by the blood / Of the crucified One"—a burst of song that, in a church setting, would be the emotional ejaculation on the part of the redeemed soul in the congregation (F, 234).

Significantly, nearly half (six) of Foote's fourteen instances of lining refer to the act of singing itself. Foote's conversion at the age of fifteen is steeped in musicality; the "song" becomes the trope representing salvation:

> The minister preached from the text: "And they sang as it were a new song before the throne, and . . . no man could learn that song but the hundred and forty and four thousand which were redeemed from the earth." . . . Something within me kept saying, "Such a sinner as you can never sing that new song." No tongue can tell the agony I suffered . . . In great terror I cried: "Lord, have mercy on me, a poor sinner!" The voice . . . ceased at once, and a ray of light flashed across my eyes, accompanied by a sound of far distant singing; the light grew brighter and brighter, and the singing more distinct, and soon I caught the words: "This is the new song—redeemed, redeemed!" . . . Such joy and peace as filled my heart, when I felt that I was redeemed and could sing the new song. (F, 180)

Foote's unapologetic association of climactic celebration with song—more specifically African shouting—seems a deliberate attempt to reclaim a disapproved form of musical celebration and to dissociate herself from that elite class of black Americans which would be embarrassed by such "primitivism." During his term of office as AME bishop in the last half of the nineteenth century, Daniel Payne consistently condemned shouting. Payne was "unrelenting in his denunciation of spirituals, which he called 'cornfield ditties,' and the ring dance [shout], which he described as 'ridiculous and heathenish.' Even James Weldon Johnson concluded that shouts were . . . 'semi-barbaric remnants of primitive African dances.' "[14] Mitchell comments on the classist nature of the rejection of expressions such as call-and-response, or ring shouts. Most blacks, "including most of the 'primitives' themselves, [look] down on the ancient culture, and, of course, on the low socioeconomic status of its practitioners . . . How often have marvellously warm black worshipers publicly apologized to bodies of White visitors, 'You'll have to excuse us. We haven't learned to worship quiet and dignified like yet.' "[15] At the climactic moment of baptism by Christ, Foote's narrative is steeped in the shouted song. Her decision to retain this pivotal scene of black "primitivity" seems a calculated one, part of her effort to present her written text in oral sermonic form. In the passage, shouting is referred to three times.

Repetition, often serving to heighten the oratorical effect of her narration, is also frequent in other parts of Foote's narrative. Foote, through the use of repetition in the following two examples, builds a sermonic passage to the climactic moment at which she introduces an important biblical idea:

> *Why was* Adam afraid of the voice of God in the garden? *It was* not a strange voice; *it was* a voice he had always loved. *Why did* he flee away, and hide himself among the trees? *It was* because he had disobeyed God. . . . Dear children, honor your parents by loving and obeying them [emphasis mine]. (F, 170).

14. Lincoln and Mamiya, *Black Church,* 354.
15. Mitchell, *Recovery,* 124.

This address to children is followed by one to parents:

> Parents *are you* training your children in the way they should go? *Are you*
> teaching them obedience and respect? *Are you* bringing your little ones
> to Jesus? *Are they* found at your side in the house of God . . . or *are they*
> roving the streets . . . ? Or, what is worse, *are they* at home reading books
> or newspapers that corrupt the heart . . . ? [emphasis mine]. (F, 172)

At other times, repetition serves to intensify an emotional incident.
The highly metaphoric description of the last moments of a dying
woman on her sick bed is full of rapture, with the words "sang" and
"glory" repeated several times:

> She sang with us in a much stronger voice than she had used for many
> days. As we sang the last verse, she raised herself up in bed, clapped
> her hands and cried: "He sets the prisoner free! Glory! Glory! I am
> free! They have come for me! . . . Don't you see the chariot and horses?
> Glory! glory to the blood!" She dropped back upon her pillow, and was
> gone. She had stepped aboard the chariot which we could not see, but
> we felt the fire. While many in the room were weeping, her mother shed
> not a tear, but shouted, "Glory to God!" (F, 195)

In addition to verse lining and repetition, Davis describes another
important element of the African American sermon as the identifica-
tion of "floating thematic bridges" (repetition and development of a
key sermon idea).[16] Foote's repeated use of the titular phrase "a brand
plucked from the fire," taken from a passage in Zechariah, establishes
the most important thematic bridge of her autobiography. Foote first
uses it to describe how God saved her as a child from drunkenness.
The initial cause of her alcoholism is her family's habit of making
"morning sling" for the children—"the bottom of the cup, where the
sugar and a little of the liquor was left, on purpose for them. It is
no wonder, isn't it, that every one of my mother's children loved the

16. Gerald L. Davis, *I Got the Word in Me and I Can Sing It, You Know*, 18.

taste of liquor?" (F, 167). A relative, observing a five-year-old Foote
taking liquor from the chest in which it was kept, "came in great haste,
and at once pronounced me DRUNK. . . . Sickness almost unto death
followed, but my life was spared. I was like a 'brand plucked from the
burning' [Zech. 3:2]" (F, 168). Foote uses the "brand" reference a total
of eight times, each reference marking a progressively more critical
moment in her autobiography, as the rebellious, drunken young girl
conquers her addiction and overcomes self-doubt, ridicule, illness,
racism, and sexism to become God's spokeswoman. In continuously
reminding her "congregation" of the many times and ways God has
plucked her from the fire, preserving her as his instrument, Foote
encourages her readers to have faith that God will do the same for
them. The biblical reference that Foote cites is, significantly, one that
again involves a stripping off and putting on of clothing (recall Foote's
trance vision). In this biblical reference, God battles Satan for Joshua,
God's high priest; Joshua is stripped of his filthy rags, and an angel of
the Lord then dresses him in "rich garments" and a "clean turban."

We might also examine how Foote adopts another important trope
of stripping—this time from the discourse of white abolition—in a
manner that problematizes and reconstitutes it for her congregational
reading audience. How Foote deals with the symbol of the "negro
exhibit" provides an excellent case in point. The fact that this trope of
the stripping off of clothes is used twice in Foote's short first chapter
merits closer examination. One of the first things Foote relates is
the brutality her mother suffered at the hands of her owner. But
in Foote's reworking of this initial story of stripping and exhibition,
Foote is "looked over" and stripped not by a lascivious master, but
by Christ himself. Brute sexuality becomes (erotic) religious ecstasy
in her description of her baptism by Christ: "My hand was given to
Christ, who led me into the water and stripped me of my clothing. . . .
Christ then appeared to wash me, the water feeling quite warm"
(F, 203). Once stripped of worldly encumbrances and oppressions,
Foote becomes able herself to wield the whip of holy castigation. In
a chapter entitled "Further Labors—A 'Threshing' Sermon," Foote
demonstrates how she, as preacher, adapts a biblical concept to suit
the context of her congregation. Asked by an "influential man in the

community" (F, 222) to preach on Micah 4:13, "Arise and thresh, O daughter of Zion," Foote explains: "[In] 710 B.C. corn was threshed among the Orientals by means of oxen or horses. . . . Corn is not threshed in this manner by us, but by means of flails, so that I feel I am doing no injury to the sentiment of the text by changing a few of the terms into which are the most familiar to us now" (F, 222). Foote then uses the metaphor of the "Gospel flail" to preach on the application of the lash to sinners. She herself stands poised, and ready to strike:

> With the help of God, I am resolved, O sinner, to try what effect the smart strokes of this threshing instrument will produce on thy unhumbled soul. . . . This Gospel flail should be lifted up in a kind and loving spirit. Many shrink at the sight of the flail, and some of us know, by blessed experience, that when its smart strokes are applied in the power and demonstration of the Holy Spirit, it causes the very heart to feel sore and painful. (F, 223)

Foote signifies upon a scene imprinted upon the memory of blacks that would be hard for her reader to overlook. But the tables are reversed, for a black Foote now bears the whip, ready to "beat in pieces many people" (F, 223). This (somewhat aggressive) affirmation is followed by references to Isaiah 23:18 and Isaiah 60:6–9, which, although Foote does not quote the passages, describe the fates of Tyre and Zion, great metropolitan cities which are destroyed by God as a result of their corruption. The profits of Tyre are set apart for God, and God mercifully allows Zion to be rebuilt by "foreigners." That Tyre and Zion are metaphors for white America, and that "foreigners" include African Americans, it would be reasonable to assume here.

Foote, then, superimposes her stripping by a loving, heavenly master upon the violent stripping scene of abolitionist narratives, and her "threshing" of sinners upon the thrashing received by her mother and other blacks in the slave narratives of her day. By this superimposition she reclaims the victimized black female body. For Foote—as well as for Rebecca Cox Jackson and Sojourner Truth—this black female body is subject to no man but is the property of God, who encourages the evangelist women not to remain confined and silent but to go

Julia Foote and the Sermonic Text

forth out of the private enclosure, loudly and publicly proclaiming
His word to all.

Interestingly, as the hellish stripping and thrashing performed in
slavery is replaced by heavenly stripping and threshing in Christ, so
does the hellish fire from which the "brand" is plucked become the
heavenly fire of spiritual baptism: "By the baptism of fire the church
must be purged" (F, 231). Fire, indeed, replaces the "great quantity of
water, which looked like silver" in which Foote was bathed by Christ,
as the medium of cleansing (F, 203). We must wonder if this is Foote's
version of the slave spiritual: "No more water, Lord (meaning the
water of the Atlantic over which the traffic of slaves and the exchange
of great quantities of silver and gold occurred); but the fire next time."
As the the Negro spiritual "I Got a Home in Dat Rock" goes: "God gave
Noah the rainbow sign, don't you see? / God gave Noah the rainbow
sign, don't you see? / God gave Noah the rainbow sign, no more water,
/ the fire next time / Better get a home in dat rock, don't you see?"[17]

Indeed, Foote writes to her "Christian Sisters": "Be not kept in
bondage by those who say, 'We suffer not a woman to teach,' . . . What
though we are called to pass through deep waters, so our anchor is cast
within the veil, both sure and steadfast!" (F, 227). Again metaphors
of slavery and the Atlantic slave trade are strong here. For Foote, the
water becomes blood—the cleansing blood of Christ. This blood is the
"sentinel, keeping the tempter without, that you may have constant
peace within; for Satan cannot swim waters" (F, 232). And Foote's final
words are silent ones as she ends her chapter with another reference
to Isaiah, this time Isaiah 30:7. Now it is not of Tyre or Zion that the
prophet speaks, but of Egypt. Foote does not quote the reference,
but it reads as follows as, again, Foote's voice becomes one with the
biblical text: "Egypt . . . is utterly useless. / Therefore, I call her /
Rahab the Do-Nothing." The metaphorical equation of white America
with Egypt, and of African Americans with the oppressed Israelites,
is an oft-reiterated theme in black Christianity. Foote's silent excerpt
is couched in a much longer biblical passage in which God castigates
the obstinacy of the sinful Egyptians:

17. James Campbell, *Talking at the Gates: A Life of James Baldwin,* 162.

Woe to the Obstinate Nation
"Woe to the obstinate children,"
declares the Lord,
"to those who carry out plans
that are not mine . . .
heaping sin upon sin;
who go down to Egypt
without consulting me;
who look for help to Pharaoh's
protection; ··
to Egypt's shade for refuge.
But Pharaoh's protection will be
to your shame.
Egypt's shade will bring you
disgrace . . .
because of a people useless to
them,
who bring neither help nor
advantage,
but only shame and disgrace." (Isa. 30:1–5)

The passage ends as God destroys the "obstinate nation," to the accompaniment of song, celebration and music: "And you will sing, / as on the night you celebrate a / holy festival; / . . . . / Every stroke the Lord lays on / them / with his punishing rod / will be to the music" (Isa. 30:29–32).

In a series of intriguing reversals, then, Foote turns the metaphorical into the political as she takes us on an inward journey into the world of soul and the shouted song. But this is no escape to the "other-worldliness" of white Christianity; rather it is a preacherly subversion of prevailing discourses of the cult of true womanhood, black elitism, and white abolitionism. Foote "converts" her spiritual autobiography into a uniquely African American, womanist work. Her text, incorporating African American storytelling, sermonizing, and music, diverges from the path taken by black, bourgeois-aspiring nineteenth-century postbellum sentimental writers. For Foote, sermonic performer, the burning fire of hell becomes the fire of the shouting Spirit; the outward stripping of the female body becomes Jesus' stripping and cleansing of the soul; the beating of slaves becomes the threshing of sinners; and the water of the Atlantic, stained with the blood of purchased human merchandise, becomes the saving blood of Christ as Foote achieves a kind of spiritual returning home.

# SIX

# Smith, Elizabeth, Broughton
## The Daughters' Departure

THE END OF THE NINETEENTH CENTURY, a period that marks one of the lowest points in the history of American race relations, is also the period in which the black women's club movement was formed. In response to white terrorism against blacks after Emancipation, the National Association for Colored Women (1896) sought to establish black education, suffrage, and community development, rejecting as it did so the black vernacular and adopting in its place a white bourgeois sensibility in the name of "racial uplift." Black club women, in a concerted pursuit of Victorian values regarding education and progress, sought to rescue their less fortunate brothers and sisters from the shackles of poverty, illiteracy, and degenerate living. With missionary zeal, thousands of black women brought a social and religious gospel of racial uplift to the black poor. We may better understand this adoption of genteel whiteness when we examine prevailing white attitudes toward black women in nineteenth-century America; black women were considered a harmful influence upon the moral values of the white population. In the minds of the majority of whites, they lacked moral fibre, possessed a woman's passions and a child's judgment, and derived from a culture whose history was steeped in savagery and benighted ignorance.

For black men and women, Emancipation had been a new beginning; where slavery had kept blacks in a position of subservience and inferiority to whites, universal freedom seemed to point the way to equality with whites, toward a sharing of the (white) American dream. Blacks, newly emancipated, traveled in search of each other, black mothers, fathers, and children hoping to be reunited as families. Most often, it was the white Victorian standard of "the family" to

which newly emancipated blacks aspired. Gen. Clinton B. Fisk, head
of the Tennessee Freedmen's Bureau, counseled black men to earn
the love of their wives by providing food and clothing for them.
The female members of the population he advised: "Do not think
of getting married until you know how to knit and sew, to mend
clothes and bake good bread, to keep a nice clean house and cultivate
a garden, and to read and write. A wife should take good care of
her person . . . and look as pretty as possible."[1] Fisk's lectures were
published as a pamphlet, and illustrated with a drawing captioned
"A Happy Family." In the foreground of the drawing are a mother
knitting and a solicitous grandmother bending over her grandchild.
Behind the child is a large burning hearth, complete with mantle.
Two busts stand upon the mantle, and a large portrait hangs above it.
Framing the drawing are a grandfather on one side, who reads a book,
and a father on the other, who sits writing at a table. "A Happy Family"
and Fisk's injunctions encapsulate what Chris Weedon refers to as the
"immensely seductive" patriarchal family dream. Indeed this dream,
was the bill of goods extended by white America to black America in
the years following Emancipation.[2]

That the first novels of nineteenth-century black women aimed
to achieve the Victorian sentimentality, melodrama, and moralistic
values of white fiction, even as they (demurely) denounced racism
and sexism, is no surprise. Shockley asserts that because the novelists
attempted to imitate the white Victorian model of fiction, the themes
of racism and sexism "were not expressed so boldly" in their works
as in the writings of black evangelist women such as Amanda Smith
(1893), Jarena Lee (1833), Zilpha Elaw (1846), Julia Foote (1876),
and Rebecca Cox Jackson (1830–1864).[3] However, even if the evangelists were bolder than their sister novelists in their condemnations of
racism and sexism, there are important and complex differences to be
found over time in both the structure and content of their individual
writings on these subjects. By examining such differences, we may
understand how, to use Houston Baker's metaphor, the evangelist

1. Sterling, *Sisters*, 320.
2. Chris Weedon, *Feminist Practice and Poststructuralist Theory*, 16.
3. Shockley, *Afro-American Women Writers*, 111.

daughters gradually departed from their mothers' southern gardens, how in their writings they steadily relinquished a sense of personal power, outspokenness, and orality in which we may locate a certain African Americanness. Nowhere in the writings of the evangelists is the departure more pronounced than in the autobiographies of Amanda Smith (1893), and Virginia Broughton (1907). Smith, an AME evangelist living and traveling mainly in Pennsylvania and New York State, was unable as a woman to receive funding for mission-ary work from the AME church. She eventually went overseas as a missionary funded by a white organization. Virginia Broughton was a southern black woman involved in what seems to be a black division of a white-administrated Baptist organization. It is the texts of these women that I want to examine here. While Broughton does not draw attention to her preaching as readily as the other evange-lists do, she does preach on occasion. I include her in my study of nineteenth-century black women's spiritual autobiographies because her text acts as a kind of liminal marker between the nineteenth and twentieth centuries. I also include the brief autobiography of "Eliz-abeth" (1889)—an evangelist of lower socioeconomic background and greater religious marginality than either Smith or Broughton. Elizabeth, born of Methodist parents, seems to have adopted an independent evangelical traveling mission of her own and spent her final days among white Quakers. Born in Maryland, Elizabeth lived in various locations, including the states of Michigan and Virginia and the cities of Baltimore, and Philadelphia. In comparing Smith's and Broughton's texts with Elizabeth's we may examine the role class distinction plays in late nineteenth-century black women's adoption of white Victorian value systems.

The autobiographies of Smith, Broughton, and Elizabeth mark an important turning point; it is in these works that we witness the black female evangelist becoming not only a spokeswoman for Christ, but also a "missionary" of Euro-Empire. Baptist Broughton speaks of Christianity as "the King's highway" and, in her work to educate "[o]ur people, en masse . . . so unaccustomed to such work, lacking the needed training to succeed without some teacher or leader to constantly stimulate and instruct them," she rejoices in "[t]he fact that the Bible is being magnified" among blacks, because "[a]ny nation is

blessed whose God is the Lord" (VB, 58, 109, 110). References to
Baptist missionary work in Africa seem equally Eurocentric:

> This meeting was specially memorable because of the presence of our
> returned [white] missionary, Miss E.B. Delaney, and the glowing report
> she brought of her experiences in that dark land. All were touched by
> her pathetic story and a liberal contribution was given her. Her native
> boy, Daniel, who had walked several hundred miles through the jungle
> of Africa to reach the coast and accompany his teacher to America to
> learn more of her Jesus, also greeted us in Chicago, and added greatly
> to the interest of our foreign mission work. (VB, 104)

With similar Euro-Christian zeal, AME evangelist Amanda Smith writes
of her own missionary experiences: "I am often asked, 'What is the
religion of Africa?' Well, where I was they had no real form of religion.
They were what we would call devil worshippers."[4] Later, she advocates
the preferability of white to black missionaries in Africa:

> When the whole work is left to [native helpers] the interest seems to
> flag, and the natives themselves seem to lose their interest. . . . [T]he
> white missionaries, as a rule, give better satisfaction, both to the natives
> and to the church or society which sends them out. . . . "Then you
> think, Mrs. Smith, it is better that white missionaries should go to
> Africa."
>
> Yes, if they are the right kind. If they are thoroughly converted
> and fully consecrated and wholly sanctified to God, so that all their
> prejudices are completely killed out, and their hearts are full of love
> and sympathy. (S, 422–23)

Independent evangelist Elizabeth, finding "a wide field of labour
amongst my own color" establishes a school for black orphans. She
"always felt the great importance of the religious and moral *agriculture*
[emphasis in original] of children, and the great need of it, especially
amongst the colored people. Having white teachers, I met with much

4. Amanda Smith, *An Autobiography: The Story of the Lord's Dealings with Mrs.
Amanda Smith the Colored Evangelist,* 383, hereinafter cited as S in the text.

encouragement."⁵ With the eye of the benevolent moralist, she writes: "Since the Benefactor of all has granted emancipation to this people, they need much to improve their morals" (Ez, 14). In spite of the fact that, as a black woman, she performs missionary work among blacks, it is black people and black vernacular modes of religious worship that seem to bear the brunt of Elizabeth's disdain: "Ah, jumping and shouting are not religion! how much there is of this, and how little *true* prayer" (Ez, 15). But interestingly, elsewhere in her narrative, Elizabeth draws attention to the fact that she has been called an enthusiast (Ez, 8) and that on at least one occasion a watchman attempts to break up one of her meetings where " 'Complaint has been made to me that the people round here cannot sleep for the racket' " (Ez, 7).

The discrepancies between this ex-slave's own self-presentation (deliberately as benevolent bourgeois missionary and inadvertently as disruptive enthusiast), as well as the evidence of an observer's description of her in her last days present a portrait of Elizabeth that is disjunctive and jarring. Working among the "degraded . . . people of color in Philadelphia" as a very old woman, the benevolent Elizabeth is herself plagued by physical ailments that, it appears, receive little medical attention: "Through months of bodily anguish, occasioned by gangrenous sores upon one of her feet, which extended from the toes to the knee, destroying in its terrible course all the flesh, leaving the bone bare and black, many sweet sayings of heavenly wisdom fell from her lips" (Ez, 13–14).

As Mary Helen Washington observes: "The literature of black women at the turn of the century is a literature frozen into self-consciousness by the need to defend black women and men against the vicious and prevailing stereotypes that mark nineteenth-century American cultural thought."⁶ The works of Smith, Broughton, and Elizabeth fall into this category of "frozenness." If, as Shockley asserts, texts such as Smith's are "bold" in comparison with the writings of

---

5. Elizabeth, *Elizabeth, A Colored Minister of the Gospel, Born in Slavery,* 12, hereinafter cited as Ez in the text.
6. Mary Helen Washington, *Invented Lives: Narratives of Black Women 1860–1960,* 73.

Smith's novelist sisters, the opposite is true when we compare these three late nineteenth-century evangelists with earlier black women writing spiritual autobiographies. The "culture of dissemblance" in which black women, to counteract negative social and sexual images of their womanhood, develop "the appearance of openness and disclosure but actually [shield] the truth of their inner lives and selves from their oppressors" prevails in the form of a polite self-conscious gentility in the writings of Smith, Broughton, and Elizabeth.[7] It is a gentility that accompanies a strange sense of dissociation from the black self. Toward the end of her life, a poverty-stricken Elizabeth locates herself among not blacks, but white Quakers, whose role in editing her text seems substantial; the writers claim to have reproduced "her simple language" as "strictly as was consistent with [white?] perspicuity and propriety" (Ez, 2). Her narrative follows a chronological and staid standard English form. Elizabeth, although born a slave, is most adamant and outspoken in her narrative not about racism but about sexism in her ministerial career; she criticizes black vernacular forms of religious worship and distances herself from black people—"It is not from the worldly, so called, that I have endured the most, but from high professors, mostly amongst my own people" (Ez, 12–13). (Perhaps it is this rejection that drives Elizabeth into the company of a white religious organization.) Northern AME missionary Amanda Smith's text, like the independent Elizabeth's, very often exhibits a lack of emotional expressivity. It also betrays a number of conflicting assertions, and (although she protests to the contrary) we are made aware of both her extreme discomfort with her own blackness and her privileging of whiteness. In a similar manner of self-dissociation, Southern Baptist Virginia Broughton refers to herself in the third person, as though her autobiography were written by another member of her Baptist Bible Band community, eager to recount the exploits of "our heroine" (VB, 23).

Throughout the "simple, unvarnished story" of Amanda Smith's life—which is in actuality a long-winded text of 506 pages—we are, in spite of Smith's verbosity, constantly made aware of her sense of

7. Hine, "Rape and the Inner Lives of Black Women," 916.

reticence and self-censorship (S, iv). Smith assures us repeatedly of her own propriety: "I was the only colored person there and I had a very keen sense of propriety; I had been taught so" she says of her experience of sanctification in a white New York City church, during which she was tempted to shout and jump for joy but refrained from doing so (S, 77). Similar statements about her propriety abound in the text: "I did not want to do anything that would not be perfectly agreeable to all" Smith declares on one occasion (S, 252). Elsewhere, her concern over others' judgment of her becomes an all-consuming preoccupation, as in the case of her inability to make payments on a house that white friends secure for her but prove unable to finance:

> I was ashamed to tell anyone, it would look to white people like bad management on the part of those who were my friends. Then I knew what some of my own people would say, and had said already, that I was a kind of a "white folks' nigger," and I knew they would say, "That is just what I told you it would all come to, can't tell me about white folks." They wouldn't see God in any of it, so here I was. What to do I didn't know. I could not speak of it publicly for the reason I have already mentioned. . . . I came home in great distress of mind. (S, 232)

On a later occasion, Smith agonizes over what bonnet to wear in England:

> I prayed and cried about it a great deal for the Lord only knows how I hate deception or sham in anything. . . . I thought if I take off my [plain Quaker] bonnet, and I did not want to do so, for I really loved it, but still if I should take it off, and see persons from America who knew me, that they would say, "Yes, that is just what we thought, Amanda Smith would take off her plain bonnet when she got to England." Then the people on this side thought I was representing myself, by wearing the Friends' dress, to be what I was not. So there I was, between two fires, and the thought of sailing under false colors, this was more than I could bear. (S, 494–95)

Appearances, and externally oriented performance then, seem all-important to Smith, who was careful not to offend the sensibilities of white people or lend fuel to the fire of black people's condemnation. On her arrival in England from missionary work in Africa, she was seriously ill but "did not go to any of my [white] friends in Liverpool, or Southport as they wanted I should do" (S, 486). Smith claims that her reason for not visiting her friends is that "I thought of the care and anxiety I would be to them, and then the extra work for the servants" (S, 486). In the next breath, surmising that no British lady would ask her servants how they felt about entertaining a black woman, she relates a story of ill-treatment received at the hands of white ladies and servants in America:

> I was at a good lady's house in Philadelphia, not long since; she was very kind to me, and wanted to ask me to stay for tea, but did not dare to do so on account of an old servant who would have been vexed if she had to serve a colored woman, whom the lady herself had asked to sit at her table. It was night, and I only had to ride two and a half hours, from Philadelphia to Newark, my home, and I got my own supper, thank the Lord.
>
> Well, I had no fears of this kind in England. But I felt that I wanted to be quiet, and simply let alone. (S, 486)

Even though she denies it, we can only wonder how much Smith's fear of humiliation at the hands of condescending British servants forced to wait on her prevented her from calling on whites in a moment of dire necessity. But it is a distanced objectivity rather than passionate expressivity that marks Smith's relating of such painful incidents. For example, in what is perhaps the most intense scene of her autobiography, Smith relates how, with forty of the fifty dollars she borrows from her employer (fifty dollars is more than eight months' pay), she buys her sister from a white man who purchased the girl. Her sister, traveling without her free-papers, had been kidnapped by whites and sold to a Mr. Hutchinson, "considered to be a very good man to his black people." However Hutchinson became "rough" when approached by Amanda:

> I cried, but he raved; he swore, and said Frances had not been of any use anyhow. At first he said he would not let her go at all. Then he went

into the house. . . . I cried, and cried, and could not stop. I was foolish,
but I could not help it. . . . [He] said he was not going to let her go
for less than forty dollars. . . . [He] walked up and down and swore."
(S, 52–53)

Amanda engaged the help of a Quaker man, but Mr. Hutchinson
could not be convinced to let Frances go without payment. Eventually, Amanda paid him the price he demanded. Her sister Frances
attempted to retrieve her shawl, but Hutchinson

said to her she should not have anything but what she had on. . . .
He flourished the horses-whip around so I didn't know but we were
both going to get a flogging before we left; but we got out without the
flogging. But oh! wasn't he mad! I thanked the Lord for the old Quaker
gentleman. But for him it would have been much worse. Then how I
prayed the Lord would bless Mrs. Hutchinson. I believe she was good.
(S, 53)

Smith's analysis of the scene then proceeds as follows:

There were a number of little black children around there, and Mr.
Hutchinson was kind to them, and played with them, and put them on
the horse and held them on to ride, and they seemed to be very fond of
him. But then they were slaves. What a difference it made in his feelings
toward them. My sister was free. He had not any business with her, and I
had no right to pay him any money; and if I had as much sense then as I
have now, I would not have paid him a cent; I would have just waited till
he went to bed, and taken the underground railroad plan. (S, 53)

The constrained, polite, and mild indignation Smith expresses as she
recalls the incident ("But oh! wasn't he mad!") and the casualness with
which she describes the course of action she would have taken had
she been wiser belie the seriousness of her dilemma and the extreme
danger involved in "just tak[ing] the underground railroad plan."
Unlike Broughton, Smith cites numerous examples of the racism she
encounters. But often, her reminiscences are delivered in a demure
tone, any indignation cooled by the sense of distance, suggestions

of humour that accompany her more intense feelings, or blatant
contradictions in the text. For example, within three pages, Smith
describes the white passengers aboard a ship she is on as "critical" and
condescending, so "curious" that she prays to God to "'make them
let me alone, for Jesus' sake,'" "all very nice," and "not even [saying]
good morning to me" (S, 250, 252, 253). The divided consciousness
of the departed daughters is certainly manifest here.

Smith's struggle to overcome her own self-consciousness about
her blackness is ongoing. The reason for this self-consciousness can
perhaps best be encapsulated in Smith's analysis of what it is like to
be black in America:

> It is often said to me, "How nicely you get on, Mrs. Smith; everybody
> seems to treat you so kindly, and you always seem to get on so well."
>
> "Yes; that is what you think," I said; "but I have much more to con-
> tend with than you may think." Then they said: "Oh, well, but no one
> would treat you unkindly." Then I said: "But if you want to know and
> understand properly what Amanda Smith has to contend with, just turn
> black and go about as I do, and you will come to a different conclu-
> sion." And I think some people would understand the quintessence
> of sanctifying grace if they could be black about twenty-four hours.
> (S, 116–17)

For Smith then, "sanctifying grace" can be best understood as a re-
lieving of the condition of anxiety that accompanies blackness. In
the passage immediately following, Smith admits wishing she were
white only once in her life. But her dialogue reveals her ambivalence about her blackness and her constant sense of inhibition and
discomfort (expressed on numerous occasions) at being routinely
scrutinized. On one occasion, while she attends a Methodist church,
she is touched by the spirit of God: "and I did want to shout, 'Praise
the Lord'; and I remember saying 'I wish I was white, and I would
shout "Glory to Jesus."'" They did not look at white people nor remark
about their shouting; for they did use to shout! I did not shout. . . .
And that was the only time in my life I ever wanted to be white."
Smith goes on to assure us that, "I shout now whenever His spirit
prompts. No, we who are the royal black are very well satisfied with

His gift to us in this substantial color. I, for one, praise Him for what
he has given me, although at times it is very inconvenient" (S, 117).
Her final word on the matter in this instance is that although she
is satisfied with her color, she might have chosen a different one,
had she been given a choice in the matter, "for when I was a young
girl I was passionately fond of pea-green, and if choice had been
left to me I would have chosen to be green, and I am sure God's
color is the best and most substantial. It's the blood that makes
whiteness. Hallelujah!" (S, 118). The last line of this statement, as
well as the hymn she quotes next seem to belie all of her previous
assertions about the "royal" nature of blackness: "The blood applied
/ I'm justified, / . . . / There is power in Jesus' blood, / To wash
me white as snow" (S, 118–19). Other black female evangelists also
employ the metaphor of whiteness as purity. Julia Foote quotes the
same hymn Smith does. Rebecca Jackson dreams about people in
spotless white garments, a common motif in Shaker literature. Indeed,
the motif of whiteness as purity is a common one. The fact that the
black evangelist women use it suggests to me a consciousness deeply
rooted in a white Christian system of symbolism struggling against the
obvious conflicts that the adoption of such a system precipitates for
black people.

As I have mentioned, sanctification relieves some of Smith's discomfort about her difference. But late in the text, she proudly quotes
a letter from a superior in the missionary field, which, even as it denies
the importance of color and status in heaven, establishes whiteness as
a metaphor for ultimate salvation:

> And now, in these latter days, you have come into our organization
> of The King's Daughters and Sons. I am so glad to see the gleam of
> the silver cross on any Daughter or Son, but when I saw it on you,
> my princely sister, I was peculiarly happy. Many jewelled hands I shall
> forget, but never your dark hand, raised so high when singing. . . . You
> are a real daughter of the King, "all glorious within. . . ." Well he has
> worked wonders through you. Many an owner of a white face would
> have been willing to have exchanged it for your white soul, but we are
> in a spiritual kingdom where there is neither bond nor free, white nor
> black. (S, 483–84)

Smith, then, occupies the uneasy ground between shame and pride in her physical blackness, always influenced by her intense awareness of that physicality. In her autobiography's final pages she expresses the courage she must sum up to cast the pearls of her gospel before a group of whites, "not the best type of English ladies and gentlemen": "They were of an 'airish' quality, and that class of English or Americans, especially when traveling, are not the class that good taste would be apt to admire or fall in love with; and to do your duty in spite of these surroundings takes a good deal of pluck, especially for a colored woman" (S, 504).

But if, as "a colored woman," Smith must demonstrate her ability to adopt the "whiteness" of Victorian Christianity and gentility, there are still (brief) moments in her text where we see remnants of her vernacular roots. These moments reside in Smith's strangely incongruous use of slang and dialect in the text and in a disruptive narrative strategy—both features that demonstrate the "recursiveness" Karla Holloway marks as a common feature of twentieth-century black women's texts. Recursion, a method of suggesting repetition even if there are no obvious repetitions of words or phrases in the text, signals "that the reflective, backwards glance . . . is significant to the strategies of revision and (re)membrance." We may witness recursion in the text's "linguistic inversions" such as dialect or redundancy: "[A] relationship between memory and experience is encouraged through linguistic recursion. Events, and the memory of events, become "multiple and layered rather than individual and one-dimensional . . . strain[ing] against the literal narrative structure for an opportunity to dissemble the text through their diffusive character."[8] In Smith's 506–page autobiography, there are several incidents of "linguistic inversion"—moments when Smith's mask of whiteface civility shifts, and orality and the vernacular (dialect) insinuate their way into the text. Such moments often accompany a situation of emotional and spiritual intensity, as in Smith's description of her distress when she believes she has missed a sermon that would have aided her sanctification: "I said, 'Oh I have missed my chance; two Sabbaths ago I had such a

8. Holloway, *Moorings*, 14, 55–6.

drawing to come here and I did not do it; O, Lord, I have disobeyed that spirit and I am so sorry; do forgive me and help me, I pray Thee.'

*O, how I wept, for I had lost my chance and I am so hungry for the blessing; but, 'Lord forgive me and help me to listen now'* [emphasis mine]" (S, 75). The emphasized words in this passage exhibit two shifts as Smith moves from formal narrative structure to what amounts to a kind of oral theatricality: her sudden shifts from the standard descriptive past tense she uses throughout the text ("O, how I wept") to the present tense ("I am so hungry for the blessing") and the urgent immediacy of directly quoted discourse ("but, 'Lord forgive me'").

At the moment of her sanctification, Smith again slips into the vernacular: "Just then such a wave came over me, and such a welling up in my heart, and these words rang through me like a bell: *'God in you. God in you,'* . . . O, what glory filled my soul! [emphasis mine]" (S, 76). The elliptical omission of the verb "to be" is common in the language of the African diaspora. As Geneva Smitherman observes: "West African languages allow for the construction of sentences without a form of the verb *to be.* . . . Such sentence patterns, without any form of the verb *be,* can frequently be heard in virtually any modern-day black community."[9]

In another example of Smith's use of the vernacular, she receives badly needed money from a kind benefactor: "I put my hand in my pocket and took it out; there was one two dollar bill and three one dollar bills. I spread it on the table and counted it. It was the first time I ever had that much money given me in my life, *just for nothing, like,* and I thought I must have made a mistake in counting it, so I counted it again" [emphasis mine] (S, 134). In a moment of acute indecision, Smith reflects: "I prayed and told the Lord how I had been asked to go [to Martha's Vineyard], that Brother P. was a good man, and he said he thought I had better not go, and *I wanted He should show me His will* [emphasis mine]" (S, 221).

Recursion in the form of narrative incongruities, in which Smith breaks her usual chronological time sequence, also signals a desire to re-present past incidents. In this reordering of events, Smith is able

9. Smitherman, *Talkin,* 16.

to make such subtle commentary upon certain issues in her life that
it goes unnoticed until subjected to closer investigation. I want to
examine three important occasions here. The first involves Smith's
sanctification, which occurs around October 1868, and the death of
her husband a year later, November 1869 (S, 97, 96). While these two
incidents occur a year apart, they become interestingly intertwined in
Smith's relation.

How her narrative structure reflects her attitudes toward her husband and the negative role he plays in her life merits investigation.
Sometime after her marriage to James Smith (her second husband),
"things began to get very unsatisfactory. . . . At times things in the
house were very unpleasant. I was greatly disappointed" (S, 57). At
one point Amanda describes James rather sympathetically as: "one of
those poor unfortunate dispositions that are hard to satisfy, and many
a day and night my poor heart ached as I wept and prayed God to help
me" (S, 68). But she gradually presents us with a few incidents that
reveal why and how James Smith was "hard to satisfy." We learn, for
example, in a chapter that describes her desperate struggle to attain
sanctification, that he stands in the way of her efforts: "I would talk to
my husband, but he had no sympathy with holiness"; she believes she
can do better out of his presence: "I told the Lord one day if He would
send James away somewhere till I got the blessing [of sanctification]
he would never get it away again, but that he hindered me from getting
it" (S, 70, 71). We learn also that Smith fears him. When James loses
his job placement, Smith writes: "I was afraid to talk too much. He was
like a fish out of water when he had no work. It was two weeks before
he got a situation" (S, 71). James's new job takes him out of town, and
he demands that Amanda accompany him:

> I reasoned every way I could, but he was determined I should go. At
> last I said, "James, I am afraid to go; you have done me so bad right
> here where I have just begun to get used to the people, and know how
> to turn around, and what will it be if I go there out in the country, no
> church near, and a stranger, and if I give up my washing what will I do.
> I can help myself a little now." But this did not please him, and I told
> him I would wait till spring. The landlady died, and a new landlord
> raised the rent,—thirteen dollars. He paid the rent, but would do no

more. . . . He came home regularly every fortnight. I said, "Now, Lord, while James is away do please give me the blessing I seek. I will be true, I will never let anything he may say or do get the blessing away from me." (S, 71–72)

In Smith's recounting of how she attained sanctification, James figures prominently as the obstacle to that attainment. Once she achieves it however, Jesus replaces James as husband, as in the autobiographies of Foote, Truth, Lee, and Jackson: "I had never felt such a soul union with Jesus before in my life, so I sang, 'I am married to Jesus / For more than one year, / I am married to Jesus / For during the war'" (S, 81). However, after Amanda's sanctification, James again figures as an obstacle, as he undermines her achievement:

He listened patiently. When I got through he began his old argument. I said, "Now, my dear, you know I can't argue."

"O well," he said, "If you have got something you can't talk about, I don't believe in it."

"Well, I said, "I have told you all I can and I cannot argue." O, how he tantalized me in every way, but God kept me so still in my soul, and my poor husband was so annoyed because I would not argue. . . . I could only weep and pray. (S, 84)

At this moment Smith goes backward in time, relating a series of incidents before her sanctification, when she was "so hungry" for the blessing, but was deterred or misguided in a number of attempts to attain it. In this backward movement, the narrative changes from one of chronological continuity to one of contiguity as Smith's mention of how her husband undermined her blessing triggers a whole array of memories that deal with blockage and frustration. (One of the memories, incidentally, is of her actual marriage to James: "After a year or two I went to Philadelphia. There I was married to my second husband, James Smith. Then I had given up seeking the blessing definitely" (S, 90). The chapter that follows returns us to chronological time, resuming with the events occurring after Smith's October 1868 sanctification. At this point in the narrative, as in her replacement of James with Jesus, Smith again returns to a position of complete empowerment. She relates two incidents in which God aids her to overcome Satan's undermining of her self-esteem. In the first incident, overcoming the fact that, in an all-white church, "I was a colored woman, [and] did not like to push myself forward," Smith boldly goes to the aid of a young white woman who is struggling to be sanctified (S, 94).

In the second incident, John Bentley, son-in-law to James's employer, castigates Amanda for coming to visit James to ask for rent money:

> So, that day in New Utrecht, John Bentley came in, as I was in the next room talking with James, my husband. I had gone over to see him. My rent was due, and [James] had not been over for two weeks, and had not sent me any money. . . . I was crying and talking. . . . So, when John Bentley cursed and swore at me, I turned to him quietly, and said: "Why, John Bentley, haven't I a right to come where my own husband is?" But he was fierce. I did not know but he was going to strike me. (S, 95)

What occurs next is tantamount to a "fixing" scene:

> He went on talking and abusing me terribly. There seemed to come an indescribable power over me, and I turned and lifted my hand toward him, and I said to him, "Mind, John Bentley, the God that I serve will make you pay for this before the year is out." He said: "Well, I don't care if He does. Let Him do it." He had not more than said the words when he seemed to tremble and stagger. There was a chair behind him, and he dropped down into the chair. I never saw him from that day. This was about two weeks before Christmas, and before the New Year came, John Bentley was dead and buried! I always feel sad when I think of it, but I believe that God was displeased with that man for cursing me that day. (S, 95)

The paragraph that immediately follows is a curious one. A seeming nonsequitur, it appears to interrupt the sequence of events concerning Amanda's triumphs after sanctification: her assistance of the white woman, her cursing of John Bentley—and after the paragraph in question—her self-conscious raising of her black hand in a white church, upon which "the power of the Spirit fell on the people and the whole congregation . . . [and] the people shouted and my own heart then filled with adoring praise" (S, 97). The paragraph in question leaps ahead in time about one year to describe nothing other than the death of Amanda's husband, James Smith: "My husband, James Smith, was formerly of Baltimore, Md. He was for many years a leader of the choir of Bethel A.M.E. Church, in that city. Afterward he moved to Philadelphia, and was ordained deacon in the A.M.E. Church. He died, in November, 1869, at New Utrecht, N.Y. Since then I have been a widow, and have travelled half way round the world, and God has ever been faithful" (S, 96).

Smith's insertion of her husband's death here, rather than thirty-six pages later where it should chronologically occur, seems to suggest again a disruption of the narrative's normal teleology; James's decease is remembered not within a chronological telling of events but as contiguous to Smith's recounting of the triumphant experiences God sent her after she attained sanctification through Him. The only event Smith mentions about the winter of 1869 (the time of James's death), once she arrives at that point in her narrative, is the conversion of her daughter, Mazie, and, subsequently, her own triumphant going out into the world to preach God's word. Smith "dissembles" the logical teleology of her narrative, subtly ordering memory in ways that create her own sense of empowerment. The seemingly polite, orderly, Victorian text masks a woman who is able with God's help to do away with those who challenge her in her own self-fashioning.

While the death of James serves as a kind of metaphor for empower-ment, the deaths of Amanda's father, Samuel Berry, and her brothers, also introduced out of chronological order, are mentioned in relation to a passage dealing with extreme spiritual angst and frustration. Amanda initially fails in her struggle to attain sanctification: "I was in such distress that I never thought about faith; I was taken up with my desire and distress when seeking the blessing. Well, I did not get it then, of course, for faith without works is dead, so works, without real faith in God, are dead also." This description is followed by a quote from a hymn: "I struggled and wrestled to win it, / The blessing that setteth me free, / But when I had ceased all my struggle, / This peace Jesus gave unto me." It is "[i]n this connection"—spiritual struggle and death—that Amanda gives "a brief account of the closing years of my father's life, as doubtless some may desire to know how he who had fought the battle of life so bravely met the last great enemy—death" (S, 63). In presenting this story, she jumps forward about two years in the narrative, explaining how, after she does attain sanctification, "my burden for my poor father increased," because he has fallen away from his church, and "lost his spiritual life" (S, 64). In worrying obsessively about her father's spiritual and physical safety (he works atop high buildings), she ultimately learns to "let go of father and [take] hold of God" (S, 64). As a result, "the Lord seemed to bring him to Himself; took all the harshness out of him; sweetened him down so beautifully," and her father's death is a peaceful one (S, 65). But if the story of Samuel Berry demonstrates the beautiful outcome of "sink[ing] into the will of God," it is also a story of terrible loss for Amanda (S, 65). In turn, it triggers the memory of three other losses:

> I had three brothers in the late war. My youngest brother came home sick, and died in the hospital at Harrisburg. . . . Oh, what a blow it was to me! He was my favorite brother. . . . My next brother, Samuel Grafton, served three years. He lived at Towanda, Pa., and about a year ago he was drowned.
> My oldest brother, William Talbert, served two years in the war, and died about eight or nine months ago. . . . But I return to the story of my experiences in New York. (S, 65)

Thus, at a nadir in Smith's spiritual career, the deaths of father and brothers, inserted out of chronological order, seem contiguous to Smith's own soul-death; it is these losses she recalls, before going on to describe even further hardships experienced in New York City— a new baby dies, and her husband, James, becomes a troublesome obstacle.

The final narrative disruption I want to examine concerns Smith's cancelled trip to Broadlands, following her arrival in England some years after the death of her husband. Again, the continuity of Smith's narrative collapses as she interrupts her chronologically arranged journal entries to re-create over and over again an incident that, we must conclude, is of great concern and anguish to her. The incident is important to Smith for two reasons, both unspoken: first, it involves the inherent racism of her white friends; second, it ultimately brings the bourgeois-aspiring Smith into the sphere of the English gentry, satisfying a vain obsession she frequently denies having. The incident occurs as follows: Smith arrives in England and is hosted by several religious people, among them a Mrs. Menzes. One or two days later, she receives an invitation to attend a religious convention in Broadlands hosted by Lord Mount Temple. Smith's new friends try to dissuade her from going on the grounds that the convention will be beyond her understanding; Smith believes God wants her to go. Ultimately, her friends arrange for her to speak at another religious convention, thus actively preventing her from attending Broadlands. A year later, Smith receives another invitation from Lord Mount Temple, which she accepts. At the home of his lordship, to her delight, she is escorted to table by Mount Temple himself. Smith introduces the Broadlands story with a description of her initial meeting with Mrs. Menzes, "a wonderful lady," in July 1878 (S, 259). At this point, the Broadlands fiasco is a future incident, not to occur until the following month. Smith then relates the entire Broadlands fiasco in detail, disrupting her chronology to skip about a week or two ahead to August 1878 when the fiasco occurs, and then further, to August 1879 (the second, happy Broadlands conference) and the gratifying completion of the story at Lord Mount Temple's. After this digression from July 1878 to August 1879, she resumes temporal chronology, reverting back a year to her very first introductions in England, in July of 1878, and the initial kindness of her white friends, who raised money for her. Following this reversion is a series of chronological entries for July and August 1878: Friday, [July] 26th, Monday, July 29, Wednesday, July 31, Thursday, August 1; Saturday, August 3, Sunday, August 4, and Monday, August 5. But what is most interesting about these entries is that they are chronological accounts of the events of the entire Broadlands fiasco, unfolded all over again. The very first one, Friday, July 26, 1878, begins: "This is a day that I had to regret. I had been invited to Lord Mount Temple's" (S, 263). This first entry tells the story, which originally took two pages, in about three paragraphs. It recounts the reluctance of Smith's friends, Smith's prayers to God about the situation, and the manner in which Smith's friends arranged

for her to be at Victoria Hall rather than Broadlands. Where the
second account differs significantly from the first is in the addition
of a new piece of rather disturbing information about the reaction of
Smith's friends to her first Broadlands invitation:

> They said the teaching at that Conference was so deep, and they were
> afraid I would be confused, and it would not be good for me. *And then,*
> *besides, for one like me to be entertained where there was so much elegance and*
> *style, it might make me proud and turn my head.* But, poor things! they
> didn't know that I had always been used to a good deal of that, though
> in the capacity of a servant; so that no style or grandeur affected me at
> all [emphasis mine]. (S, 263)

Smith's is a gradual and pained revelation of the racist attitudes of
her white friends. Subsequent to this new revelation, she disembarks
from the train (as in the first account) and stands before the sign that
advertises her. The dated entries that follow go into further detail
about the incident, repeating its unfolding a *third* time. It is only in
this third telling that we are able to learn what the sign advertising
Smith actually says: "The first thing that struck me when I got out of
the carriage was large bills pasted up, beautiful pink paper, with black
letters: '*Mrs Amanda Smith, the Converted Slave from America, will give*
*Gospel Addresses and Sing in Victoria Hall for so many days.*' My knees felt
very weak, but there I was in for it" (S, 264). (In actuality Smith was
born of staunchly Christian parents and had been a Christian all her
life.) I have quoted the moment of disembarkment and confrontation
with the sign in each of its three re-creations by Smith because it seems
to me that there is a progressive narrowing down of events from a kind
of factual first report, complete with directly quoted discourse, to a
shorter, denser, more accusatory summation of the event ("they so
arranged it . . . they had advertised me beyond the date I was to go
to Broadlands . . . I knew nothing about the advertisement myself . . .
but that I could not explain") to a final synecdoche in which the
entire event is represented in the offending sign in stark black and
pink, jarring as a slap (S, 263).

Ten pages later, in an entry dated "Monday, August 11th [1879]," 
Smith recounts her happy visit to Lord Mount Temple's yet again, and

she follows this last telling with another story of "honor conferred upon me," this time "in America"—belying her earlier protestation to readers that "no style or grandeur affected me at all": "Dr. Newman, who is now Bishop Newman, was pastor of the Metropolitan Church in Washington. . . . When we got down into the parlor Dr. Newman came and said, 'Take my arm, Mrs. Smith,' and we led the way; and he gave me the seat of honor at his right. . . . Of course, this was all before Dr. Newman was Bishop." (S, 274, 263, 275–76).

Smith's telling and retelling of certain events, and the manner in which that telling disrupts the chronological narrative structure, seem a kind of reiterative catharsis, as though repeatedly recounting the injury will somehow purge her of the damaging effects the occasion had upon her. The disruptive repetition is also a healing balm—just as she must reiterate the thoughtless treatment she receives at the hands of her friends, it is equally important to reiterate *lavish* treatment received from white men much more important than her insulting friends could ever be.

If Amanda Smith's narrative is a kind of genteel saying without saying, Southern Baptist Virginia Broughton's *Twenty Year's Experience of a Missionary* is even more genteel, her emotions even more disguised. The autobiography begins with a stilted and sentimental encomium to the South: "In a certain city of the fair South Land of the United States of America there was born a wee little girl baby, whom her father named Virginia, in honor of the state of her nativity, which he never ceased to praise" (VB, 7). Later, Broughton speaks of the southern slaveocracy in fond, familiar, and romantically self-inclusive terms: "[On one of her missionary travels] she [Virginia] was cozily tucked to bed in one of the old-time typical high soft beds that prosperous farmers have on our southern plantations"; she describes black sharecroppers in the following manner: "It was cotton-picking time and the people were having a merry time weighing their cotton when Virginia rode up to the settlement" (VB, 16, 17). In this "fair" south, Virginia's father, an "industrious, intelligent man" improves himself by his own determination to succeed, and Virginia is thus able to "enjoy the privileges of education that only very few of our race could enjoy at that time" (VB, 8). In Broughton and Smith, the female autobiographer's often troubled relationship to literacy is no longer of importance as it was in the texts of several black female evangelists (Belinda, Lee, Foote, Truth, Jackson); basic literacy as an issue is replaced by the pursuit of institutional education and upward social mobility as "the new day of freedom dawned upon the race [bringing] with it the glorious light of education for all who would receive it" (VB, 7). Broughton's education does not consist of a young black woman's difficult rite of passage in her ability to master (or reject) the (dangerous) lettered text. The illiterate Belinda and Truth reject Western letters; Lee almost drowns in a book/brook; Foote experiences several traumatic disillusionments at the same time that she learns to read; Jackson is pitted against her black brother at the moment of her attainment of literacy. But Virginia Broughton is able to attend a private school in the manner of any privileged white American girl. Later, she attends a black postsecondary institution founded by white philanthropists. If Broughton's sister evangelists critique the harmful effects of racism and sexism in America, we are given no evidence of Broughton's awareness of such oppressions early on in her text. Broughton later describes the sexism she encounters in the formation of Baptist female Bible bands, but racism seems an issue she is completely unwilling to examine. Race relations in America boil down to a kind of Washingtonian portrait of black self-improvement: "after all the salvation and education of the Negro depended largely upon himself, and men and women of the race should be helped and trained for leadership along all lines of religious and educational work as well as industrial pursuits" (VB, 22).[10] In

10. With the aid of white philanthropists, Booker T. Washington (1856–1915) organized the Tuskegee normal and industrial school for blacks in 1881. He was condemned by more militant blacks for his famous Atlanta Exposition speech of 1895, in which he advocated blacks forgoing equality and integration in favor of education and economic assistance. The speech's most memorable line was, "In all things that are purely social we can be as separate as the fingers, yet one as the hand in all things essential to mutual progress." It garnered rave reviews from Southern whites who would have welcomed anything that delayed the end of segregation. See Fred Powledge, *Free at Last? The Civil Rights Movement and the People Who Made It,* 13.

this program of black betterment, whites are universally supportive and approving. Broughton describes a Trenton district meeting to set up Bible classes and socioeducational uplift programmes at which the "good white people of Trenton" provide food and other supplies for the convention: "Large numbers of the white citizens attended this meeting and expressed themselves as pleased with our effort" (VB, 27). Indeed, Broughton's reason for writing her autobiography hinges on her desire to improve her race: "we send forth this booklet as our contribution to the history of a race, whose true story must yet be told by members of the race would we give our young people the needed encouragement to make their lives what they should be" (VB, 3). In this desire to set an example, to live according to the dictates of how one "should" live, Broughton aspires to write a polite, unaggressive, and feminine text. There are echoes of the genteel Richard Allen here, whose 1833 autobiography is also informed by his own desire to impress those who might criticize him. Broughton seems to be the female equivalent of what William Andrews has termed an "institution man"—her autobiography, like Allen's, is the genteel story of the development not of the writer herself so much as the Baptist Bible groups and programs she establishes. In Broughton, as in Allen, there is a sense of "we," a communality of spirit that represents the writer as a leader and member of an order larger than herself. Indeed, Broughton's text seems to follow a trend prevalent in black male autobiographies that privileges communal black solidarity rather than individualism. But, as an "institution" woman, Broughton can never establish institutions or head them; instead, downplaying her own womanism, she focuses upon her community involvement as an auxiliary worker—a "missionary," cooperating within "bands" of other women to accomplish "woman's work." At Fisk University she is eager to let us know that she might have taken the principal's examination but "declined to do [so], as she did not wish to be a rival of her male classmate who was aspiring for that position" (VB, 8). Giddings notes that many nineteenth-century black women felt male pressure to put aside individual aspirations in deference to auxiliary work for the cause of freedom and race equality: "In periods of Black radicalism, which always includes a self-conscious quest for manhood, Black men attempt to exercise their male prerogatives more vigorously. . . .

Following the Civil War, men attempted to vindicate their manhood largely through asserting their authority over women."[11]

Interestingly, it is as "man's helpmeet in the church as well as in the school and home" that Broughton is able to establish a strong community of other black women, unlike her sister evangelists before her. What she often terms "this woman's work" does not involve overt preaching or ministerial callings as it does in the case of her historically obscure maverick evangelist sisters, but rather, the much better known and documented efforts of many black church women as religious and moral educators, church mothers, preachers' wives (VB, 24, 26).[12]

But even this work is met with the disapprobation of male church members suspicious of their wives' "associating with that mannish woman which many called Virginia" (VB, 60). Why the ingratiating Broughton should be singled out for disapproval is a question that deserves some investigation. Black male church leaders normally sanctioned the auxiliary work done by church women. The reason for the male resistance Broughton receives perhaps lies in the threatening fact that she is not content to keep her place but preaches on occasion—and, indeed, is often well received by her audiences:

> The news of a woman missionary being in town soon spread, and the small church house was filled to over-flowing; both white and colored people came out. Evidently God used the missionary to give the right message, from the many expressions of joy and God bless you heard from all sides. The white and colored people stood on the roadside to bid us farewell, as we began our return trip the next morning. Throughout this section Virginia was received warmly and the messages she bore were heard gladly. (VB, 17)

It is significant that nowhere in this passage, or throughout Broughton's entire text, does she state that she actually preaches to gath-

11. Giddings, *When and Where I Enter,* 60–61.
12. See Cheryl Townsend Gilkes, "The Politics of 'Silence': Dual-Sex Political Systems and Women's Traditions of Conflict in African-American Religion," in *African-American Christianity: Essays in History,* ed. Paul E. Johnson, 80–110. Also Lincoln and Mamiya, *Black Church,* 274–5.

ered congregations of people. But the suggestion, as it is presented in the above passage, seems clear, especially when we consider the aggressive male resistance Broughton later faced in a church that normally encouraged the work of women. Broughton describes this resistance in the same distanced tones with which she addresses other issues. A chapter entitled "A Period of Stern Opposition" goes on to relate violent incidents in which: "[a] brother who opposed our work said . . . 'I would rather take a rail and flail the life out of a woman than to hear her speak in the church' "; "a certain minister . . . came . . . with the expressed intention to throw Virginia out of the window"; "violent hands [were] even laid upon some"; and "Brother F. P. became so enraged he drew a gun on his wife . . . and threatened to take her life" (VB, 37, 38, 39).

Broughton's response to this violence is to express a complete and optimistic trust in God. It is God who permits Virginia to abandon her maternal duties in pursuit of her religious work, giving her license to relinquish her calling as a mother. Broughton deftly introduces the subject by putting the concerns and accusations of her male detractors, into her own mouth: "After the service one of the good women approached [Virginia] and said, 'God surely sent you to us at this time; our hindrances are so great and so numerous that we could not possibly carry on our Bible Band work without an occasional visit from you.' Virginia replied, 'I don't know when I'll come again, for it seems that I ought to be at home with my children.' " Broughton then counters her own supposed concern with a message from God: "Immediately there on the spot, this revelation was made to Virginia's innermost soul, 'What if God should take all the children away.' " She proceeds to relate the story of how, called home to her sick daughter's bedside, she nurses the girl day and night, only to watch her die. The lesson that Broughton learns is this: "Through this affliction Virginia was made to see plainly that she could stay home and sit by the bedside of her children and have all the assistance that medical skill could render, and yet God could take her children to himself if he so willed it." Thus the "darling" child is buried on Friday afternoon, and "Virginia went on her mission Saturday morning. So mightily did God use her on that occasion that her bitterest opposers said: 'Let that woman alone, God is truly with her.' She has ever since been enabled to trust God for the care of her home and her children; nothing has been allowed to hinder her from doing her Master's bidding" (VB, 43–45). Broughton is completely confident in the guidance of God: "While men opposed and Satan strove our progress to retard, God was with us and was only permitting those trials our dross to consume and our gold to refine. Those oppositions proved to be stepping stones to nobler and more extended endeavors" (VB, 39).

Significantly, her language at this moment is the language of biblical hymn-singing—for example, a popular Methodist hymn begins "God moves in mysterious ways his wonders to perform." In the hymn, the object ("his wonders") of an infinitive of purpose ("to perform") is inserted between the verb ("moves") and the infinitive ("to perform"), rather than after the entire verbal construction, as is normally the case ("God moves to perform his wonders"). We discover that it is in hymn-singing that Broughton's sense of resistance lies; as Broughton herself writes in her final chapter: "God has taught her many lessons through songs" (VB, 119). Perhaps this is the seed that Broughton carries from her African American mothers' gardens, for as she asserts: "Virginia well knew at this time her Master's voice when he spoke to her in song," and often she describes sung messages from God as "ringing in her soul" (VB, 122, 124, 15, 47). In a strangely nonemotional text, hymns and songs occasionally seem the only mode of expression through which "her great conflict[s]" are resolved (VB, 83).

The turn-of-the-century daughters, then, frozen into self-consciousness, only rarely exhibit returns to the ancestral places of their mothers—the vernacular, the circular, the contiguous, the power of song. By the time Virginia Broughton wrote her autobiography in 1907, Zora Neale Hurston was six years old. Hurston's first short story "Drenched in Light" (1924) remembers the exuberance of childhood; but more important, it is a spiritual recuperation not of the southern Christian mothers, but of their African mothers before them. In a movement of circularity, then, it is to Belinda that we begin to return as we examine how Hurston effected a "conversion" that changed the face of African American women's literature.

# SEVEN

# Zora Neale Hurston
## The Daughter's Return

THE POTENTIAL POWER of black women's voices, passed down by communities of mothers to daughters, was for Zora Neale Hurston an intensely personal, spiritual, and mythical phenomenon. In "Drenched in Light," one of her earliest writings, we see Hurston shaping that myth in tropes and characters that would appear in her later works. The short story was published in *Opportunity*, a black magazine, in 1924. The religious undertone of the title becomes more apparent as "Drenched in Light" develops. In the story, a mischievous and exuberant young black girl named Isis—whom her repressive grandmother refers to as " 'dat limb of Satan' "—sits atop her grandmother's gatepost, yearning to partake in the excitement of the world that passes by her lookout. Hurston's descriptions of Isis as "perched upon the gate" and, later, of Janie in *Their Eyes Were Watching God* as commencing her life "at Nanny's gate" strongly echo the manner in which she describes her own child self in her autobiography: "I used to take a seat on top of the gate-post and watch the world go by. . . . My grandmother worried about my forward ways a great deal. . . . 'Git down offa dat gate-post! You li'l sow, you! Git down! Setting up dere looking dem white folks right in de face! They's gwine to lynch you, yet. And don't stand in dat doorway gazing out at 'em neither. Youse too brazen to live long.' "[1]

Dressing herself in costumes ranging from "trailing robes and golden slippers with blue bottoms" to her grandmother's "brand new

---

1. Zora Neale Hurston, "Drenched in Light," 371, hereinafter cited as "Drenched" in the text; *Their Eyes Were Watching God*, 10, hereinafter cited as *Eyes* in the text; *Dust Tracks on a Road*, 45–46, hereinafter cited as *Dust* in the text.

red tablecloth," the girl "[rides] white horses with flaring pink nostrils to the horizon. . . . She [pictures] herself gazing over the edge of the world into the abyss." ("Drenched," 371, 373). Both the repressive grandmother and the trope of the horizon figure prominently in *Their Eyes Were Watching God.* Isie, the goddesslike creatrix of "Drenched in Light" becomes the object of a white philanthropist's curiosity. The white woman is significantly called Helen, a name that suggests that which is Hellenic, white, and appropriating in relation to that which is Egyptian and black. As George James has cogently argued, the intellectual conquest of Egypt by Greece began as a result of the Persian invasion around 525 B.C., during which time Greeks began to travel to Egypt "for the purpose of their education" and continued to do so until the Greeks gained possession of Egypt, and access to Egypt's renowned centers of learning through the military conquests of Alexander the Great.[2] In this way, many of Egypt's myths were appropriated by Greece and Egyptian mythical characters assigned Greek names. White "adoption" of black art, black artists, and black culture during the Harlem Renaissance may have carried for Hurston a certain sense of historical déjà vu. Black artists often found themselves competing for favor among white patrons. Hurston herself often wrote and researched under the aegis of whites such as Franz Boaz and Fannie Hurst and, by her own admission to black friends, was not above self-ingratiation in her relationships with them. Hurston's familiarity with Egyptian history, myth, and culture would have derived from her training as an anthropologist. She began this work under the supervision of Boaz and later studied under Charlotte Osgood, collecting data that related to black history, music, folklore, poetry, and hoodoo. In her essay "Characteristics of Negro Expression," she compares black modes of expression to non-"Occidental," Egyptian ones: "So we can say the white man thinks in a written language and the negro thinks in hieroglyphics."[3]

In "Drenched in Light," Helen becomes enthralled by Isie and wants to adopt the child. The story ends with Helen's "hungrily"

2. George James, *Stolen Legacy,* 42.
3. Zora Neale Hurston, "Characteristics of Negro Expression," in *The Sanctified Church,* 50.

uttered admission: " 'I want a little of her sunshine to soak into my soul. I need it' " ("Drenched," 374). Hurston's construction of the creative black girl as Egyptian Isis makes "Drenched in Light" an ironic story of spiritual conversion—not the traditional conversion of blacks to whiteness and/or Christianity, but of a soul-starved white woman to the joy of blackness: "The lady went on: 'I want brightness and this Isis is joy itself, why she's drenched in light!'" ("Drenched," 373). Thus, Zora becomes Isie, who in *Jonah's Gourd Vine* is refigured as another girl-child named Isis, who in *Their Eyes* appears as Janie, who becomes Isis again, as the Egyptian goddess trope introduced in "Drenched in Light" is finally completed in Tea Cake's burial scene. In Egyptian myth, the goddess Isis is mother to her son-consort Osiris, whose death-and-resurrection story, prefiguring that of Christ by thousands of years, symbolizes two processes: the continuous cycles of earth's vegetation, and the ancient matrilinear tradition by which successive kings came to Egypt's throne.[4] If Janie is Isis, then the boyish Tea Cake becomes Osiris—"son of Evening Sun," who rides in death, "like a Pharaoh to his tomb" (*Eyes*, 180). It is Janie who buries Tea Cake, Egyptian style, with all his earthly possessions about him, and then returns full circle home: "So the beginning of this was a woman and she had come back from burying the dead" (*Eyes*, 1). Tea Cake is indeed the resurrected god who returns to life through the intense power of spiritual witnessing and prayer: "The day of the gun . . . and the courthouse came and commenced to sing a sobbing sigh out of every corner in the room. . . . commenced to sing, commenced to sob and sigh, singing and sobbing. Then Tea Cake came prancing around her. . . . Tea Cake with the sun for a shawl. Of course he wasn't dead" (*Eyes*, 183).

In all of Hurston's Isis myths ("Drenched in Light," *Jonah's Gourd Vine, Their Eyes*) the transmission of spiritual power from mother (or, in more troubled scenarios, from grandmother) to daughter figure prominently. In "Drenched in Light," Isie converts her grandmother's legacy of God-fearing "Thou shalt nots" into her own powerful black female magnetism. In *Jonah's Gourd Vine*, Isis is one of Lucy Pear-

4. Monica Sjoo and Barbara Mor, *The Great Cosmic Mother: Rediscovering the Religion of the Earth*, 168.

son's daughters. Lucy, married to a philandering preacher husband, subordinates her dreams to her husband's ambitions. However, she refuses to let such a fate befall her daughter Isis. Lucy's poignant death scene is reminiscent of the exchange that occurred between Hurston and her own dying mother. In *Dust Tracks,* Hurston's autobiography, Hurston writes: "I thought that [my mother] looked to me. . . . Her mouth was slightly open, but her breathing took up so much of her strength that she could not talk. But she looked at me, or so I felt, to speak for her. She depended on me for a voice" (*Dust,* 86–87). In *Jonah's Gourd Vine* the dying mother speaks, imparting important advice to her daughter and entrusting young Isis with last wishes to fulfill—get an education, love no one more than herself, keep the pillow under her dying mother's head, and cover up the clock and the mirror after her mother's death: "Ahm tellin' you in preference tuh de rest 'cause Ah know you'll see tuh it."[5] But like Hurston at the bedside of her own mother, Isis is powerless to prevent her elders from performing the rituals she knows Lucy would not have wanted, and the moment of maternal loss is a traumatic one. Hurston writes of the death of her own mother as a loss of spiritual direction: "But life picked me up from the foot of Mama's bed, grief, self-despisement and all, and set my feet in strange ways. . . . That hour began my wanderings. Not so much in geography, but in time. Then not so much in time as in spirit" (*Dust,* 88–89). This quest for a matrilineal spiritual past finds its culmination in the character of Janie in *Their Eyes Were Watching God.* Like the initial Isis of "Drenched in Light," Janie rejects the fear-based admonitions of a grandmother raised in slavery. Yet in spite of that rejection, Janie and Nanny are deeply connected on a mythical level. Hurston figures Nanny as a Medusa figure, her head and face resembling "the standing roots of some old tree that had been torn away by storm. Foundation of ancient power that no longer mattered" (*Eyes,* 12). In Egyptian myth, the goddess Isis was also Medusa in another aspect, a serpent goddess representing infinite female wisdom, signifying past, present, and future. Presiding over the principles of both creation and destruction (as Medusa also did), Isis

---

5. Zora Neale Hurston, *Jonah's Gourd Vine,* 130, hereinafter cited as *Jonah's* in the text.

was, metaphorically, the throne of Egypt; Pharaohs were depicted as
diminutive figures sitting in her lap, protected by her arms or wings.
She carried a symbol on her crown called the mu'at, which proclaimed
her as "foundation of the throne" and which also represented her "*alter ego* Maat, the motherhood-principle called Right, Justice, Truth, or
the All-seeing Eye."[6] Nanny, as "foundation," emerges from a Christian
framework—one she desires to pass on to her grandchild:

> Ah wanted to preach a great sermon about colored women sittin' on
> high, but they wasn't no pulpit for me. Freedom found me wid a baby
> daughter in mah arms, so Ah said Ah'd take a broom and cook-pot and
> throw up a highway through de wilderness for her. She would expound
> what Ah felt. But somehow she got lost offa de highway and next thing
> Ah knowed here you was in de world. So whilst Ah was tendin' you of
> nights Ah said Ah'd save de text for you. (*Eyes,* 15–16)

Nanny's aspirations to attain a powerful voice for herself as a woman
have failed. The dream of the woman preacher has been subsumed,
altered beyond all recognition by life's harsh contingencies. Now
all Nanny can hope for is to protect Janie from sexual and racial
degradation. The significance of this sermon of sorts becomes clear
in light of the importance of preaching for Hurston's literary foremothers. While Hurston may or may not have read the texts of the
black preacher women, she was certainly knowledgeable about the
womanist preacherly traditions that bred the texts. In *The Sanctified
Church,* Hurston describes the "calls" to preach received by several
black women, and it is likely that she would have read at least the
autobiography of Sojourner Truth, whose name appeared in many
a newspaper and whose narrative enjoyed several reprints in the
nineteenth century.[7]

Indeed, Sojourner Truth's narrative may have been a palimpsest
upon which Hurston placed her story of Janie. Certain tropes and
pivotal moments in Truth's autobiography may be precursors upon
which Hurston signifies, creating a parallel fictional narrative of

6. Barbara Walker, *Woman's Encyclopedia of Myths and Secrets,* 454, 629.
7. Hurston, *Sanctified Church,* 23–29, 85–90.

Janie's spiritual development. For example, in Truth's autobiography Truth is descended from a treelike parent, as Janie is in Hurston's novel. Of Truth's father, Olive Gilbert writes: "Isabella's [Truth's] father was very tall and straight, when young, which gave him the name of 'Bomefree'—low Dutch for tree . . . and by this name he usually went" (TGT, 15). Sojourner herself is described by her amanuensis as follows: "Her finely molded form is yet unbent, and its grand height and graceful, wavy movements remind the observer of her lofty cousins, the Palms, which keep guard over the sacred streams where her forefathers idled away their childhood days." On another occasion she is referred to as "calm and erect, as one of her own native palm-trees waving alone in the desert" (TGT, vi, 153). Truth describes herself in her old age as one who has "'budded out wid de trees, but may fall wid de autumn leaves'" (TGT, 145). Correspondingly, in *Their Eyes,* Hurston creates an animistic belief system that is reflected in tropes of vegetation and fertility throughout the novel. Leafy is the name by which Janie's mother comes to be known. Tea Cake is a Christ figure whose birth name is Vergible Woods, a conflation of two root words: the Latin "veritas," meaning truth, and "virgeus," meaning green twig, slip, or rod. Janie herself experiences an early spiritual/sexual awakening amidst a veritable eruption of bloom:

> Janie had spent most of the day under a blossoming pear tree in the back-yard. She had been spending every minute that she could steal from her chores under that tree for the last three days. . . . She was stretched on her back beneath the pear tree soaking in the alto chant of the visiting bees, the gold of the sun and the panting breath of the breeze when the inaudible voice of it all came to her. She saw a dust-bearing bee sink into the sanctum of a bloom. . . . She had glossy leaves and bursting buds and she wanted to struggle with life. (*Eyes,* 10–11)

We may compare this spiritual awakening with Truth's account of her own experience in which she, convinced that if she

> were to present her petitions under the open canopy of heaven, speaking very loud, she should the more readily be heard; consequently, she sought a fitting spot for this, her rural sanctuary. . . . [S]he improved

it by pulling away the branches of the shrubs from the centre, and weaving them together for a wall on the outside, forming a circular arched alcove, made entirely of the graceful willow. To this place she resorted daily." (TGT, 60).

The natural setting of both experiences, and the description of each resort as sacred space, a "sanctum" or "sanctuary," prepares the way for the epiphanic scene to follow—in the case of Truth, it is her first personal encounter with Jesus. In Hurston's novel, Janie has another kind of spiritual encounter—that of her initial sexual knowledge of herself. As Audre Lorde explains, such erotic self-knowledge becomes the spiritual basis for an all-encompassing knowledge, creativity, and love:

> The very word *erotic* comes from the Greek work *eros,* the personification of love in all of its aspects—born of Chaos, and personifying creative power and harmony. When I speak of the erotic, then, I speak of it as an assertion of the life-force of women; of that creative energy empowered, the knowledge and use of which we are now reclaiming in our language, our history, our dancing, our loving, our work, our lives.[8]

I am interested in the ways Hurston's text seems to echo Truth's—Jesus/Johnny/Tea Cake, familiar-looking, the "glorious" and "transcendently lovely," appearing to the previously blind young female supplicant out of a "beglamored" world "clad in new beauty," has the power to transform, to create in both Truth and Janie a "jealousy" that sweetly torments, and a knowledge of God and self gained through a strong sense of natural being in the world. At the height of her own epiphany, Truth has a vision of Jesus:

> "Who are you?" she exclaimed, as the vision brightened into a form distinct, beaming with the beauty of holiness, and radiant with love. She then said, audibly addressing the mysterious visitant—"I *know* you and I *don't* know you." Meaning, "You seem perfectly familiar." . . .

8. Audre Lorde, "Uses of the Erotic," in *Sister Outsider: Essays and Speeches,* 55.

Now he appeared to her delighted mental vision as so mild, so good, and so every way lovely, and he loved her so much! . . . [T]he world was clad in new beauty, the very air sparkled as with diamonds, and was redolent of heaven. . . . Jesus, the transcendently lovely as well as great and powerful; for so he appeared to her, though he seemed but human; and she watched for his bodily appearance, feeling that she should know him, if she saw him; and when he came, she should go and dwell with him, as with a dear friend.

It was not given her to see that he loved any other; and she thought if others came to know and love him, as she did, she should be thrust aside and forgotten. . . . and she felt a sort of jealousy, lest she should be robbed of her newly found treasure. (TGT, 66–68)

I want to compare this scene with three passages in *Their Eyes*. In the first, Janie, after her sexual/spiritual awakening, sees "shiftless Johnny Taylor" in an entirely new light—the young man assumes divine proportions: "Through the pollinated air she saw a glorious being coming up the road. In her former blindness she had known him as shiftless Johnny Taylor, tall and lean. That was before the golden dust of pollen had beglamored his rags and her eyes" (*Eyes*, 11). In the second passage, Janie encounters another tall, shiftless, and equally bewitching man—Tea Cake: "At five-thirty a tall man came into the place. Janie was leaning on the counter making aimless pencil marks on a piece of wrapping paper. She knew she didn't know his name, but he looked familiar" (*Eyes*, 90). The Gospel of Luke 24:15, 31 recounts the manner in which the resurrected Jesus appears to two followers on their way to Emmaus. The men "were kept from recognizing him," and it is only after Jesus breaks bread with them that "they recognized him, and he disappeared from their sight." While the sense of this encounter is that the men were "familiar" with Jesus without initially recognizing him, the actual word *familiar* is not used in Luke, as it is in both Truth and Hurston—along with the assertion in both cases that the women did not know the name of their visitors. Finally, while Truth uses sexual jealousy as a metaphor with which to describe her initial possessiveness in her relationship with Jesus, Hurston literalizes the metaphor: "Janie learned what it felt like to be jealous" (*Eyes*, 130). So begins Janie's life with Tea Cake, whose resemblance to Osiris, the resurrected Egyptian god, precursor to Christ, is too striking to be overlooked here.

If Hurston is signifying on the Christianity of her literary foremothers, refiguring the power they found in God as a pagan, animistic power, how are we to interpret the apocalyptic flood scene? The echoes of the Flood in which Noah builds an ark while his pagan neighbours blithely ignore the coming of the deluge are too loud to ignore. In a scene of reversal, the Christians become the fools while the pagans are the "saved" ones. Ironically, it is Janie and Tea Cake who become these foolish Christians, as they ridicule the (pagan) Indians who have observed the natural signs of the coming disaster and have headed out of the hurricane area. Janie and Tea Cake are descendants of a white economy of slavery—an economy undergirded by a religious system based upon a slavelike adherence to the dictates of a master-god. As such, in the crucial moment of the hurricane, they revert to a dependence on white/Christian knowledge and can only passively "question God." It seems that we may interpret this scene in two ways: we can see Janie's experience in the flood as (Christian) divine punishment for her "womanish" self-assertion or as the result of Janie's refusal to heed natural signs as her pagan Indian brothers and sisters do. Janie, Tea Cake, and Motor Boat can only wait helplessly for the storm to reach them: "They huddled closer and stared at the door. . . . The time was past for asking the white folks what to look for through that door. Six eyes were questioning God" (*Eyes*, 150–51). But the powerful and punitive Christian God of white men will provide no answer: "They sat in company with others in other shanties, their eyes straining against crude walls and their souls asking if He meant to measure their puny might against His. They seemed to be staring at the dark, but their eyes were watching God" (*Eyes*, 151). In the ultimate analysis, for Hurston, the Christian God must be replaced by a belief in the power of human beings who, as part of the ecosystem, are able to read natural signs and live by them. Such a lifestyle is the essence of Vodou, which means "life force" and from which the Western corruption "voodoo" derives.[9] In the instances of

9. Luisah Teish, *Jambalaya: The Natural Woman's Book of Personal Charms and Practical Rituals,* x-xi.

both Truth and Janie, it is Christ and Tea Cake, respectively, who help the women to find their voices as black female emissaries of the word. For Hurston, that word is an African American woman's experience of herself, handed down from mother to daughter, from female friend to female friend, a sensuous eruption of funk where, in the midst of the communal telling, the "kissing young darkness [becomes] a monstropolous old thing" and "the night-time put[s] on flesh and blackness" (*Eyes*, 7–10). In the famous courtroom scene, we hear not Janie's individual words but those of the nameless narrator reiterating the legendary scene for us: "She tried to make them see how terrible it was. . . . She made them see how she couldn't ever want to be rid of him. She didn't plead to anybody. She just sat there and told and when she was through she hushed" (*Eyes*, 178). Critics have long debated the vexed issue of Janie's voice in the courtroom scene. Alice Walker, Robert Stepto, and Mary Helen Washington feel that the relation of the scene by the narrator suggests Janie's silence. Washington relates a debate she witnessed between Walker and Stepto, in which Walker argued that "women did not have to speak when men thought they should, that they would choose when and where they wish to speak because while many women *had* found their own voices, they also knew when it was better not to use it." Both Washington and Stepto, however, are "uncomfortable with the absence of Janie's voice in the courtroom scene."[10] I argue that the relating of events by the narrator suggests not silence on Janie's part but the exact opposite—a communication of stories between women so that, by the time the story comes to be told by the narrator, Janie's courtroom experience has become a legendary tale, handed down from one woman to another over time. The telling begins with Janie's relation of her story to Pheoby, who by her own proclamation, "'done growed ten feet higher from jus' listenin' tuh you, Janie'" (*Eyes*, 182). In the narratives of Foote, Elaw, and Truth there are references to the biblical messenger Phoebe, whom, in the words of St. Paul in Romans 16:1: "I commend to you, our sister . . . I ask you to receive her in the Lord in a way worthy of the saints and to give her any help she may need from you, for she has been a great

10. Mary Helen Washington, foreword to *Their Eyes Were Watching God*, by Zora Neale Hurston, xii.

help to many people, including me." Hurston's Pheoby is indeed the bearer of good news, but rather than the Good News of the Gospel, she carries the message of female power and continuity that the nameless narrator also conveys to us. Perhaps the increasingly vernacular free indirect discourse of the novel is not that of Janie but of that narrator, the "sister" who becomes more and more identified with the story she is telling and the woman she is telling about. As Janie acquires a stronger sense of integrated black female self, so does the narrator, who, in listening and telling, becomes one with Janie, Pheoby, and a common black sisterhood.

In the courtroom scene, it is the white women who "cried and stood around [Janie] like a protecting wall, and the Negroes, with heads hung down, shuffled out and away" complaining: " 'Yeah, de nigger women kin kill up all de mens dey wants tuh, but you bet' not kill one uh dem. . . . Well, you know whut dey say "uh white man and uh nigger woman is de freest thing on earth." Dey do as dey please' " (*Eyes*, 179–80). While we may question the motives of crying white women who "applaud when the black (male) community is controlled," we cannot dismiss the fact that Janie yearns to tell her story to women, "instead of those menfolks" or that while Janie as black woman is isolated at the intersection of race, class, and gender, she ultimately chooses to tell her entire life story to a black woman, Pheoby (*Eyes*, 176).[11] Janie hopes Pheoby will represent her before the harsh jury of her own black townsfolk. Thus, we must question whether the orality of the novel represents that of the general black community or of a community of outspoken, own-mind black women who occupy the troubled spaces of interstitiality between a number of communities, never quite fitting into any of them—very much like Hurston herself.

In 1937 Hurston had alienated herself from her black male contemporaries by daring to do what they would not—speak in the vernacular of her own blackness. During and after the Harlem Renaissance, foremost black writers such as Alain Locke and Richard Wright viewed "characteristics of Negro expression" and the emphasis on folklore

11. Rachel Blau DuPlessis, "Power, Judgment and Narrative in the Work of Zora Neale Hurston: Feminist Cultural Studies," in *New Essays on* Their Eyes Were Watching God, ed. Michael Awkward, 103.

that marked Hurston's work as storytelling identified with the un-cultured, intellectually lacking, passive, minstrelish—perhaps "femi-nine." At a time when neither the womanist voice nor strong black folk forms were being particularly valorized by black male literary aspirants to "legitimacy," Hurston boldly claimed both. Thus, it is both a black and a female-valorised metaphorical/oral language that she develops in her bold creation of *Their Eyes* as a speakerly text.

Hurston's novel, then, stands between the profoundly spiritual works of Hurston's descendant daughters—women such as Morrison, Walker, and Bambara—and the equally powerful spiritual autobiogra-phies of her ancestral mothers—Belinda, Lee, Elaw, Jackson, Truth, Foote, Smith, Elizabeth, and Broughton, the first black women to inscribe an African American spirituality on American shores. The narratives of the nineteenth-century black women evangelists record a literal struggle to speak as preachers and as women. It is in the power of a vernacular, sermonic speech that these early women writers most often defend their rights as women—and that speech is very often reflected in their written narratives. Unlike nineteenth-century black male autobiographers, who increasingly replace religious with secular concerns, black preacher women continue to cling to God as the directing and legitimizing force behind their voices. Replacing God with a female sense of power derived from Egyptian goddess worship and vodou, Hurston accomplishes an astounding chiasmus; she carries on the oral tradition of her Christian foremothers, but as they increasingly left Africa and the vernacular behind, Hurston effects a *return* to African ways of knowing and saying. In her develop-ment of an oral text, she challenges respectable white/male "literacy" with the black vernacular, creating a new tradition (or reviving an old one?) that Alice Walker would rescue from obscurity many years later. In that tradition the vernacular voices of black women can be heard in their own right. Belinda, standing before the Massachusetts Legislature in 1787, is nowhere more close to us than she is in the writings and the dreams of her granddaughters—Hurston and the contemporary African American women novelists. It is to these con-temporary women that I turn now.

# EIGHT

# The Blues Bad Preacher Women
## (Per)forming of Self in
## the Novels of Contemporary
## African American Women

THE FICTIONAL WORKS of contemporary African American women demonstrate the existence of a spiritual-literary lineage that connects contemporary writers to their spiritual mothers writing before them. While some of the connections between early and contemporary works are deliberate significations on the part of the modern writers (for example, Walker's significations in *The Color Purple* on Hurston's *Their Eyes Were Watching God,* or Hurston's significations on the nineteenth-century Christian black preacher women), there are times when the connections are *not* deliberate but, rather, seem to derive from a powerful commonality of shared histories, discourses, and ways of seeing and knowing that have been passed down among African American women over time. It is to these commonalities that I finally turn, focusing here on (1) the figure of the "unnatural" preacher woman, (2) scenes of communal trial, and (3) the issue of black female performance both as thematic and rhetorical device in the text. How contemporary novels signify on the literary configurations of nineteenth-century black evangelist women demonstrates what Karla Holloway, Barbara Smith, and other black theorists have asserted—that "black women's literature reflects its community—the cultural ways of knowing as well as ways of framing that knowledge in language." Indeed, in theme and form, "Black women writers manifest common approaches to the act of creating literature as a direct result of the specific political, social, and economic experience they have been obliged to share."[1]

*The Blues Bad Preacher Women*

In contrast to their white female counterparts, the early black spiritual mothers present almost unanimously in their autobiographies an outspoken preacherly self negotiating the public realm. This figure of the preacher woman recurs with astonishing frequency in the fictional works of contemporary black American women. I am interested in how the figure recurs because, rather than the holy woman called by a patriarchal Christian God, she increasingly appears as whore, madwoman, blues performer, conjure woman, priestess, or any combination of these. Interestingly, in black American literature, the figure of the black preacher woman has been viewed with suspicion and disapproval by those subscribing to patriarchal Christian religion. As Betty J. Overton observes in her discussion of black female ministers in African American literature:

> What one does garner from the few women ministers in black literature
> is a half view, a view characterized by an attitude that women do not
> belong in the pulpit and that they earn their suffering and problems
> by daring to take on this role. For the most part they are not admirable
> characters but stereotypes of the worst that is in religious ministry. They
> often become normal people only after leaving the ministry.[2]

The suspicion with which black women ministers are viewed may be extended to all black women who question prevailing hegemonies,

---

1. Holloway, *Moorings*, 1; Barbara Smith, "Toward a Black Feminist Criticism," in *The New Feminist Criticism: Essays on Women, Literature, and Theory*, ed. Elaine Showalter, 174.

2. Overton, "Black Women Preachers," 165. Overton examines Sterling Brown's *Manchild in the Promised Land* (1965), Kristin Hunter's *The Soul Brothers and Sister Lou* (1968), Langston Hughes's *Tambourines to Glory* (1968), James Baldwin's *The Amen Corner* (1968) and *Just above My Head* (1979), and Ann Shockley's *Say Jesus and Come to Me* (1982).

taking on roles traditionally reserved for (white and/or black) men, and living outside of male power systems. I want to examine several contemporary novels in which the figure of the "blues bad preacher woman" appears: Zora Neale Hurston's *Their Eyes Were Watching God,* Alice Walker's *The Color Purple,* Toni Cade Bambara's *The Salt Eaters,* and Toni Morrison's *Beloved* and *Paradise.* All five titles are spiritual in reference, conflating both Christian and animistic notions of the divine. Some other titles that reflect the deep spiritual preoccupation of contemporary African American women are *Song of Solomon* by Toni Morrison; *The Healing* by Gayl Jones; *Jonah's Gourd Vine,* and *Moses, Man of the Mountain* by Zora Neale Hurston; and *The Temple of My Familiar* by Alice Walker.

If the modern blues bad holy woman exists outside of Christianity, what I will call the blues *good* holy woman (still wrapped in controversy and perhaps the original blues woman) is to be found inside of it. The nineteenth-century evangelists (some more so than others) are such women. Sterling Stuckey argues that Truth is "a kind of priestess . . . one who, like a great Blues singer, embodied and helped sustain a number of the most essential values of her people."[3] According to Esther Terry, Truth is a blues singer in the traditional African American grain—one who gives voice to or calls up "the harsh experiences of her life . . . in order to confront them and thereby gain dominance over them. The great need to sing the Blues is the need to survive a reality that threatens to pull one down to annihilation. Sojourner's moans, so utterly connected with her memory of slavery, *are* her Blues."[4]

If Janie succeeds Truth as blues holy woman, in Alice Walker's *The Color Purple* it is Shug Avery, blues performer, who takes on this role. Bernard Bell observes the manner in which Walker uses the black vernacular, black American religion, and Shug as blues singer to signify on a long tradition of blues "bad" women such as Bessie Smith. Shug Avery "embodies and evokes the moral ambivalence of many black Americans toward music and behavior that they feel make the best of a bad situation by being as raw, mean, and wild as human

---

3. Sterling Stuckey, introduction to *Narrative of Sojourner Truth,* vii.
4. Terry, "Sojourner Truth," 431.

existence itself frequently is."[5] It is Shug who introduces Celie to an animistic belief system. Shug is religious in the manner of the blues bad holy woman, explaining to Celie: "'Just because I don't harass it like some peoples us know don't mean I ain't got religion.' "[6] As such, she speaks outside of the traditional African American system of religious mores. She asks Celie: "'[T]ell the truth, have you ever found God in church? I never did. I just found a bunch of folks hoping for him to show' " (*Color*, 200). The ultimate blues holy woman, Shug preaches:

> God is inside you and inside everybody else. You come into the world with God. But only them that search for it inside find it. And sometimes it just manifest itself even if you not looking, or don't know what you looking for. Trouble do it for most folks, I think. Sorrow, lord. Feeling like shit. . . . I believe God is everything. . . . Everything that is or ever was or ever will be. And when you can feel that, and be happy to feel that, you've found it. . . . But more than anything else, God love admiration. . . . I think it pisses God off if you walk by the color purple in a field somewhere and don't notice it. (*Color*, 202–3)

Bernard Bell seems vaguely uncomfortable with Walker's lack of moral and political sympathy toward traditional black institutions. His description of what Walker intends to be celebratory in *The Color Purple* rings strangely terse and hollow: the novel is "a contemporary rewriting of Janie Crawford's dreams of what a black woman ought to be and do. But rather than heterosexual love, lesbianism is the rite of passage to selfhood, sisterhood, and brotherhood for Celie, Walker's protagonist"; or later: "The color purple signifies a metaphysical, social, and personal rebirth and a celebration of lesbianism as a natural, beautiful experience of love." Bell finally feels able to articulate his discomfort directly as he addresses what he calls the "problematic" nature of the "implied author and protagonist's hostility toward black men, who are humanized only upon adopting womanist principles of sexual egalitarianism."[7] Indeed, it is this very discomfort that we see

5. Bell, *Afro-American Novel*, 264.
6. Alice Walker, *The Color Purple*, 199, hereinafter cited as *Color* in the text.
7. Bell, *Afro-American Novel*, 263–66.

manifested over and over again when the gatekeepers of (black and white) male hegemony—both inside and outside of black women's texts—are confronted with what I have termed the cult of "unnatural" womanhood—the Sojourners, Rebeccas, Celies, Shugs, Tashis, Pilates, Sulas, Janies, Sethes, Violets, Minnie Ransoms, Velmas, Mama Days, and all the convent women of *Paradise.*

The women I examine here—Janie Crawford (*Their Eyes Were Watching God*), Minnie Ransom and Velma Henry (*The Salt Eaters*), and Consolata Sosa and the convent women (*Paradise*)—as "unnatural" holy women and figures of communal scrutiny, stand outside of their communities, spectacles put on trial by (often skeptical) juries of their peers. For these black women self-determination can be a dangerous undertaking in which they must pit themselves against hegemonic moral and ethical systems often completely contrary to their own.

### Trials of the Spirit and the Blues Bad Women

As I have mentioned, the trial scene first appears in one of the earliest precursors to date of African American female autobiography—Belinda's petition to the Legislature of Massachusetts, dated 1787. Standing resolutely outside of a Euro-American ontological system, she challenges that system with the fierce oppositionality of one who is more African than American, more pagan than Christian. The fictional works of Zora Neale Hurston, Alice Walker, Toni Morrison, and Toni Cade Bambara, written two centuries after Belinda's petition, seem a return to that original point of arrival (or is it departure, in the legendary manner of the enchained Ibo who, arriving on American soil, took one look and walked off upon the water, saying they were going home?) of defiant African and Africentric women upon America's shores.[8] It is the conflation of the scene of the trial with what I will call the departure of the African daughters from Eurocentric mores that I want to examine here.

8. Julie Dash, *Daughters of the Dust: The Making of an African American Woman's Film,* xi.

Between Belinda and these modern novelists, however, there stand several black women who also undergo trial, and it is perhaps in the autobiographies of the nineteenth-century African American evangelical women that we first observe how trial of the spirit is mapped upon trial of the black woman (as black and as woman) by her peers. Autobiography after autobiography recounts trial scenes in which a black female evangelist, convinced of her powers to speak the Word of God, must answer to a jury (official or unofficial) of those who would condemn her for speaking as African American and as woman. Concerning the long history of black women on trial for speaking up and speaking out, in particular the trials of Phillis Wheatley (1772) and Anita Hill (1991), Karla Holloway points out that "skepticism, outright disbelief, and implied derision surrounded both events, and the powerful presence of the judiciary stalked both the margins and the centers." Holloway observes that because Wheatley was audacious enough to claim she had written a small volume of poems, and because Anita Hill dared to accuse black judge Clarence Thomas of sexual harassment, the women found themselves positioned "at the center of a conflict over credibility . . . attempt[ing] a negotiation of racial and gender politics within which neither had a stable or legitimized presence."[9] Speaking out becomes a public event, and the black woman a spectacle, a doubly negative example (as black, as woman) for all other black women who might attempt similar action. Thus, it is silence that seems safest; in fact, it is silence that is *demanded* of black women. In the case of Anita Hill, some who believed her testimony also believed that she should have been silent rather than publicly disparage a black male and disrupt the unity of the African American community. Holloway goes on to cite other contemporary examples of black women who were faced with the injunction to be silent—for example, Robin Givens and Diseree Washington, victims of prizefighter Mike Tyson's violence, were accused of hurting black men with their testimonies. The inspection to which black women have found it necessary to subject themselves in order

9. Karla Holloway, "The Body Politic," in *Subjects and Citizens: Nation, Race and Gender from* Oroonoko *to Anita Hill,* ed. Michael Moon and Cathy N. Davidson, 481–82.

to gain the "inalienable rights" that others often take for granted is still widely operative in America today. The autobiographies of Virginia Broughton, Amanda Smith, "Elizabeth," Julia Foote, Sojourner Truth, Rebecca Cox Jackson, and Jarena Lee, and the petition of Belinda have all recorded the spiritual and secular trials of black women doubly scrutinized in the public realm. Hurston's *Their Eyes Were Watching God,* Morrison's *Paradise* and *Beloved,* Bambara's *Salt Eaters,* and Walker's *Color Purple* turn these trials into heightened scenes of crisis where black women, in facing communal juries, act as catalysts for individual and communal transformation.

Repeatedly, the spiritual autobiographies of black women chronicle the disbelief and disapprobation that meet their efforts to speak publicly, to preach the word of God. Such disapprobation comes from friends, superiors, brothers, and husbands, but I am most interested in the public condemnations the women face, since these set the stage for the trope of the trial by communal jury we see in later black women's works of fiction. In a chapter entitled "Public Effort—Excommunication," Julia Foote (1879) describes the sneering ridicule she receives from a minister, Mr. Beman, of the AME church. As she begins to hold meetings in her own home, Mr. Beman forbids church members from attending them, since "they were breaking the rules of the church." Foote continues to hold the meetings, and Beman sends a number of church officials to question her and her motives. He finally summons Foote to meet with him: "He asked me a number of questions. . . . The next evening, one of the committee came to me and told me that I was no longer a member of the church, because I had violated the rules of the discipline by preaching." Foote then personally delivers a letter to the AME Conference (governing body) in which she presents her case. The result is as follows: "My letter was slightingly noticed, and then thrown under the table. Why should they notice it? It was only the grievance of a woman, and there was no justice meted out to women in those days. Even ministers of Christ did not feel that women had any rights which they were bound to respect" (F, 206–7). Foote's final comment purposely echoes the edict of Supreme Court Chief Justice Roger B. Taney in the Dred Scott Decision of 1857—that African Americans "had no rights which the white man was bound to respect." In conflating her own experience before several committees of sexist AME ministers with the racism of the Dred Scott edict, Foote comments loudly upon her complex situation at the intersection of blackness and femaleness. As Holloway asserts, it is these very identities that have created implicit and explicit legal, political, and cultural contracts in America that enforce silence on black women, and encourage black women to themselves exercise "vocal constraint."[10] But it is in facing a public jury (official or unofficial) and in breaking silence that some black women achieve a sense of selfhood, ironically, often at great cost to themselves.

Sometimes, as we have seen in the case of Belinda, Truth, and Jackson, black women *request* a court hearing, purposely attempting to enter the public sphere in order to sue for justice—a dangerous action, indeed, since the very judiciary to which they appeal has been instrumental in the oppression of blacks and/or women. For example, the black Lucy Terry Prince (1730–1821), roughly a contemporary of Belinda, came to be known not only for her poem "Bars Fight" but also for her shrewd and bold oratorical ability before the courts. Prince came into "national prominence" when she brought a suit against Colonel Eli Bronson, her neighbor, for encroaching on her property. Her suit reached the Supreme Court, where the future governor of Vermont, Issac Ticknor, represented her. Dissatisfied with his representation, Prince dismissed him and argued her own case. Justice Samuel Chase commented that "Lucy's plea surpassed that of any Vermont lawyer he had ever heard."[11]

But in the public space of the courtroom or community, it is the black woman who goes on trial, regardless of the fact that she is often the one suing for justice. Rebecca Cox Jackson, for example, repeatedly requests that the male ministers of the AME church publicly try her instead of privately attempting to sabotage her preaching efforts; but for this request, Jackson is ridiculed, condemned, and made the object of community rumor. Finally, she receives the savage indictment of her own brother. In a chapter entitled "Occasion Sought against Me. A Trial of Faith," she writes:

10. Ibid., 489.
11. Shockley, *Afro-American Women Writers*, 14.

[T]hey had stoned me out of the Jersey [*sic*], and . . . they were going to stone me to death in Philadelphia. . . . I went to Brother Peterson, asked him who gave me the appointment in the Presbyterian church. He said he did not know. I told him I thought it was him, as his wife brought it to me. "However, I have just come from New York. I heard there that they were agoing to stone me here for preaching an awful doctrine. . . . Now, Brother Peterson. . . . [i]f I have preached a false doctrine, I wish to be tried by your Bishop and five or six of your ministers, men that can read and that are spiritual, and four or five of the ministers of Big Wesley Church, two or three of the Little Wesley Church, and the minister of the Presbyterian church, and yourself. . . ." . . . . So I left and went home. On the next morning, my brother came around. He seemed as if he could tear me in pieces. He was like a lion. I told him the same as I told Brother Peterson. He said, "Try thee?—Ah, *that* thee will never get, me girl!" (RCJ, 150–51)

Thus, *not* being granted the legitimacy of a trial becomes a continuing trial in itself, as Jackson doggedly continues to speak publicly in the face of savage condemnation and resistance. Such resistance to the self-assertion of black women amounts to what Jackson calls a "cut[ting] and carv[ing]" of the self (RCJ, 103). Jackson recounts a brutal dream in which an intruder carves out her entrails. Her dream seems a manifestation of Jackson's fear of the abusive treatment she experiences in her waking life—for example, a group of male ministers uttering death threats and intimidating Jackson with promises of incredible violence, such as tarring and feathering, burning, and various other modes of torture and humiliation.

If the autobiographies of Foote and Jackson recount trials of the spirit, Sojourner Truth's narrative straddles both the spiritual world of religious preaching and the secular arena of abolition and women's rights. In Truth, spiritual trial ultimately produces the strength for her to sue in a secular court for custody of her son. It is a strong belief in God and the power of resistance, maintained against the derision of her mistress, that drives Truth to legal action. With the help of God and a kind Quaker, Truth "was taken and set down near Kingston, with directions to go to the Court House, and enter complaint to the Grand Jury" (TGT, 47).

Truth's opposition to everything the U.S. court system represents is perhaps best captured in her supposedly naive understanding of legal discourse:

> By a little inquiry, she found which was the building she sought, went into the door, and taking the first man she saw of imposing appearance for the *grand* jury, she commenced her complaint. But he very civilly informed her there was no Grand Jury there; she must go up stairs. When she had with some difficulty ascended the flight through the crowd that filled them, she again turned to the "*grandest*" looking man she could select, telling him she had come to enter a complaint to the Grand Jury. (TGT, 47–48)

In these scenes of naïveté, which we see also in the works of male autobiographers such as Gronniosaw, Marrant, and Jea, the "simple savage" encounters European "civilization," only to be found deplorably and comically ignorant of its sophistications. But where the male writers contrast these portraits of their past savage selves with the men of (Euro) culture they have now become, Truth never achieves metamorphosis into a pseudowhite sophisticate. Instead, she remains forever the naïf. On the one hand, this tactic on the part of Truth encourages a "black-as-ignorant-primitive" stereotype that amused and entertained whites while erasing Truth's status as respected and respectable "woman." On the other hand, I would argue that Truth's refusal to become "woman" (do whites not also define the parameters of "womanhood" and female respectability?) keeps her on the margins of hegemonic discourse, forever able to ridicule it, even as it ridicules her. As her experience in court demonstrates, Truth in her naïveté (and she uses this naïveté in similar ways on many other occasions) exposes the racist and sexist workings of a white court system that professes fairness and objectivity but permits only white males of a certain class and order to sit in judgment over plaintiffs and defendants. Literally speaking, Truth knows very well whom she should seek out— the grandest looking (white) men she can find. When she eventually locates the proper group of white males, they can only "burst into an uproarious laugh" at her further naïveté; when ordered to "'swear by this book'" that the boy she desires to retrieve is indeed her son,

Truth raises the "book, which she thinks must have been the Bible . . . putting it to her lips [and] began to swear it was her child" (TGT, 48). This image, of Truth putting her lips to the Bible, is strikingly reminiscent of what Gates describes as "the trope of the (un)talking book" in his study of early black male autobiographers. But where Gronniosaw and Marrant raise the Bible to their ears, expecting that it will "speak" to them, Truth's action seems a reverse one. Gronniosaw and Marrant are disappointed by the text's refusal to "speak." The silence in which their symbolic action occurs is indeed deafening, as Gates comments; and it is only much later that they obtain the knowledge of Euro-culture necessary to combine oracy with literacy, to interact with and produce the written text. Their acquisition of literacy goes hand in hand with their acquisition of grand clothes, European manners, and Christianity. However, Truth—who refuses to acquire literacy, or any other European accoutrements—revises the scene of the (un)talking book by privileging oracy only. Whether her revision was intentional or only coincidental we will never know. Truth literally talks all over the (un)talking book, and while her white audience (both the grand jurors and the implied reader) may laugh "uproariously" at her, Truth (unlike her black male counterparts) achieves her intended purpose. Early black male autobiographers remain ineffectual until they acquire the necessary Euro-characteristics, literacy being foremost among these. But Truth—without literacy, in the manner of her foremother Belinda—effects legal action in her own favor: "When the pleading was at an end, Isabella understood the Judge to declare, as the sentence of the Court, that the 'boy be delivered into the hands of the mother—having no other master, no other controller, no other conductor, but his mother' " (TGT, 53). Thus, utilizing hegemonic systems, while being subjected to and scrutinized by them, Truth and other black women who find themselves subject to public judgment or communal trial attain a voice with which to assert themselves.

    In the twentieth-century novels of black women, trial scenarios, whether communal or courtroom-based, become a secular literalization of the spiritual trials of the evangelist foremothers. For example, the trial in *Their Eyes Were Watching God* serves to exonerate Janie in the eyes of the (white) American judiciary, but ironically, in the estimation of her black community, she remains guilty of the "crimes" of spiritual self-assertion and of killing a black man in self-defence. In *The Color Purple* Shug Avery, as blues bad woman, comes under scrutiny and judgment of the entire town: "Shug Avery sick and nobody in this town want to take the Queen Honeybee in" (*Color*, 45). Interestingly, in this same passage, Celie describes the manner in which *she* feels scrutinized by the town women who "look at me there struggling with Mr. _____ children. . . . [T]hey stare at me. Puzzle. I keep my head up, best I can" (*Color*, 45). The passage connects Celie and Shug— both of whom undergo communal examination for different reasons entirely—and demonstrates the hypocrisy of the "jury" that passes judgment on both women. That jury of townswomen would smile at Celie's husband (Shug's lover) Mr. _____ while "say[ing] amen against Shug." Celie's sentiment, "[s]omebody got to stand up for Shug," allies her with this blues bad woman and marks the beginning of a liaison in which Celie and Shug, along with Nettie and "our children" build a matriarchal community of their own within the larger township (*Color*, 46).

In *The Salt Eaters* the voice of black preacherly female assertion, linked strongly to African animistic belief systems, is put on trial as the last alternative in the healing of one woman, Velma Henry, and her entire Southern black community. Minnie Ransom, like Janie Starks, Shug Avery, and many other blues bad preacher women, derives from Christian roots; "sent off to Bible college" in her youth, she performs upon the psychically wounded Velma "the miracle of . . . laying on the hands" within an apostolic "circle of twelve" that functions as a "prayer group."[12] I use the words *perform* and *performance* here mainly in the sense of enactment ultimately resulting in what I have already described as "(per)formance"—a profound self-fashioning that demystifies and challenges the empty performances of black womanhood prescribed as "natural" by hegemonic discourses. When I use the word in the latter hegemonic sense, I specify that usage.

My usages, especially my use of hegemonic "performance," are somewhat different from those of J. L. Austin, Judith Butler, or Henry

---

12. Toni Cade Bambara, *The Salt Eaters*, 53, 9, 11, 12, hereinafter cited as *Salt* in the text.

Louis Gates, Jr. Austin and Butler write of performance as specifically a speech act, and of the performative as that act of speech that results in a desired action. Gates's use of "performance" centers around signifyin(g)—in the African American tradition, an act accomplished with other members of the community as audience looking on, a theatrical, sometimes musical, always communal act, such as the story-telling that unfolds on Joe Starks's porch. My use of "(per)formance" certainly contains echoes of the usages employed by Austin, Butler, and Gates, in that (per)formance, once accomplished, "makes things happen"; (per)formance is the ultimate artistic act; (per)formance is necessary as self-healing before communal healing can begin.

Minnie Ransom, blues bad preacher woman, in her dialogue with Christianity, in her (per)formance of self, must always find her own voice, her own story to tell: " 'They packed me off to seminary thinking helping and healing and nosing around was about being good. . . . No, good ain't got a blessed thing to do with it" (*Salt*, 54–55). Minnie becomes a figure of communal scrutiny in the text because the community of Claybourne, while struggling to embrace ways of black be-ing, must reconcile such strategies with inherited white belief-systems:

> The visiting interns, nurses and technicians stood by in crisp white jackets and listened, some in disbelief, others with amusement. Others scratched around in their starchy pockets sceptical, most shifted from foot to foot embarrassed just to be there. . . . There seemed to be, many of the visitors concluded, a blatant lack of discipline at the Southwest Community Infirmary that made suspect the reputation it enjoyed in radical medical circles. (*Salt*, 9–10)

Thus, Minnie Ransom, whose very name suggests the spiritual con-tribution that will be demanded of Velma once she is finally psychi-cally well (" 'Can you afford it, is what I'm asking you, sweetheart,' Minnie persisted" [*Salt*, 106]), is by turns a figure of veneration and vilification—"fabled healer of the district," the "legendary spinster of Claybourne, Georgia" "finally into her dotage" " '[l]ooking more like a monkey every day' " (*Salt*, 3, 4, 16, 17). Minnie, the rather zany healer of Claybourne, is affectionately if skeptically granted recognition by the Infirmary fathers as a practitioner of alternative healing practices;

but there was a time when she was feared and ostracized by her community, as all females who belong to the cult of unnatural womanhood and blues bad women must be: "They called her batty, fixed, possessed, crossed, in deep trouble. . . . [T]he sight of full-grown, educated, well-groomed, well-raised Minnie Ransom down on her knees eating dirt, craving pebbles and gravel, was too much to bear. . . . [W]ho could know then that the message wasn't about death coming to sting her but about a gift unfolding?" (*Salt,* 51–53).

Minnie goes on trial as a healer woman in the first pages of the text; the jury and the judged stand and sit assembled in order to learn if Minnie can bring Velma Henry (also deemed an unnatural woman—" 'Crackpot,' " " 'predisposed to strife and conflict and crises,' " " 'Always going against the grain',," " 'Always . . . contrary' ") back from the brink of suicide into the circle of black community and redemption (*Salt,* 100, 236, 252). Velma's healing, however, far surpasses any redemption this community is able to offer, for it is a community wrestling with its own psychic pain—welfare mothers, black "boy-men," "veterans of the incessant war—Garveyites, southern Tenant Associates, trade unionists, Party members, Pan-Africanists—remembering night riders and day traitors and the cocking of guns" (*Salt,* 15). And Velma's breakthrough into wellness under the hands of Minnie Ransom, conjure woman, becomes an epiphanic moment, in which the ecosystem responds synchronically to the power of the event. Not only Velma is affected, but all the people of Claybourne: "*Fear and dread at the unspeakable level puts thunder in the air.* The zig-zag strike between the clouds crackling down. Would Velma find an old snakeskin on the stool? *The sky is lit by tomorrow's memory lamp.* Slate rained clean, a blessing. . . . Twenty-four more hours to try and pull more closely together the two camps of adepts still wary of the other's way" (*Salt,* 293).

If Minnie Ransom, Shug Avery, and Janie Starks are blues bad preacher women who undergo communal trial but ultimately precipitate community healing and/or the formation of new communities, Baby Suggs, holy, and the convent women of Toni Morrison's *Beloved* and *Paradise* also form healing communities. However, at the hands of the larger township, both Baby Suggs and the convent women become catalysts for communal catharsis of a completely different kind. In Morrison's novels, community can turn sinister. For example, in *Sula* the townspeople of "the Bottom" (a black Ohio community) lapse into despair after Sula's death, not because they have loved her, but rather, because their common spitefulness when it came to Sula, sustained and united them. The bad blues preacher woman is also the communal sacrifice. Although she may bring good things to her people—as in the case of Baby Suggs, holy, powerful preacher woman, and communal healer, her fate is Christ-like; she is figuratively crucified. Baby Suggs is an "unchurched preacher," visiting pulpits and "open[ing] her great heart to those who could use it. In winter and fall she carried it to AME's and Baptists, Holinesses and Sanctifieds, the annointed. . . . When warm weather came, Baby Suggs, holy, followed by every black man, woman and child who could make it through, took her great heart to the Clearing."[13] Morrison's depiction of this bad blues preacher woman is one of the most powerful and moving of all the contemporary renditions. We may note also, the (per)formative power of this preacher's speech; Baby Suggs can make things happen with her words:

> After situating herself on a huge flat-sided rock, Baby Suggs bowed her head and prayed silently. The company watched her from the trees. They knew she was ready when she put her stick down. Then she shouted, "Let the children come!" And they ran from the trees toward her.
>
> "Let your mothers hear you laugh," she told them, and the woods rang. . . .
>
> Then "Let the grown men come," she shouted. They stepped out one by one from among the ringing trees.
>
> "Let your wives and your children see you dance," she told them, and groundlife shuddered under their feet.
>
> Finally she called the women to her. "Cry," she told them. "For the living and the dead. Just cry." And without covering their eyes the women let loose. . . . "Here," she said, "in this here place, we flesh. . . . Love it. Love it hard . . . *You* got to love it, *you!*" (*Beloved*, 88–89)

13. Toni Morrison, *Beloved*, 87, hereinafter cited in the text.

However, Baby's power is one that her community comes to resent. She can "smell" the disapproval of her people like a bad odor: "She was accustomed to the knowledge that nobody prayed for her—but this free-floating repulsion was new. It wasn't whitefolks—that much she could tell—so it must be colored ones. And then she knew. Her friends and neighbors were angry at her because she had overstepped, given too much, offended them by excess" (*Beloved*, 138). It is the town's resentment of Baby Suggs's bounty and generosity that leads them to spitefulness. Nobody warns Baby Suggs about the arrival of the slave-catchers, and it is their arrival that precipitates Sethe's butchering of her children. Stamp Paid, one of the elder men of the community, believes that it is not exhaustion from feasting at Baby Suggs's home, but "some other thing—like, well, like meanness—that let them stand aside, or not pay attention, or tell themselves somebody else was probably bearing the news already to the house on Bluestone Road. . . . Maybe they just wanted to know if Baby really was special, blessed in some way they were not" (*Beloved*, 157).

In Morrison's *Paradise*, Ruby becomes a spiritually bankrupt town, where the virtually all-black "eight-rock" inhabitants take the lives of a group of blues bad women as their sacrifice. "Eight-rock" refers to the pure African blood lines preserved in the town of Ruby— "eight-rock, a deep deep level in the coal mines. Blue-black people, tall and graceful, whose clear, wide eyes gave no sign of what they really felt about those who weren't 8-rock like them."[14] I will focus on the figure of Consolata in *Paradise* because, while all of the convent women are blues bad women, it is Consolata who, by virtue of her position as "heiress" to the duties of Mother Mary Magna, becomes a Christ figure, a spiritual leader of the other women. In a ritual very much resembling a Last Supper rite, Consolata calls the women to her as disciples. Consolata, who goes blind as she develops the gift of healing through "seeing in," was nine when Sister Mary Magna rescued her along with two other orphans from the streets in South America (*Paradise*, 247). Her roots, then, are planted firmly in the soil of the convent life to which Sister Mary Magna brought her—in

14. Toni Morrison, *Paradise*, 193, hereinafter cited in the text.

Christianity, and more specifically, in Roman Catholicism. Her carnal
relationship with Deek Morgan "the living man" is what precipitates
Consolata's metamorphosis from docile pseudonun to a woman of
the flesh, literalizing the figurative nature of the Last Supper, eating
the body of the god and drinking his blood in the much more
ancient version of Christ's sacrament of Communion, an "unnatural"
woman: "Consolata had lost him. Completely. Forever. . . . Not when
she bit his lip, but when she had hummed over the blood she licked
from it. He'd sucked air sharply. Said, 'Don't ever do that again.'
But his eyes, first startled, then revolted, had said the rest of what
she should have known right away. . . . [W]ho would chance pears
and a wall of prisoner wine with a woman bent on eating him like
a meal?" (*Paradise*, 239). The ancient religious practice of eating a
god sacrifice may be traced at least as far back as the Greek cult of
Dionysus. The myth follows a common "savior" story in which a king is
ritualistically killed and eaten to provide the earth and the wombs of
women the fecundity of his virile blood. Later the king was replaced
by a surrogate—a criminal, a young man, an animal, and finally,
in Roman Catholicism, the body and blood became the bread and
wine of the Holy Sacrament of Communion. Consolata, the unnatural
"cannibalistic" woman, must be tried and exterminated by those who
uphold the male hegemonic order. It is her ability to form liaisons with
other women independently of men, to instill in other women a sense
of their own power that frightens the men of Ruby most of all. The
women, led by Consolata, embark upon a number of healing rituals
that culminate in a spontaneous, sacred, and sensual dance of self
(re)membering. What the Christian men of Ruby perceive when they
raid the convent, however, are indications of diabolism—in the cellar,
the women's chalk drawings become "filth carpet[ing] the stone
floor" (*Paradise*, 287). Perception becomes a trope in the text, where
what is seen and judged is also what is (mis)taken—which is to say
misperceived—but also "taken" as God's Truth, "taken" in the sense
of meanings, goods, lives appropriated. And rushing to judgment
can be a dangerous act indeed. The men of Ruby, ignorant of the
healing rites in which the convent women have immersed themselves,
see in the untended mason jars of the women only evidence of
their laziness, a neglecting of proper women's tasks: "Slack, they

think. August just around the corner and these women have not even sorted, let alone washed, the jars." Tiny statues that the women have used as icons are also misjudged by the hysterical men: "Holding a baby or gesturing, their blank faces fake innocence." A letter—which we learn only much later, in Seneca's acts of (re)membering and recursion, was a sister's message of love written in red lipstick—the men interpret as "a letter written in blood so smeary its satanic message cannot be deciphered" (*Paradise*, 5, 9, 7). Such acts of (mis)taking on the part of the men would seem almost comical—childish, the imagination-run-wild of little boys, boys who perceive with eyes as "innocent" as those of the brothers Deacon and Steward—if we were not cognizant of the sinister consequences of such misperceptions (*Paradise*, 12). What follows these (mis)takings is the hunting and shooting of the women. The men take it upon themselves to try the women, in a series of shared (mis)takings in the absence of the accused:

> But there was no pity here. Here, when the men spoke of the ruination that was upon them—how Ruby was changing in intolerable ways—they did not think to fix it by extending a hand in fellowship or love. They mapped defense instead and honed evidence for its need, till each piece fit an already polished groove. . . . Remember how they scandalized the wedding? What you say? Uh huh and it was that very same day I caught them kissing on each other in the back of that ratty Cadillac. Very same day, and if that wasn't enough to please the devil, two more was fighting over them in the dirt. Right down in it. Lord, I hate a nasty woman. Sweetie said they tried their best to poison her. . . . All I know is they beat Arnette up some when she went out there to confront them about the lies they told her. . . . They don't need men and they don't need God. Can't say they haven't been warned. . . .
> (*Paradise*, 275–76)

Tried and found wanting by the men of Ruby, the convent women of *Paradise*—"unnatural" women—do not fare as well as Janie, Celie, and Shug, or Velma Henry and Minnie Ransom. Indeed, their fate is ironically that of countless black men and women before them who were "tried" in the kangaroo courts of white lynch mobs. Morrison's

final pronouncement on the fate of "unnatural" black women at the
hands of their own communities is indeed a sobering one.

*Performance and (Per)formance:*
*"Something Inside Me That Banishes Pain"*

Finally, I would like to investigate the manner in which black women
(through their rhetorical strategies as the writers of texts, or as characters within texts) become consummate performers. I have already
examined this aspect of the black women evangelists, especially Jarena
Lee, Zilpha Elaw, Sojourner Truth, and Amanda Smith, and I suggest
that self-conscious performance in the narratives of the contemporary black women I examine—either the performance of the writer
herself, or of some significant character in her text—is of considerable
significance in any study of a tradition of African American women's
writing. As Houston Baker observes, black performance in America
involves negotiating a fine line between minstrelsy and integrity:

> As [Ralph] Ellison suggests, Afro-Americans, in their guise as entertain-
> ers, season the possum of black expressive culture to the taste of their
> anglo-American audience, maintaining, in the process, their integrity
> as performers. But in private sessions—in the closed circle of their own
> community . . . everybody knows that the punch line to the recipe and
> the proper response to the performer's constrictive dilemma is, "Damn
> the possum! That sho' is some good gravy!" It is just possible that the
> "gravy" is the inimitable technique of the Afro-American artist, a tech-
> nique (derived from lived blues experience) as capable of "playing
> possum" as of presenting one.[15]

In contemporary black American women's novels, formal and rhetorical strategies of performance comment upon tropes and themes
of performance within texts. In *The Color Purple* pleasing God and
Mr. _____ implies for Celie a performance based on self-negation. But
this God, Celie comes to realize much later, "is a man. And act just like

15. Baker, *Blues, Ideology*, 194.

all the other mens I know. Trifling, forgitful and lowdown" (*Color,* 199).
If Celie must perform the duties of a "good wife" for such a man/God,
(per)forming—a self-fashioning directly opposed to "performing"—
requires not that she *do* anything—her only requirement is to *be:* "I'm
pore, I'm black, I may be ugly and can't cook, a voice say to everything
listening. But I'm here" (*Color,* 214). To *this* (per)formance of self,
Shug enjoins in true church style: "Amen, say Shug. Amen, amen."
Thus, (per)formance seems to be a function of not only self, but other;
it is only in relation to another black woman—first Shug, and later in
writing letters to Nettie—that Celie is able to achieve selfhood at all.

Performance as (per)formance operates in *The Color Purple* in a
number of powerful ways. Gates has observed that Walker performs
rhetorical acts of signification upon her maternal ancestor Hurston's
text, most notably Walker's signifyin(g) use of Hurston's free indirect
discourse. Where the language of Hurston's unnamed narrator is
initially that of standard English, becoming more and more marked
by African American dialect as the novel develops, the language in
*The Color Purple* is almost completely in dialect. In addition to this
observation of Gates's, I suggest that Walker's tropes of performance
support her own rhetorical use of performance in her text. That
is, the manner in which Walker lovingly signifies on the narrative
strategy of her foremother Hurston is reflected in Walker's performance metaphors—"oral hieroglyphics" (to use a theoretical term of
Hurston's) depicting various forms of black performance as the power
of shared influence, as black mentorship. Shug, blues bad woman,
becomes a performance mentor for both Squeak and Celie. It is Shug
who transforms Celie's razor-wielding anger into art:

> [Shug] say, Times like this, lulls, us ought to do something different.
> Like what? I ast.
> Well, she say, looking me up and down, let's make you some
> pants. . . . [E]veryday we going to read Nettie's letters and sew.
> A needle and not a razor in my hand, I think. (*Color,* 152–53)

And it is directly after Shug's "sermon" about God that Celie (with
further instigation from Shug) is able to conduct her own surprising
oppositional performance against Mr. _____ at the communal dinner

table. In this same dinner table scenario, Mary Agnes (Squeak) announces her decision to leave Harpo, as well as to rename herself once and for all. Performance works as a domino effect:

> I need to sing, say Squeak.
> Listen Squeak, say Harpo. You can't go to Memphis. That's all there is to it.
> Mary Agnes, say Squeak.
> Squeak, Mary Agnes, what difference do it make?
> It make a lot, say Squeak. When I was Mary Agnes I could sing in public. (*Color,* 209–10)

Singing, writing, speaking the self as (per)formance becomes an act accomplished not alone, but publicly, in the company of other black (per)formers: "Shug like Squeak too, try to help her sing. . . . Shug say to Squeak, I mean, Mary Agnes, You ought to sing in public" (*Color,* 120). The manner in which other African Americans have encouraged Walker herself to perform becomes clear when we read the quotation that follows Walker's dedication of the book. That dedication is

> To the Spirit: Without whose assistance
> Neither this book
> Nor I
> Would have been
> Written.

"Assistance," what I have already called the power of shared influence, or inspiration, brings both text and author into being through the act of writing. A quotation from Stevie Wonder then reads: "Show me how to do like you / Show me how to do it." Performance becomes (per)formance, text becomes author, student becomes teacher, and congregation becomes preacher in Walker's sermonic work. A church-like "Amen" is the penultimate signification of the novel, written by Celie; and the final words, written by Walker, are: "I thank everybody in this book for coming. A.W., author and medium." This note of thanks on the part of the "medium"—she who brings the spirits of the dead (the characters as well as the literary foremothers) before a collective audience of the living—is directed toward the reader also, who, like God, Celie, Shug and Nettie, reads all the missives of this (per)formance-text.

In *Their Eyes Were Watching God,* Janie's (per)forming of self occurs first through her relationship with Tea Cake, and finally in the communal story-telling setting of the porch, in the presence of Pheoby Watson, as she relates the drama of her life to her friend, who will "tell it" to others. The (per)formance of Janie's life counters the empty performance of it that Nanny demanded—to marry early, to be a "good" wife to a respectable black husband. As in *The Color Purple,* the initial performance of "goodness"—that hollow, external presentation of self that Janie instinctively knows she must (per)form against—is inspired by fear based upon Nanny's experience of black women's double oppression at the hands of white and black men. Nanny's past is figured as the theatrical, as performance: "Old Nanny sat there rocking Janie like an infant and thinking back and back. Mind-pictures brought feelings, and feelings dragged out dramas from the hollows of her heart" (*Eyes,* 16). Indeed, the metaphor for both Nanny's and Janie's search for voice, as I have observed in Chapter Seven is the sermon—itself a performance: "'Ah wanted to preach a great sermon about colored women sittin' on high, but they wasn't no pulpit for me" (*Eyes,* 15). As Smitherman observes, the sermon is a highly performative act:

We're talking, then, about a tradition in the black experience in which verbal performance becomes both a way of establishing "yo rep" [your reputation] as well as a teaching and socializing force. This performance is exhibited in. . . . black folk sermons. . . . [W]hoever speaks is highly conscious of the fact that his personality is on exhibit and his status is at stake. Black raps ain bout talkin loud and sayin nothin, for the speaker must be up on the subject of his rap, and his oral contribution must be presented in a dazzling, entertaining manner. Black speakers are flamboyant, flashy, and exaggerative; black raps are stylized, dramatic, and spectacular; speakers and raps become symbols of how to git ovuh.[16]

16. Smitherman, *Talkin,* 79–80.

In *The Salt Eaters* and *Paradise,* (per)formance becomes a trope
for the recursive process of (re)membering black women's lives. As
in *Their Eyes* and *The Color Purple,* performance as "good" or socially
acceptable action gives way to (per)formance as self-fashioning. In
both *Salt Eaters* and *Paradise,* this (per)formance becomes a form
of audience-witnessed art in a most profound sense. "Good" is a
word that Minnie Ransom, legendary conjure woman of the black
community of Claybourne, has had to ponder deeply in her journey
from young Christian seminarian to "fabled healer" (*Salt,* 3), for
it is a strange combination of African vodun and Christianity that
Minnie practices, and her conversations with Old Wife on goodness
as dutiful performance are interspersed with addresses to the "Lord"
concerning a (per)formance for which Minnie has been divinely
chosen: " 'Old Wife, good and bad and deserve and the rest of that
stuff have got nothing, I'm telling you, nothing to do with it' " (*Salt,*
63). Minnie Ransom's (per)formance is an iterative act; the ultimate
(per)former, her self-fashioning becomes her public healing power
to help others fashion themselves also:

> Rumor was these sessions never lasted more than ten or fifteen minutes
> anyway. It wouldn't kill [Velma] to go along with the thing. Wouldn't kill
> her. She almost laughed. She might have died. *I might have died.* It was
> an incredible thought now. She sat there holding on to *that* thought,
> waiting for Minnie Ransom to quit playing to the gallery and get on
> with it. . . . [Velma] understood she was being invited to play straight
> man in a routine she hadn't rehearsed. (*Salt,* 7–8)

If Minnie's (per)formance of self as African healer becomes a challenging of the performance of what is "good" in the Western Christian
sense, Velma Henry undergoes a similar transformation. Caught up
in the magic of her own healing, and approaching a crucial moment
of recursive remembrance central to the text, Velma, in her utter-
ance of the word *good,* approaches a crossroads of meaning: "There's
nothing that stands between you and perfect health, sweetheart. Can
you hold that thought?" "Nothing can hold me from my good,"
Velma drawled, reciting a remembered Sunday school lesson, "neither
famine, nor evil, nor . . ." (*Salt,* 104). Although she uses the word *good*

as something remembered in a Christian context, Velma—and the reader—sit poised on a threshold, on one side of which words such as *good* and *afford* are imbued with Western Christian and Western economic connotations, respectively, but on the other side of which they signify something else altogether:

> "Can you afford to be whole?" Minnie was singsonging it. . . .
> "Afford . . . Choose . . ."
> Velma groaned, sore and sodden. . . . "But I thought . . ."
> "You think I mean money? Mmm." (*Salt,* 106–11)

For Velma, the performance of "goodness" has been secular—social activism. She engages in this performance not with a sense of the oppressiveness of the performance (like Celie of *The Color Purple* or Janie of *Their Eyes*), but rather, with a sense that she is *resisting* oppression. Velma's initial performance of self is conducted with an intensity, a conviction, a "wildness" in which she clings tenaciously to past pain—

> It's got to be costing you something to hang on to old pains. Just look at you. Your eyes slit, the cords jump out of your neck, your voice trembles, I expect fire to come blasting out of your nostrils any minute. It takes something out of you, Velma, to keep all them dead moments alive. Why can't you just . . . forget . . . forgive . . . and always it's some situation that was over and done with ten, fifteen years ago. But here you are still all fired up about it, still plotting, up to your jaws in ancient shit. (*Salt,* 22)

Not until her encounter with Minnie is she able to relinquish performance as frenetic social activism for (per)formance as a spiritual self-centeredness. Frenetic social activism (as opposed to an activism deriving from an internal centeredness) is a hollow performance in which Velma keeps her interiority from others and from herself. She is an absence: "Velma . . . had down cold the art of being not there when the blow came"; a Velma who "withdraw[s] the self to a safe place where husband, lover, teacher, workers, no one could follow, probe" (*Salt,* 4, 5). Indeed, it is centeredness and presence—the presence, initially, of self to the self—that heals and makes way for communal revitalization in the novels of African American women. In Bambara's novel, a sense of "orientation" is what Velma and the black community of Claybourne need in order to be healed: "Then James standing, turned toward the window, arms wide to the sun, then turned toward her and the baby. 'I orient myself,' he smiled. 'I de-occident myself,' she answered. A private joke whose origins they'd forgotten" (*Salt,* 119).

In a novel in which tropes of musical, sermonic, and theatrical performances abound, I am interested in the way in which Bambara as African American storyteller (per)forms her own acts of formal orientation—de-Occidenting and centering in the text. While self-conscious (per)formance figured prominently as an issue in the auto-biographies of some of the nineteenth-century black women evange-list autobiographers, and Zora Neale Hurston and Alice Walker use free indirect discourse and the vernacular as ways of performing a return to African American modes of saying and signifying, similarly, Bambara creates a text that is literally centered on non-Western ways of telling and being. *The Salt Eaters* seems to spin on an Afri-centrality. It encompasses many senses of the word *spin:* "The strands that flowed from her to Minnie Ransom"; "spinning in the music"; the spin of "the pottery wheel"; and finally to finish spinning and (per)forming, in the sense of the closing lines of the text: "No need of Minnie's hands now so the healer withdraws them, drops them in her lap just as Velma, ris-ing on steady legs, throws off the shawl that drops down on the stool a burst cocoon" (*Salt,* 267, 114–15, 295)—Bambara's tale is spun/woven in a multilayered, nonchronological metamorphosis. The tumultuous climax of this remembering is Bambara's orchestration of a number of characters and events in a theatrical and carnivalesque scene of epiphany—a communal spring festival of drumming performance, drama, and political demonstration in Claybourne—where nature itself is caught in the grip of a shuddering, apocalyptical storm of renewal. Bambara's text spins on a number of epiphanic axes, but the principal centrifugal point occurs roughly at the center of the novel. That point of orientation is rife with tropes of spinning, performance and centeredness, and comprises a series of remembered scenes, the central trope of which is the art of pottery spinning, Velma herself having become "a lump of clay . . . [t]he healer's hands steadying her, coaxing her up all of a piece" (*Salt,* 115–16). The last scene of remembrance in this moment of centrifugality revolves around Velma, Obie, and their newly adopted, still nameless son. "[T]urning slowly on the stool," Velma watches her husband: "'I orient myself,' he smiled. 'I de-occident myself,' she answered" (*Salt,* 119). Bambara performs an act of de-Occidentation, in a theatrical novel in which (per)formance, the seen (scene), the (re)cognized, is everything. It is a kind of bearing witness, which, just before the cataclysmic moment of her healing, Velma almost cannot accomplish.

We find this (per)formative act of healing in Toni Morrison's *Paradise* also. The convent women defy the performance of "true womanhood" demanded of them by the men of Ruby such as Steward, who upholds a boyhood memory of "nineteen Negro ladies" dressed in pastel colors and smelling of verbena as what black women should be. Instead of this performance which shapes the vaguely empty lives of "ladies" such as Dovey, Soane, and Sweetie, the convent women heal themselves through (per)formance rituals of memory, art and incantation. How Morrison herself comments upon her own act of (per)formance in the text is to be found, as in Bambara and also in Walker, roughly in the center of the novel. Walker, in *The Color Purple,* presents Nettie's letters as a crucial centering force of her text. The letters are located at roughly the center of this work. It is the presence of these long-deferred letters in Celie's life that prompts Celie to completely reassess her existence and the events of her history. Morrison's self-commentary as artistic "performer" occurs in the chapter of *Paradise* entitled "Patricia," which describes that character's attempt as (significantly) teacher, writer, and historian, to make sense of the fragmented remembrances of the people of her town. Morrison's commentary is embedded in a scene that details the yearly Christmas performance enacted by the children of Ruby. That performance depicts the "Disallowal"—the barring of the then-homeless black founders of Ruby from a town of yellow men they encounter—and the subsequent founding of their own all-black town. The children of Ruby perform the Disallowal and the black town fathers' retaliatory cursing of the yellow men, as an act of catharsis, iterated and reiterated. Indeed, it is this reiterated act, this churchlike, sermonic, amen-saying performance of cursing in self-defense that so hardens the hearts of the citizens of Ruby that in the final analysis, they kill the convent women:

> Pointing forefingers and waving fists, they chant: "God will crumble you. God will crumble you." The audience hums agreement: "Yes He will. Yes He will."
>
> "Into dust!" That was Lone DuPres.
>
> "Don't you dare to mistake Him. Don't you dare."
>
> "Finer than flour he'll grind you."
>
> "Say it, Lone."
>
> "Strike you in the moment of His choosing!"
>
> And sure enough, the masked figures wobble and collapse to the floor, while the seven families turn away. Something within me that banishes pain; something within me I cannot explain. (*Paradise*, 211)

This last sentence I suggest is the centrifugal point of the novel. In it, Morrison (per)forms an act of authorial intervention with such sleight of hand that her audience might easily miss it: "Something within me that banishes pain; something within me I cannot explain;" this sudden shift to first-person in a passage written entirely in third-person seems to me to be Morrison's commentary on the reason she as black artist performs at all. What "banishing pain" means, however, is the question this novel asks. For the men of Ruby, the pain of the history of African Americans is to be looked at down the barrel of a gun. For the convent women—and for Morrison—the unnameable "something" that heals is not the performance of communal violence as banishment of the painful, but communal (per)formance as healing, art, writing, and remembering against pain. The blues bad preacher woman has always (re)membered herself against pain. (Per)forming her self out of the initial negation of her existence, she becomes—through various strategies of oppositionality, rememory, recursion and resistance—a figure who stands trial before a jury of her communal peers. This sense of communal judgment of individual (per)formance is one that permeates the earliest black women's life writings, from Belinda's petition to Jarena Lee's insistence upon her own truthfulness, to Sojourner Truth's self-fashioning, to the self-conscious (per)formances of black women both as writers of and characters in contemporary black women's fiction. The spiritual trials of nineteenth-century African American women become a metaphor for trials of another order—over and over again, black women's writings attest to the fact that it is under scrutiny by the public eye that "womanish" black women have always found themselves in America. And it is before that gaze that they have (per)formed themselves into blues bad being.

# Conclusion
## Bone by Bone

AFRICAN AMERICAN WOMEN'S affirmation in letters of a highly spiritual black self began with the 1787 petition of Belinda, continued throughout the 1800s in the spiritual autobiographies of eight black preacher women, and can be identified today in some of the most powerful fictional works of contemporary black women writers in America. The nineteenth-century autobiographies demonstrate the manner in which African American women uniquely inscribed themselves in the American literary consciousness. Challenging the collective brotherhood of black men that purported to speak for all black people or the sacred tenets of the cult of true (white) womanhood, the black evangelist women defined themselves. They publicly questioned the nature of white/male "truth," problematized the value of literacy, employed black sermonality and song, and (per)formed astounding feats of self-fashioning and community formation in the face of virulent resistance and an alienation so profound that they often stood strangely apart from the very communities in which they ministered. Theirs was a setting down of spiritual experience which began with Belinda's strong Africentricity and ended as the twentieth century dawned, with the genteel Victorian sentimentality of Virginia Broughton's missionary narrative. Yet, if the seeds of the mothers' gardens were dispersed upon the winds of a Christian Eurocentricity that exerts its influence in varying degrees (according to class, chronology, and religious denomination) over all the narratives, those seeds were never lost. The texts of the black mothers were not forgotten. The contemporary daughters recall the mothers in some of the very same themes, figurations, and narrative strategies that had their origins in the nineteenth-century works: themes of spiritual and communal trial, figurations of the "unnatural woman," and multivoiced narrative strategies of recursion and revision that describe the cultural negotiations and profound spiritual transformations that all these women experienced. What became of Belinda, or of all the nineteenth-century evangelist women with the exception of Sojourner Truth, we will never know; their existence, in a white/male hegemonic system that failed to honor them, was ephemeral. But their texts remain, and bone by bone, we may recover their works. That task is as necessary as ever, for black women in America continue to struggle to be heard above a cacophony of discourses that speak about them but are often not produced by them. In the literary works of black women the resolutely articulate power of the ancestral spirit has been, and perhaps always will be, present in some form; as in the case of Belinda, she stands before a jury of her peers—"and she will ever pray."

# BIBLIOGRAPHY

Abrams, M. H. *A Glossary of Literary Terms.* Toronto: Holt, Rinehart, & Winston, 1988.

Allen, Richard. *The Life Experience and Gospel Labors of the Rt. Rev. Richard Allen . . . Written by Himself and Published by His Request.* New York: Abingdon Press, 1833.

Andrews, Edward Deming. *The Gift to Be Simple: Songs, Dances and Rituals of the American Shakers.* New York: Dover, 1940.

———. *The People Called Shakers: A Search for the Perfect Society.* New York: Dover, 1963.

Andrews, William. Introduction to *African American Autobiography: A Collection of Critical Essays,* ed. William Andrews. Englewood Cliffs, N.J.: Prentice Hall, 1993.

———. "The Politics of African-American Ministerial Autobiography from Reconstruction to the 1920s." In *African-American Christianity: Essays in History,* ed. Paul E. Johnson. Berkeley: University of California Press, 1994.

———. *Sisters of the Spirit: Three Black Women's Autobiographies of the Nineteenth Century.* Bloomington: Indiana University Press, 1986.

———. *To Tell a Free Story: The First Century of Afro-American Autobiography, 1760–1865.* Chicago: University of Illinois Press, 1986.

Ashcroft, Bill et al., eds. *The Post-Colonial Studies Reader.* New York: Routledge, 1995.

Baker, Houston A., Jr. *Blues, Ideology, and Afro-American Literature: A Vernacular Theory.* Chicago: University of Chicago Press, 1984.

———. *Workings of the Spirit: The Poetics of Afro-American Women's Writing.* Chicago: University of Chicago Press, 1991.

Bambara, Toni Cade. *The Salt Eaters.* New York: Random House, 1980.

Belinda. "Petition of an African Slave, to the Legislature of Massachusetts." *The American Museum or Repository of Ancient and Modern Fugitive Pieces, Prose and Poetical* vol. 1, no. 6: 538–40.

Bell, Bernard. *The Afro-American Novel and Its Tradition.* Amherst: University of Massachusetts Press, 1987.

Bereton, Virginia Lieson. *From Sin to Salvation: Stories of Women's Conversions, 1800 to the Present*. Bloomington: Indiana University Press, 1991.

Boime, Albert. *The Art of Exclusion: Representing Blacks in the Nineteenth Century*. Washington: Smithsonian Institution Press, 1990.

Braxton, Joanne. *Black Women Writing Autobiography: A Tradition within a Tradition*. Philadelphia: Temple University Press, 1989.

Brent, Linda [Harriet Jacobs]. "Incidents in the Life of a Slave Girl, Written by Herself." In *The Classic Slave Narratives*, ed. Henry Louis Gates, Jr. New York: Penguin Books, 1987.

Brodzki, Bella, and Celeste Schenck. Introduction to *Life/Lines: Theorizing Women's Autobiography*. Ithaca, N.Y.: Cornell University Press, 1988.

Broughton, Virginia. "Twenty Year's Experience of a Missionary." In *Spiritual Narratives*, ed. Henry Louis Gates, Jr. New York: Oxford University Press, 1988.

Browning, Elizabeth Barrett. "Hiram Powers' 'Greek Slave.' " In *The Norton Anthology of Literature by Women*, ed. Sandra M. Gilbert and Susan Gubar. New York: W. W. Norton & Co., 1996.

Bruce, Dickson D., Jr. *Black American Writing from the Nadir: The Evolution of a Literary Tradition 1877–1915*. Baton Rouge: Louisiana State University Press, 1989.

Burns, Amy Stechler. *The Shakers: Hands to Work, Hearts to God*. New York: Aperture Foundation, 1987.

Butler, Judith. *Bodies That Matter: On the Discursive Limits of "Sex"*. New York: Routledge, 1993.

———. *Excitable Speech: A Politics of the Performative*. New York: Routledge, 1997.

Campbell, James. *Talking at the Gates: A Life of James Baldwin*. Boston: Faber & Faber, 1991.

Carby, Hazel. *Reconstructing Womanhood: The Emergence of the Afro-American Woman Novelist*. New York: Oxford University Press, 1987.

Christian, Barbara. "The Race for Theory." *Feminist Studies* 14, 1 (spring 1988): 67–79.

Cone, James. *The Spirituals and the Blues: An Interpretation*. New York: Orbis Books, 1972.

Connor, Kimberly Rae. *Conversions and Visions in the Writings of African-American Women.* Knoxville: University of Tennessee Press, 1994.

Cook, Blanche Wiesen. "'Women Alone Stir My Imagination': Lesbianism and the Cultural Traditions." *Signs: A Journal of Women in Culture and Society* 4, 4 (1979): 718–39.

Crenshaw, Kimberle. "Whose Story Is It, Anyway? Feminist and Antiracist Appropriations of Anita Hill." In *Race-ing Justice, Engendering Power: Essays on Anita Hill, Clarence Thomas, and the Construction of Social Reality,* ed. Toni Morrison. New York: Pantheon Books, 1992.

Cuguano, Ottobah. *Thoughts and Sentiments on the Evil and Wicked Traffic of the Slavery and Commerce of the Human Species, Humbly Submitted to the Inhabitants of Great-Britain. . . .* London, 1787.

Dash, Julie. *Daughters of the Dust: The Making of an African American Woman's Film.* New York: New Press, 1992.

Davidson, Phebe. *Religious Impulse in Selected Autobiographies of American Women (c. 1630–1893): Uses of the Spirit.* Lewiston, Idaho: Edwin Mellen Press, 1993.

Davis, Gerald L. *I Got the Word in Me and I Can Sing It, You Know: A Study of the Performed African-American Sermon.* Philadelphia: University of Pennsylvania Press, 1985.

Douglass, Frederick. *Narrative of the Life of Frederick Douglass, an American Slave.* New York: Signet, 1968.

Dove, Rita. Foreword to *Jonah's Gourd Vine.* New York: Harper & Row, 1990.

Du Bois, W. E. B. *The Souls of Black Folk: Essays and Sketches.* New York: Bantam, 1989.

DuPlessis, Rachel Blau. "Power, Judgment and Narrative in a Work of Zora Neale Hurston: Feminist Cultural Studies." In *New Essays on* Their Eyes Were Watching God, ed. Michael Awkward. Cambridge: Cambridge University Press, 1990.

Edkins, Carol. "Quest for Community: Spiritual Autobiographies of Eighteenth-Century Quaker and Puritan Women in America." In *Women's Autobiography: Essays in Criticism,* ed. Estelle Jelinek. Bloomington: Indiana University Press, 1980.

Elaw, Zilpha. "Memoirs of the Life, Religious Experience, Ministerial

Travels and Labours of Mrs. Zilpha Elaw, an American Female of Colour." In *Sisters of the Spirit*, ed. William Andrews. Bloomington: Indiana University Press, 1986.

Elizabeth. *Elizabeth, A Colored Minister of the Gospel, Born in Slavery.* Philadelphia: Tract Association of Friends, 1889.

Equiano, Olaudah. *The Interesting Narrative of the Life of Olaudah Equiano, or Gustavus Vassa, the African. . . .* New York: 1791.

Etter-Lewis, Gwendolyn. *My Soul Is My Own: Oral Narratives of African American Women in the Professions.* New York: Routledge, 1993.

Evernden, Neil. *The Social Creation of Nature.* Baltimore: Johns Hopkins University Press, 1992.

Farley, Reynolds, and Walter R. Allen. *The Color Line and the Quality of Life in America.* New York: Oxford University Press, 1989.

Fielder, Leslie A. *The Return of the Vanishing American.* New York: Stein & Day, 1968.

Fishburn, Katherine. *The Problem of Embodiment in Early African American Narrative.* Westport, Conn.: Greenwood Press, 1997.

Foote, Julia A. J. "A Brand Plucked from the Fire: An Autobiographical Sketch." In *Sisters of the Spirit*, ed. William Andrews. Bloomington: Indiana University Press, 1986.

———. *A Brand Plucked from the Fire: An Autobiographical Sketch by Mrs. Julia A. J. Foote.* New York: George Hughes & Co., 1879.

Foster, Frances Smith. *Written by Herself: Literary Production by African American Women, 1746–1892.* Bloomington: Indiana University Press, 1993.

Friedman, Susan Stanford. "Women's Autobiographical Selves: Theory and Practice." In *The Private Self: Theory and Practice of Women's Autobiographical Writings.* Chapel Hill: University of North Carolina Press, 1988.

Gates, Henry. "Afterword: A Negro Way of Saying." *Their Eyes Were Watching God.* New York: Harper & Row, 1990.

———. *The Signifyin(g) Monkey: A Theory of African-American Literary Criticism.* New York: Oxford University Press, 1988.

———. Foreword to *Narrative of Sojourner Truth.* Oxford: Oxford University Press, 1991.

Giddings, Paula. "The Last Taboo." In *Race-ing Justice, En-gendering Power: Essays on Anita Hill, Clarence Thomas, and the Construction of Social Reality,* ed. Toni Morrison. New York: Pantheon Books, 1992.

—————. *When and Where I Enter: The Impact of Black Women on Race and Sex in America.* New York: Bantam, 1984.

Gilbert, Sandra M., and Susan Gubar. "Infection in the Sentence: The Woman Writer and the Anxiety of Authorship." In *Feminisms: An Anthology of Literary Theory and Criticism,* ed. Robyn R. Warhol and Diane Price Herndl. Piscataway, N.J.: Rutgers University Press, 1991.

Gilkes, Cheryl Townsend. "The Politics of 'Silence': Dual-Sex Political Systems and Women's Traditions of Conflict in African-American Religion." In *African-American Christianity: Essays in History,* ed. Paul E. Johnson. Berkeley: University of California Press, 1994.

Gilman, Sander. "Black Bodies, White Bodies: Toward an Iconography of Female Sexuality in Late Nineteenth-Century Art, Medicine, and Literature." *Critical Inquiry* 12 (autumn 1985): 204–42.

Gooze, Marjanna E. "The Definitions of Self and Form in Feminist Autobiography Theory." *Women's Studies* 21, 4 (1992): 411–29.

Graves, Robert. *The Greek Myths.* Toronto: Penguin Books, 1992.

Gronniosaw, James Albert Ukawsaw. *Narrative of the Most Remarkable Particulars in the Life of James Albert Ukawsaw Gronniosaw, an African Prince.* Newport, R.I.: 1774.

Gubar, Susan. "'The Blank Page' and the Issues of Female Creativity." In *The New Feminist Criticism: Essays on Women, Literature, and Theory,* ed. Elaine Showalter. New York: Pantheon Books, 1985.

Hall, Jacquelyn Dowd. *Revolt against Chivalry: Jessie Daniel Ames and the Women's Campaign against Lynching.* New York: Columbia University Press, 1979.

Hammon, Briton. *A Narrative of the Uncommon Sufferings, and Surprizing Deliverance of Briton Hammon, a Negro Man. . . .* Boston: 1760.

Hammonds, Evelynn. "Black (W)holes and the Geometry of Black Female Sexuality." *Differences: A Journal of Feminist Cultural Studies* 6, 2–3 (summer-fall 1994): 126–45.

Harrison, Daphne Duval. "Black Women in the Blues Tradition." In *The Afro-American Woman: Struggles and Images,* ed. Sharon Harley and Rosalyn Terborg-Penn. New York: National University Publications, 1978.

Hawes, Clement. *Mania and Literary Style: The Rhetoric of Enthusiasm from the Ranters to Christopher Smart.* Cambridge: Cambridge University Press, 1996.

Hemenway, Robert. *Zora Neale Hurston: A Literary Biography.* Chicago: University of Illinois Press, 1977.

Hine, Darlene. "Rape and the Inner Lives of Black Women in the Middle West: Preliminary Thoughts on the Culture of Dissemblance." *Signs: A Journal of Women in Culture and Society* 14, 4 (1989): 912–20.

Hodges, Graham Russell. *Black Itinerants of the Gospel: The Narratives of John Jea and George White.* Madison, Wis.: Madison House, 1993.

Holloway, Karla. *Moorings and Metaphors: Figures of Culture and Gender in Black Women's Literature.* Piscataway, N.J.: Rutgers University Press, 1992.

————. "The Body Politic." In *Subjects and Citizens: Nation, Race and Gender from* Oroonoko *to Anita Hill,* ed. Michael Moon and Cathy N. Davidson. Durham: Duke University Press, 1995.

hooks, bell. *Sisters of the Yam: Black Women and Self-Recovery.* Toronto: Between the Lines, 1993.

Howard, Lillie P. *Zora Neale Hurston.* Boston: Twayne Publishers, 1980.

Hurston, Zora Neale. "Characteristics of Negro Expression." In *The Sanctified Church.* Berkeley, Calif.: Turtle Island Press, 1981.

————. *Dust Tracks on a Road.* Philadelphia: J. B. Lippincott, 1942.

————. "Drenched in Light." *Opportunity* (December 1924): 371–4.

————. *Jonah's Gourd Vine.* New York: Harper & Row, 1990.

————. *Their Eyes Were Watching God.* New York: Harper & Row, 1990.

Jackson, Rebecca Cox. [untitled autobiography] *Gifts of Power: the Writings of Rebecca Jackson, Black Visionary, Shaker Eldress,* ed. Jean McMahon Humez. Amherst: University of Massachusetts Press, 1981.

James, George. *Stolen Legacy.* San Francisco: Julian Richardson Associates, 1988.

Jelinek, Estelle. *The Tradition of Women's Autobiography: From Antiquity to the Present.* Boston: Twayne, 1986.

Kaplan, Sidney, and Emma Nogrady Kaplan. *The Black Presence in the Era of the American Revolution.* Amherst: University of Massachusetts Press, 1989.

Katrak, Ketu H. "Decolonizing Culture: Toward a Theory for Postcolonial Women's Texts." In *The Post-Colonial Studies Reader,* ed. Bill Ashcroft, Gareth Griffiths, and Helen Tiffin. New York: Routledge, 1995.

Langer, William L., ed. *An Encyclopedia of World History.* Boston: Houghton Mifflin Company, 1968.

Lee, Jarena. "The Life and Religious Experience of Jarena Lee, a Coloured Lady, Giving an Account of Her Call to Preach the Gospel." In *Sisters of the Spirit,* ed. William Andrews. Bloomington: Indiana University Press, 1986.

————. *The Religious Experience and Journal of Mrs. Jarena Lee.* 1849. Rpt. Nashville: AMEC Sunday School Union/Legacy Publishing, 1991.

Lincoln, C. Eric, and Lawrence H. Mamiya. *The Black Church in the African American Experience.* Durham: Duke University Press, 1990.

Livermore, Harriet. *A Narration of Religious Experience in Twelve Letters.* N.H.: Jacob B. Moore, 1826.

Lorde, Audre. "Uses of the Erotic." In *Sister Outsider: Essays and Speeches.* Freedom, Calif.: Crossing Press, 1984.

Lubiano, Wahneema. "Black Ladies, Welfare Queens, and State Minstrels: Ideological War by Narrative Means." In *Race-ing Justice, En-gendering Power: Essays on Anita Hill, Clarence Thomas, and the Construction of Social Reality,* ed. Toni Morrison. New York: Pantheon Books, 1992.

Mabee, Carlton, and Susan Mabee Newhouse. *Sojourner Truth: Slave, Prophet, Legend.* New York: New York University Press, 1993.

Marrant, John. *A Narrative of the Lord's Wonderful Dealings with John Marrant, a Black (Now Going to Preach the Gospel in Nova-Scotia) Born in New-York. . . .* London: 1785.

McCaskill, Barbara. "'Yours Very Truly': The Fugitive as Text and Artifact." *African American Review* 28, 4 (winter 1994): 509–29.

Mitchell, Henry H. *The Recovery of Preaching.* London: Hodder & Stoughton, 1977.

Morrison, Toni. *Beloved.* New York: Alfred A. Knopf, 1987.

————. "Introduction: Friday on the Potomac." *Race-ing Justice, En-*

*gendering Power: Essays on Anita Hill, Clarence Thomas, and the Construction of Social Reality.* New York: Pantheon Books, 1992.

———. *Paradise.* New York: Alfred A. Knopf, 1998.

Neimark, Philip John. *The Way of the Orisa.* San Francisco: Harper, 1993.

Oden, Thomas C. *Phoebe Palmer: Selected Writings.* New York: Paulist Press, 1988.

Olney, James. *Tell Me Africa: An Approach to African Literature.* Princeton, N.J.: Princeton University Press, 1973.

———. "The Value of Autobiography for Comparative Studies: African vs. Western Autobiography." In *African American Autobiography: A Collection of Critical Essays,* ed. William Andrews. N.J.: Prentice Hall, 1993.

Overton, Betty J. "Black Women Preachers: A Literary View." *Southern Quarterly: A Journal of Arts in the South* 23, 3 (spring 1985): 157–66.

Painter, Nell Irvin. "Difference, Slavery, and Memory: Sojourner Truth in Feminist Abolitionism." In *The Abolitionist Sisterhood: Women's Political Culture in Antebellum America,* ed. Jean Fagan Yellin and John C. Van Horne. Ithaca, N.Y.: Cornell University Press, 1994.

Palmer, Phoebe. *The Way of Holiness, with Notes by the Way; Being a Narrative of Religious Experience Resulting from a Determination to be a Bible Christian.* Toronto: G. R. Sanderson, 1855.

Payne, Daniel A. *Recollections of Seventy Years.* New York: Arno Press, 1968.

Powledge, Fred. *Free at Last? The Civil Rights Movement and the People Who Made It.* Boston: Little, Brown & Co., 1991.

Reynolds, Donald Martin. *Hiram Powers and His Ideal Sculpture.* New York: Garland Publishing, 1977.

Sasson, Diane. *The Shaker Spiritual Narrative.* Knoxville: University of Tennessee Press, 1983.

Shockley, Ann Allen. *Afro-American Women Writers 1746–1933: An Anthology and Critical Guide.* New York: Penguin Books, 1989.

Sjoo, Monica, and Barbara Mor. *The Great Cosmic Mother: Rediscovering the Religion of the Earth.* San Francisco: Harper & Row, 1987.

Smith, Amanda. *An Autobiography: The Story of the Lord's Dealings with*

*Mrs. Amanda Smith the Colored Evangelist.* Chicago: Meyer & Brother, 1893.

Smith, Barbara. "Toward a Black Feminist Criticism." In *The New Feminist Criticism: Essays on Women, Literature, and Theory,* ed. Elaine Showalter. New York: Pantheon Books, 1985.

Smith, Sidonie. "Resisting the Gaze of Embodiment: Women's Autobiography in the Nineteenth Century." In *American Women's Autobiography: Fea(s)ts of Memory,* ed. Margo Culley. Madison: University of Wisconsin Press, 1992.

Smith, Venture. *A Narrative of the Life and Adventures of Venture, a Native of Africa. . . .* Conn.: 1798.

Smitherman, Geneva. *Talkin and Testifyin: The Language of Black America.* Detroit: Wayne State University Press, 1977.

Southern, Eileen. "The Religious Occasion." In *The Black Experience in Religion,* ed. C. Eric Lincoln. New York: Anchor Books, 1974.

Stanton, Domna. *The Female Autograph: Theory and Practice of Autobiography from the Tenth to the Twentieth Century.* Chicago: University of Chicago Press, 1987.

Sterling, Dorothy. *We Are Your Sisters: Black Women in the Nineteenth Century.* New York: W. W. Norton & Company, 1984.

Stewart, Jeffrey C. Introduction to *Narrative of Sojourner Truth.* New York: Oxford University Press, 1991.

Stuckey, Sterling. Introduction to *Narrative of Sojourner Truth.* Chicago: Johnson Publishing Co., 1970.

Swaim, Kathleen M. " 'Come and Hear': Women's Puritan Evidences." In *American Women's Autobiography: Fea(s)ts of Memory,* ed. Margo Culley. Madison: University of Wisconsin Press, 1992.

Teish, Luisah. *Jambalaya: The Natural Woman's Book of Personal Charms and Practical Rituals.* San Francisco: Harper & Row, 1985.

Terry, Esther. "Sojourner Truth: The Person behind the Libyan Sibyl . . . with a Memoir by Frederick Douglass: 'What I Found at the Northampton Association.' " *Massachusetts Review* 26, 2–3 (1985): 425–44.

Truth, Sojourner, Olive Gilbert, and Frances Titus. *Narrative of Sojourner Truth.* New York: Arno Press, 1968.

Walker, Alice. *In Search of Our Mothers' Gardens: Womanist Prose.* New York: Harcourt Brace Jovanovich, 1983.

————. *The Color Purple.* New York: Simon & Schuster, 1982.

Walker, Barbara. *The Woman's Encyclopedia of Myths and Secrets.* New York: Harper & Row, 1983.

Wall, Cheryl A., ed. *Changing Our Own Words: Essays on Criticism, Theory, and Writing by Black Women.* Piscataway, N.J.: Rutgers University Press, 1991.

Washington, Joseph, Jr. "The Black Holiness and Pentecostal Sects." In *The Black Experience in Religion,* ed. C. Eric Lincoln. New York: Anchor Press, 1974.

Washington, Mary Helen. Foreword to *Their Eyes Were Watching God,* by Zora Neale Hurston. New York: Harper & Row, 1990.

————. *Invented Lives: Narratives of Black Women 1860–1960.* New York: Doubleday, 1987.

Webster, J. Carson. *Erastus D. Palmer.* Newark: University of Delaware Press, 1983.

Weedon, Chris. *Feminist Practice and Poststructuralist Theory.* Cambridge, Mass.: Blackwell Publishers, 1987.

Welter, Barbara. *Dimity Convictions: The American Woman in the Nineteenth Century.* Athens: Ohio University Press, 1976.

West, Cornel. "Nihilism in Black America." In *Black Popular Culture,* ed. Michele Wallace. Seattle: Bay Press, 1992.

White, Charles Edward. *The Beauty of Holiness: Phoebe Palmer as Theologian, Revivalist, Feminist, and Humanitarian.* Mich.: Francis Asbury Press, 1986.

White, George. "A Brief Account of the Life, Experience, Travels, and Gospel Labours of George White, an African; Written by Himself, and Revised by a Friend." In *Black Itinerants of the Gospel: The Narratives of John Jea and George White,* ed. Graham Russell Hodges. Madison, Wis.: Madison House, 1993.

Whitefield, George. "A Short Account of God's Dealings with George Whitefield from His Infancy to His Ordination, 1714–1736." In *George Whitefield's Journals.* London: Billing & Sons, 1960.

————. "A Further Account of God's Dealings with George Whitefield from the Time of His Ordination to His Embarking for Georgia, June, 1736–December, 1737 (Age 21–22)." In *George Whitefield's Journals.* London: Billing & Sons, 1960.

Williams, Raymond. *The Country and the City.* New York: Oxford University Press, 1973.

Willis, Susan. "Histories, Communities, and Sometimes Utopia." In *Feminisms: An Anthology of Literary Theory and Criticism,* ed. Robyn R. Warhol and Diane Price Herndl. Piscataway, N.J.: Rutgers University Press, 1991.

Yellin, Jean Fagan. "Text and Contexts of Harriet Jacobs' 'Incidents in the Life of a Slave Girl: Written by Herself.'" In *The Slave's Narrative,* ed. Charles T. Davis and Henry Louis Gates, Jr. Oxford: Oxford University Press, 1985.

Youngs, Benjamin S. *Testimony of Christ's Second Appearing.* Lebanon, Ohio: 1808.

# INDEX